Age of Invisible Machines

REVISED AND UPDATED SECOND EDITION

Age of Invisible Machines

A guide to orchestrating AI agents and
making organizations more self-driving

Robb Wilson
with Josh Tyson

Published by John Wiley & Sons, Inc., Hoboken, New Jersey.
Published simultaneously in Canada.

For general information on our other products and services or for technical support, please contact our Customer Care Department within the United States at (800) 762-2974, outside the United States at (317) 572-3993 or fax (317) 572-4002.

Wiley also publishes its books in a variety of electronic formats. Some content that appears in print may not be available in electronic formats. For more information about Wiley products, visit our website at www.wiley.com.

Library of Congress Cataloging-in-Publication Data is Available:
ISBN: 9781394321551 (Cloth)
ISBN: 9781394321568 (ePub)
ISBN: 9781394321575 (ePDF)

Cover Design and Image: by north.no & Daryna Moskovchuk
Author Photos: Courtesy of Mandraketheblack.de
SKY10099735_031025

Contents

Part IV Conclusion 277

Preface

By Josh Tyson

Much has changed since the first edition of *Age of Invisible Machines* was released back in the fall of 2022. I give Robb credit for astutely predicting the incoming adoption of conversational technologies, as ChatGPT was unleashed on a largely unsuspecting world a couple of months after our book was published. We both watched with excitement and awe as OpenAI's public-facing large language model (LLM) sent shockwaves through every industry and prompted more and more individuals to take a deeper look at the technologies associated with conversational AI, and decide how they might use them in their own lives.

Robb and I also watched with excitement and awe as *Age of Invisible Machines* quickly became the first bestseller about conversational AI. That unexpected success has afforded us the opportunity to put together this second edition in paperback. While the core information in the first edition remains practical and strategically sound, there have been many radical new developments that we were eager to put into context. Without fully realizing it, we were preparing for the task when we launched the *Invisible Machines* podcast shortly after the first edition came out.

We wrote the first edition of this book over the course of many hours of conversation, and we decided to hit record and continue our investigations, inviting in the smartest people we could find who are working with, or thinking deeply about, these technologies. You'll see that insights and commentary from episodes of *Invisible Machines* have made their way into the pages of this second edition. There's also a new kind of digital experience connected with this tangible one you're holding in your hands that can connect you with content from the podcast, as well as the many other resources we reference throughout.

Using the practical information we've been sharing (and with Robb's help) I've done some AI agent orchestration of my own. Follow any of the QR codes in these pages and you'll begin a journey with an intelligent digital worker (or IDW) that has a nuanced understanding of the ideas we talk about in this book. Think of it as a revolutionary sidecar experience: as you read, you can have a conversation with Invisible Machines (literally and figuratively).

Along with updates throughout the text, we've completely rewritten chapters 11, 12, and 13 to better align with the current marketplace. And while we've been told this book is a pretty good read straight through, you can get something useful from reading any one of the chapters herein. One last note, most of the chapters are written from a "we" perspective to mirror the tone of the *Invisible Machines* podcast that Robb and I co-host. There are other chapters, however, where Robb is sharing his direct perspective on his decades-long journey with conversational AI, so the narrative shifts to his "I" perspective.

With that, welcome to the exciting, expanding universe of Invisible Machines!

Follow the QR codes found at the end of each chapter to continue your learning journey with an intelligent digital worker (or IDW) that has a nuanced understanding of the ideas expressed throughout this book as well as insights uncovered on the Invisible Machines podcast.

Acknowledgments

I've been collecting the many ideas, experiences, and stories that went into this book for decades, and getting them wrestled out of my head and onto bookshelves fell on the capable shoulders of Elias Parker, this project's producer and developmental editor. Many thanks for your commitment to seeing this project through. Thank you also to Josh Tyson for helping give these many ideas, experiences, and stories structure and a voice on paper.

Hearty high-fives to Alison Harshberger, Alla Slesarenko, Vira Prykhodko, Mykhailo Lytvynov, Daryna Moskovchuk, Cole Gentile, Katie Tymchenko, Michael Salamon, Henry Comes-Pritchett, Julie Kerr, the wonderful team at Wiley, and The Editrice, Kirsten Janene-Nelson. Additional thanks to Melody Ossola for your visual designs and bynorth.no for your cover designs. My journey in conversational AI has brought me into contact with so many great people, incredible opportunities, and sizable challenges, and *Age of Invisible Machines* isn't the product of just one person, it's the sum of many parts.

To that end, I'd like to thank the many people who have joined the ongoing conversation on the *Invisible Machines* podcast. We've been fortunate to welcome many of the world's brightest minds into the fold and the ideas they shared were instrumental in shaping the revised version of this book. Special thanks to Cassie Kozyrkov, Jeff McMillan, Ben Goertzel, Cathy Pearl, Annie Harshberger, Blaise Agüera y Arcas, Rebecca Evanhoe, James Bridle, Ovetta Sampson, Richard Saul Wurman, Tom Gruber, Adam Cheyer, Laura Herman, Tim Wood, Lou Rosenfeld, Dr. Lee Hood, Dr. Nathan Price, Don Scheibenreif, Greg Vert, Don Norman, Seth Godin, and Professor Daniel Lametti.

A special thank you to my business partners, Daisy and Rich Weborg, and Kevin Fredrick. Huge thanks all around to Michael Bevz, Lance Christmann, Jonathan Anderson, Petro Tarasenko, Helen and Antony Peklo, Natalia and Andrey Nikitenko, and the entire family of amazing people at OneReach.ai (who've been diligently building the best AI agent orchestration platform in the world for many, many years now). Thank you to our customers and partners for recognizing the power of our approach long before Gartner, Forrester and others came along—especially Sherry Comes, former IBM Watson Distinguished

Engineer and CTO, and Jordan Ratner, Senior Generative AI Strategist at AWS. Thank you also to the old Effective UI crew and the community of authors and readers we've built up at *UX Magazine* over the years.

My eternal gratitude goes to the powerful women I've known throughout my life, including my beautiful daughters: Sid, Cole, Katie, Melly, and Quinn. Opa ("Billing"), you rock. Mom, thank you for everything. Sasha, thank you for doing this with me. I love you. Thank you to my amazing siblings: Holly, Burt, and Ernie. Finally, thank you Marshall McLuhan, for setting my evolving worldview into motion so many years ago.

—*Robb Wilson*

Along with Robb and the many wonderful people mentioned above, I'd also like to thank my mom for everything. Eternal gratitude to Elias, Arius, Obie, Scout, and my amazing partner in life, Nicole. LYF!

—*Josh Tyson*

Introduction

Agentic AI, My White Whale

By Robb Wilson

Call me Ishmael.

Actually, please don't.

Like Captain Ahab in *Moby Dick*, I've spent many a waking hour in the heated pursuit of a powerful and elusive white whale: agentic AI. For lingering days, months, and years I've chased this steely beast on the horizon. I was frequently knocked off course by the complexity and newness of the various associated technologies, but I kept up the chase on both sides of land and over all sides of earth (as Melville would say).

Several years ago now, Josh Tyson and I started the surprisingly conversational experience of turning my journey into a practical guide for organizations that were ready to take the plunge early on in an inevitable shift in our relationship with technology. When the book quickly became a business bestseller, we created the *Invisible Machines* podcast to continue our conversations about these explosive technologies with the smartest people we could think of (including Cassie Kozyrkov, Dan Goldin, Ovetta Sampson, Richard Saul Wurman, Ben Goertzel, Laura Herman, Kara Swisher, Lisa Feldman Barrett, Jaron Lanier, Paul English, Cathy Pearl, Jim Webber, Seth Godin, Tim O'Reily, Adam Cheyer, Tom Gruber, and Tim Wood). So while this book is about a journey in technology, I don't think of it as mine alone.

When ChatGPT revealed to the general public just how revolutionary the act of conversing with a machine could be, Josh and I expected businesses to do some self-reflection and make moves toward adopting AI in earnest. Instead, there's been a fair amount of hand wringing by organizations while tech giants looked for the fastest ways to bolt large language models (LLMs) onto existing products. It's been disheartening, but that's not to say that there aren't forward-thinking leaders, designers, researchers, developers, and product designers pushing their companies in the right direction. We've had the good fortune to work with many organizations that are taking this moment seriously.

The biggest surprise has been watching everyday users out in the world really putting this technology to the test. In a way, consumers are leading the charge, and I'm starting to wonder if rather than AI in the hands of companies eliminating jobs, it might be AI in the hands of people eliminating companies. That might sound drastic, but it would be easy for customers to express their dissatisfaction with a company by orchestrating some AI agents to totally overrun their call center. At present that wouldn't even be an illegal action. Those aren't the kinds of applications we're talking about in this book, but it's getting easier to imagine consumer-led activities sending disruptive ripples through any industry.

Organizations that see the bigger picture are already finding ways to make their operations more nimble, so that they can meet new challenges across unpredictable terrain. There are golden opportunities for people to collaborate in designing a future where technology is a partner that's helping us forge a more balanced and equitable world for all humans. AI won't erase our many mounting problems, but we can let it help us make more efficient decisions in responding to the fallout from something as unpredictable and complex as climate change.

My journey in conversational AI began as an early practitioner in the field of experience design. I noticed that the absolute worst experiences people were routinely having with machines were conversational in nature: purgatorial voice-automated call centers and feeble chatbots trying to solve problems online and wreaking havoc on user trust with their inefficiency. Lifting users and organizations out of the seemingly infinite shitbot doldrums seemed like the true calling of experience design.

It seemed like nothing could make interactions with machines easier than using our most natural forms of communication—effectively masking the machinations, making the machine invisible.

As you'll discover in these pages, not only can agentic AI running behind the scenes in an organization handily obscure the mess of systems (and graphical UIs), it also binds your ecosystem by standardizing communications, creating a feedback loop that can evolve automations for all your users—customers and employees.

In the course of building a platform for orchestrating AI agents, I've come to realize that success is really based on a combination of three key technologies: conversational user interfaces, composable architecture, and no-code rapid application programming. In essence, this trinity is truly the white whale of experience design. It furthers the frictionless conversational interface to a point where software creation becomes democratized. Instead of focusing on the experience of using software, code-free allows us to elevate our efforts to designing the conversational experience of creating software using composable architecture. Not only do these component technologies elevate UX design to new heights, they can do the same for humanity, ensuring everyone has access to technology and can easily put it to use: **technology that doesn't leave anyone behind**.

The requirements for this level of automation—hyperautomation—create a scenario where the various elements of experience design become part of a rapidly moving feedback loop. For lack of a more creative term, this represents a kind of hyperUX. The energy previously poured into designing around the limitations of graphic UIs now gets poured into designing for an infinitely scalable conversational interface. The architecture of these experiences requires extensive journey mapping, and those maps become living documents that evolve alongside the experiences. Extensive research and analytics can happen in real time as the people inside your organization watch users moving through experiences as they unfold. This creates an environment that's more agile than Agile, where code-free interactions with machines allow for iterations and improvements being made constantly.

This might sound far-fetched to anyone who's been held hostage by the sluggish development cycles of their key vendors, but in an ecosystem built for orchestrating AI agents, you can pull in any piece of technology and make significant changes to any aspect of a user's experience at a moment's notice. Taking the wrong approach to integrating the technologies associated with AI feels eerily like Ahab's fate: his ship split in two by a forceful beast he never properly reckoned with, he finds himself tied to that force and dragged out to sea. Getting it right involves recognizing the true nature of this swirling mass of tools and strategies, as something beautiful and monstrous and beguiling.

This endeavor doesn't amount to pursuing a trophy you win with a hundred harpoons. Those who try to conquer these technologies will find their schemes smashed to bits. The trick is to be nimble and swift, riding the waves alongside them as everything churns madly around you. Learn to harness and ride AI agents, composable architecture, and no-code creation by creating a strategic environment where everyone in your org can use technology effectively and no one is left behind (or out to sea).

In the pages to follow, we'll take a deep dive into the complexity of this new realm. By sharing with you everything I've learned, I want to help you and your organization swim with the speed, strength, and flexibility necessary to propel itself forward in choppy waters. This will be an arduous and complex journey fraught with difficult decisions, but it will also give you the chance to reflect on the outdated processes and systems that have been holding you back. Regardless of whether this sounds appealing to you or horrifying, the bottom line is it's time to take the plunge. If you're going to drop into uncertain and icy waters, it's incredibly helpful to have a point of view, so I'll lend you mine.

PART I

Imagining an Ecosystem of Orchestrated AI Agents

C reating an ecosystem that supports the orchestration of AI agents is a monumental task, and you'll want to approach it with solid foundational knowledge. In Part I, we'll take a look at the current landscape (as of this writing), dispel some of the common myths associated with conversational technologies, and start to paint a picture of what successfully achieving organizational artificial general intelligence (or OAGI) looks like. With technology this all-encompassing and powerful, it's also crucial to bear in mind the myriad ethical concerns that will arise. These orchestrated technologies will upend our world in rather sudden ways, transforming established chunks of our daily routines. This work must be done with more than just good intentions; we must pay close attention to the shifting outcomes of those good intentions as things begin to accelerate. And accelerate they will. Despite the massive reverberations ChatGPT sent through the world, we are more or less at the starting point; from here we can set a trajectory that benefits everyone, leaving no one behind.

Massive opportunities are waiting for the organizations that take these efforts seriously, and that are willing to make the sacrifices of letting go of outdated systems and structures. There is a world within reach where everyone has access to technology—where soul-sucking jobs are a thing of the past, and companies are increasingly self-driving. In this world, people are free to work together on the most interesting, creative problems, and not only within the confines of large companies. The strategic orchestration of AI agents in pursuit of OAGI is just a means to that end—to that place where technology benefits everyone equally.

This is the book about how to get to that world. It's about how to get your team and company to organize and operate in ways that are highly conducive to achieving and maintaining a self-driving state. A company that reaches OAGI is a bit like someone in a state of ketosis—having starved a body of carbohydrates to burn for energy so it starts burning fat for fuel instead. The artificial general intelligence at the heart of OAGI represents a system that has self-awareness. A smaller version of the broader concept of AGI or singularity, OAGI refers to a system that knows enough to understand and contextualize everything that's happening at any given moment inside and across an organization. OAGI means you've reorganized your organization's insides (likely starving it of outdated tools and processes) so that it can exist in a far more potent and efficient state. To whet this new appetite, we'll also explore some scenarios of where hyperautomation can take your organization (and the world).

CHAPTER 1

Organizational Artificial General Intelligence Is Already Upon Us

W e don't want to scare you, but the revised edition of this book comes with the same ominous warning as the first edition: the status quo is a death sentence. Most modern organizations are still run using systems and strategies that will likely seem comically outdated a few short years from now. That's because the strategic orchestration of technologies described in this book, like AI agents, generative AI, deep learning, blockchain, and code-free development tools, will do a lot more than disrupt the ways we're accustomed to dealing with technology. The strategic orchestration of these technologies will obliterate existing models.

Back in 2010, former Google CEO Eric Schmidt claimed that humans were creating as much data every two days as we had in our entire history up until 2003, pointing to "user-generated content" as the main source.[1] This was more than a decade before users started turning generative models loose, creating exponentially more content. While Schmidt's stat was contentious, there's no doubt that we're creating and capturing more data than ever.[2] In many ways, however, this wealth of information represents a failure. To say it's being poorly leveraged is a bit of an understatement, but all of this is changing.

The technologies surrounding conversational artificial intelligence are heading toward a point of convergence that is already fundamentally altering our relationship with machines. We all experienced the early stages of these changes with the arrival of OpenAI's ChatGPT in the public sphere. The experiences customers and employees have with businesses are being reshaped by the hallmarks of this convergence— putting those massive stores of data into action in ways that have upended entire industries. In the first edition of this book, we said that this might sound hyperbolic given the substandard chatbot experiences endemic to much of the automation happening in the world. We now live in a world where most of the people you walk past on the street have engaged in conversations with machines, either by prompting any of the widely available large language models (LLMs) like ChatGPT or through interactions with companies leveraging LLMs in automated experiences.

These technologies are becoming more and more sophisticated, but that hasn't changed the fact that people don't like task-switching between a whole host of different software solutions.

For example, let's say you log on to your home security system website to cancel service. Asking their chatbot a question drops you down a funnel of FAQ menus where you learn, five minutes in, that cancellations can't be handled online. When you call the accounts department, you're confronted by a series of voice automations that feels like another funnel drop, so you start stamping "0" hoping for a shortcut to a live agent. Crap experiences like this can feel less productive than just waiting on hold and hoping you can remember the security PIN you created five years ago.

The "I don't have time—I'll do it the long way" mindset is symptomatic of the lackluster conversational experiences users are accustomed to having with machines. But that's starting to change. One of the key elements of this convergence of technologies surrounding agentic AI involves intelligent and evolving ecosystems designed for accelerated automation powered by one of humankind's oldest adaptations: conversation. Make no mistake, agentic AI isn't going anywhere. In fact, it's going *everywhere*.

Groundbreaking as they've been, innovations such as Alexa and Google Home hardly qualify as conversational AI, or AI agents. Asking smart speakers to issue weather reports, set a timer, or play a song are very limited and immature applications of agentic AI, though they hint at its nascent power. Smart speakers have completely upended the speaker industry, to the point where it might become difficult to find a new speaker for sale that doesn't have built-in conversational capabilities. But how powerful does a smart speaker become when it's not limited to the things that Siri or Alexa can do? What happens when you can ask your speaker to play "Mr. Roboto" by Styx and then follow up with another request: "I want to buy a copy of the book that Marc Maron mentioned during the intro to his podcast today. I don't remember the title but see if there's a copy available from Powell's before looking on Amazon."

What will happen is, a few minutes later, a text message could appear on your phone with a link showing a hardcover copy of *Camera Man* by Dana Stevens available on Powells.com. By replying, "Yes. Please buy" via text, you'd be communicating with the same AI agent that you initially spoke to—an umbrella conversational interface that has become your primary interaction point with most of the technology in your life.

Apple is making moves to improve Siri, and Amazon has coupled Alexa with generative AI, allowing users to request chat sessions. This is a step closer to the scenario described above, but chatting with an LLM is a different experience than talking to a system that can automate any number of tasks. Once scenarios like this are possible, you won't think of technology in terms of different apps, because you'll rarely need to open and interact with an app. *Domo arigato, Mr. Roboto.*

Take this a step further and imagine how different the experience of work would be if employees could ask a smart speaker for help and instantly engage with a conversational operating system for their company that connected them to all the relevant departments and data needed to make their work less tedious and more impactful. This is the essence of organizational artificial general intelligence, or OAGI (it's kind of fun to pronounce it, *oh-ah-gee*).

We've spent a lot of time talking about this concept on the *Invisible Machines* podcast (with guests Ben Goertzel and Aaron De Smet of McKinsey) and believe it's a central concept for forward-thinking businesses to understand. Give an organization a shared conversational interface that can communicate across channels and leverage data in various forms and organizational self-awareness is likely to emerge. Really, the "organization" part is the context that a generally intelligent machine needs to do things the way a team or company wants them done. With OAGI, a technology ecosystem is in place that can perform all sorts of tasks without needing to involve humans unless necessary.

OAGI represents a systemic understanding of the inner workings of a brand. This awareness allows technology to operate as an extension of the brand for those inside the company as well as customers. Such a technology ecosystem would also be able to identify patterns within an organization and make predictions about all aspects of operations. Obviously, this kind of functionality goes far beyond what LLMs alone are capable of, and we will discuss numerous aspects of LLMs that bear sober consideration.

Human conversation is broader than the spoken word, as we have many ways of communicating our thoughts and needs. Humans frequently incorporate gestures, facial expressions, visual aids, and sounds in conversation. As such, conversational AI encompasses a full breadth of what we call "multi-turn" or "multimodal" interactions. Because they are part of an interconnected ecosystem, these multimodal interactions can leverage those massive stores of data we're continually creating—unearthing massive opportunities for personalization and precision.

Having a text conversation with an invisible machine might include that machine showing you part of a video to illustrate a point. If you're asking it to analyze a spreadsheet or data, it can draw you a graph on the fly to help visualize data points. If the interaction is ongoing and you're about to start driving, the interface can move to voice command. Multimodal experiences mirror normal parts of conversations between people, and that sophistication enables humans to wield technological functions and capabilities using our most natural interface. These bite-sized user interfaces, or micro UIs as we call them, are dialogue-driven and, just like human conversations, they can include all kinds of audio and visual aids and even haptic cues.

You could never have an experience this seamless and efficient while digging through nested tabs or apps—and many of the world's leading companies are coming around to this fact. Salesforce didn't just acquire Slack back in 2021. Their CEO openly admitted that they were rebuilding their entire organization around Slack, and that work continues as of this writing.[3] They're betting that an integrated communication platform and a unifying conversational interface—one machine that connects to everything—will benefit customers, employees, and organizations in big ways. Slack has added generative AI to the mix, leaning on LLMs to summarize activity on users' channels. Microsoft's Copilot offers similar capabilities, but again, as of this writing, these amount to bolt-on applications that fall short of the advanced orchestration of technologies detailed in these pages.

It's critical to establish an understanding of the difference between bolt-on applications of AI technologies and real systemic change. Bolting things like LLMs onto existing systems can yield short-term results that can easily fool those who haven't unpacked the concept of OAGI. Copilot users might save a little bit of time using generative tools to write emails, but many of those same people would save just as much time using publicly available tools, like ChatGPT. The other issue is that a conversational interface that's limited by the amount of information and autonomy provided by a point solution can only do a limited amount of real work.

Systemic change means that a conversational interface becomes a portal into something much more vast and meaningful. It's not impossible for point solutions to become part of systemic change, but only if they aren't locked into partial solutions like Copilot, Salesforce, or Workday. AI agents can manipulate our current software through APIs, using both graphical user interfaces and command lines—interfaces originally designed for human interaction. Over time this approach allows point solutions to cohere and evolve into systemic changes.

This transition from point solution to systemic change won't be abrupt but will occur progressively, bringing significant value at each stage. The organizations that make the leap first will likely build an insurmountable lead. This requires careful consideration, however, as many point solutions are not flexible enough to become part of systemic change and will lead to technology dead ends.

We'll dig deeper into the relationship between point solutions and systemic change in Chapter 12, but it should become clear quickly that having agentic AI operate our old software makes sense. Continuing to invest in the antiquated wares of software providers that are either threatened by systemic change or unaware of the inevitable is a major dead end.

The systemic change described in this book utilizes conversational AI to let users leverage natural modes of communication and engage in experiences that can orchestrate all of an organization's existing software and data. Any feasible strategy for integrating agentic AI into an organization has to hinge on systemic change. Beware: anything less amounts to random acts of automation that won't lead anywhere substantial.

Most Companies Are Dying Young

According to Yale professor Richard Foster, the average lifespan of an S&P 500 company has decreased by more than 50 years in the last century. As he told the BBC in 2018, their life span had dropped from 67 years in the 1920s to just 15 years, describing the rate of change as moving at "a faster pace than ever."[4]

In an article from around the same time in *Forbes* titled "Why Some Companies Die Young," Jeff Stibel makes an astute point that relates to the pursuit of OAGI. "What is missing in business—what everyone is missing—is that the unit of measure for progress isn't size, it's time. Business owners need to start thinking more about survival than size. Bigger isn't better. And growth for growth's sake is downright dangerous."[5]

With those things in mind, we started thinking of this as a longevity book for companies, analogous to something like Peter Attia's *Outlive: The Science and Art of Longevity*. The practical strategies we've outlined for integrating the technologies associated with agentic AI have the key benefit of making organizations far more flexible and futureproof.

In the BBC article mentioned above, author Kim Gittleson points to an emphasis on innovation and reinvention (i.e., flexibility) as a heavy factor in the longevity of companies, reminding us that Nokia was a pulp manufacturer before it moved into electricity and, eventually, mobile phones.

Gittleson notes that Japan is home to more than 20,000 companies that are more than 100 years old (as well as a few that are aged more than 1,000). There's a specific word that describes these long-lived companies in Japanese: *shinise*.

"Professor Makoto Kanda, who has studied *shinise* for decades, says that Japanese companies can survive for so long because they are

(continued)

Most Companies Are Dying Young (*continued*)

small, mostly family-run, and because they focus on a central belief or credo that is not tied solely to making a profit," Gittleson writes.

The organizations that thrive during the age of invisible machines are likely to focus on a central belief that technology can move them beyond the experiences that humans alone can provide. What makes this belief compelling to the people inside these organizations is that they are the ones directly benefiting from the implementation of OAGI. A key component of our strategy involves putting employees at the center of innovation—ahead of customers and shareholders.

While this strategy won't make orgs family-run, it does borrow from a prominent feature of a family-run business: everyone has a stake in its success. Using technology to make better experiences for employees makes a business a better place to work. The work of creating these experiences moves you closer to OAGI.

It's impossible to ignore the fact that this level of automation will likely lead to fewer people working inside of organizations, making them smaller and perhaps boosting their longevity. That said, the goal isn't to replace people inside of orgs; it's to augment their skills and make their experiences better.

As such, these strategies require us to think about organizations differently. The good news for companies is that they no longer need to be confined by rigid software (and the exhausting process of building it). Orgs can stop retrofitting their work processes and start taking a new, more dynamic shape capable of making it in the long run.

As natural conversation becomes the primary interface between machines and the humans using them, the machine becomes invisible as the interface disappears. This line of thinking should be familiar to most experience design practitioners. One of the hallmarks of successful experience design is an interface that gets out of the way. The further the interface recedes into the background during an experience, the more frictionless that experience becomes. This lightens a user's cognitive load and helps them to get what they need from the technology more effectively (though it also represents a massive amount of orchestration behind the scenes).

With agentic AI, interfacing with machines no longer requires that we adapt to the way they communicate, which dramatically reduces friction in our experiences with machines and software. As we've said, agentic AI will go anywhere and everywhere—meaning that invisible machines will be, for lack of a less grandiose term, omnipresent. You'll be able to turn to your phone, any nearby smart speaker, or any voice-enabled appliance and enlist the help of an invisible machine. This ties into another element of this convergence, which involves sequencing technology so that it can react and adapt to individual situations. Invisible machines galore, connected to ecosystems built for optimized problem solving. Using agentic AI to operate our existing software for us moves away from brittle approaches like robotic process automation (RPA). OAGI puts organizations in a position to write their own software that's far more agile and customizable than the wares of third-party vendors— software that doesn't require scripts or specific instructions to complete objectives.

Some Are Calling This Hyperautomation

Sequencing disruptive, advanced technologies to work in concert is something Gartner calls hyperautomation, and it's as intense as it sounds. Gartner coined the term in 2019; by their estimation, "Technology is now on the cusp of moving beyond augmentation that replaces a human capability and into augmentation that creates super-human capabilities." We find Gartner's definition to be a bit loose. If you tighten the definition to specifically require that automation results in producing beyond human experiences, then there's less confusion around how hyperautomation is different from automation. Presume hyperautomation to result in better experiences, not just automated experiences, and that's how we'll be using the term in this book. For the most part it's also analogous to OAGI, though you could argue that OAGI is the direct result of being in a state of hyperautomation. As with broader AGI, there's also the idea of some kind of awareness, which would be a likely result from the activities surrounding hyperautomation. As an ecosystem is trained by humans to automate increasingly sophisticated tasks across an organization (i.e., hyperautomation), it develops deeper contextual awareness and can be trained to make all kinds of high-value predictions. We'll make an effort to use the best term given the context of the information presented throughout these pages.

Implementing a strategy for hyperautomation (that will lead you toward OAGI) is a massive undertaking that requires cooperation from every department within your organization. But you're not helpless in the face of this massive change. You can't succeed by resigning yourself to this disruptive era of technology. It's not something you have to succumb to. You can take charge, but first you have to surrender many of the old ways of doing things.

Organizational AGI doesn't materialize because of concrete plans laid well in advance of action. Flexibility is the name of the game. Organizations need to forge a cognitive architecture that affords you control of the tools and software you use when automating experiences (something we will dig deeper on in Chapter 12). If you think of the broader goal being establishing OAGI, the idea of flexibility comes into focus. For humans, intelligence, or learning, is a lifelong process—an evolution. It's no different when it comes to OAGI.

Robb has been working on this stuff for decades, breaking down agentic AI into patterns that can be sequenced to automate real work. It's part of a deeper passion—for the majority of his life Robb has been trying to improve the ways people and machines communicate with each other. We've come to believe that the orchestration of AI agents will level the playing field. The many technologies associated with AI represent a massive leap forward on both sides of these interactions. These tools present the potential for disruption on a scale that will eclipse the advent of the printing press, the industrial revolution, and the dawn of the computer age itself. On top of that, the rate of change will be much faster.

Hyperautomation is really an application strategy that goes beyond the development of AI and into how you sequence it with other disruptive technologies to solve complex problems as part of an organization-wide experience strategy. As you'll discover in Chapter 11, "How to

Architect Tools Like LLMs, Agents, and Generative AI," technology exists right now that can help you move toward hyperautomating business processes, workflows, conversations, and tasks to go beyond standard UX and into new territory. We think of it as going Beyond Human Experience (BHX). This means creating experiences that don't just use machines to replicate tasks the way humans currently perform them.

BHX is all about finding new ways to create experiences that surpass what humans alone are capable of. This doesn't mean that humans have to be in competition with machines. While there are certain roles that will undoubtedly disappear, ideally, machines will augment our abilities in ways that let them act as connective tissue between humans. Freed from tedium, we can extract more value from our interactions with others.

It's common for organizations to focus on disruptive technology in myopic ways—in this case, seeing automation as a means to handle simple tasks on human terms, such as automating a coffee maker so that it brews a fresh pot of coffee at 8:45 a.m. What if, instead, the coffee pot was part of a better-than-human experience that not only adjusts the time it brews coffee and the amount it brews, but also cross-references company calendars and brews an extra-strong pot of coffee in anticipation of a client coming straight to the office from an international flight.

To expand on this idea from the first edition of this book, the AI agent that manages the experience of making the coffee might swarm with other agents to automate the purchasing of the coffee—continually looking for the best price, following up to see if people like the coffee, and creating a feedback loop to hone a better coffee experience for everyone over time. This agent can obsess over the coffee experience, getting as granular as the amount of caffeine in different offerings.

This brings up the concept of AI agents as customers, something we'll explore further later on. We discussed the subject on the *Invisible Machines* podcast episode with Don Scheibenreif, a Distinguished VP Analyst at Gartner and co-author of *When Machines Become Customers*. His book says that CEOs believe up to 20% of their companies' revenue will come from machine customers by 2030. Companies will need to rewire themselves to appeal to AI agents as buyers. Among many other adjustments, traditional marketing hyperbole will be a waste of money and time. Genuine user reviews will be critical. Truth will become nearly impossible to hide. This is systemic change.[6]

OAGI, Baby Steps Toward Singularity

When we think about AI we often think about the notion of singularity—the hypothetical point in time when a powerful superintelligence will surge past all human intelligence. There's also the notion of machines gaining artificial general intelligence (AGI) and, thus, the ability to learn any intellectual task that humans can. These versions of superintelligence won't be the product of some super algorithm.

The perception of singularity or AGI is more likely to emerge from an ever-evolving ecosystem of algorithms and technologies sequenced in intelligent ways to work in concert. This singularity likely would be made up of contributions from different pieces of software engineered all over the world. These systems will likely speak to each other using human language, making APIs a thing of the past. These ecosystems of algorithms and sequenced technologies are very similar to the ones we describe in this book. It seems likely that organizational AGI might represent the early pieces of a broader, decentralized AGI (sometimes called "singularity"). That is to say that, across industries, the organizations that reach a state of hyperautomation will set the tone for their respective industries while also interacting with other companies in a similarly advanced state. The choices business leaders make in these early moments will set a mighty trajectory.

While the arrival of singularity could be decades away, we've already quietly passed a significant milestone. Users are beginning to have experiences with AI agents that are far more rewarding than what their human counterparts can offer (BHX). We recently worked directly with an enterprise retailer in the United States that, over the course of a year, used the strategies described in the first edition of this book to reduce the number of calls to stores by 47% and achieve an NPS (or Net Promoter Score) of 65 on their automated customer service experience. The initial pilot in 2022 led to a $3 million increase in gross profit, with a projected annual increase of $80 million. That's just a glimmer of the potential buried in these explosive technologies.[7]

Let Orchestrated AI Agents Run Things

In the spring of 2024, Google put a spotlight on AI agents, prediction machines that can be put to work on all sorts of tasks. These are integral to the intelligent digital workers (IDWs) concept that we introduced in the first edition of our book. Unlike typical AI agents, however, IDWs operate within carefully designed ecosystems that can easily incorporate existing software and current best-in-market solutions. Put more succinctly, IDWs are agents that orchestrate other AI agents. We'll explore all sorts of scenarios (both favorable and unfavorable) in the "How Organizational AGI Can Change the World" chapter of this section. But for now, imagine this kind of reality playing out in another context: your router goes down. You place a call to your service provider and are guided through all the necessary system checks quickly and elegantly by a conversational app.

Or, better yet, their hyperautomated ecosystem detects that your router is down and their conversational app reaches out to you before you even notice that you're offline. This is the work of an IDW. More capable than a typical AI agent, the IDW is connected to this service provider's ecosystem, which is a network of interdependent technologies, processes, people, and, of course, other AI agents.

To simplify things in this second edition, rather than continually drawing the distinction between IDWs and AI agents we'll just communicate these ideas in terms of "AI agents" and "orchestrated AI agents." IDWs are really a collection of AI agents working together to complete tasks and solve problems, driven by a conversational interface. Customers and employees can ask an IDW for help and it can orchestrate AI agents behind the scenes to deliver reliable, actionable information, or to complete tasks on the user's behalf.

The orchestration of AI agents from the example above reaches out to you to follow up on an alert from a fellow machine in the maintenance department that your location had lost coverage. These AI agents can swarm around the task, isolating and troubleshooting the issue by running background tasks while it speaks with you to verify your account and location. An AI agent could ask you to send a video of the blinking lights on your router that can be analyzed using computer vision. This AI agent swarm simultaneously looks internally at your connection status, assessing and course-correcting in seconds.

Your router is back up and running within five minutes, and you didn't have to wait on hold for a human operator, because there are unlimited AI agents at the ready—or because they called you, having detected the issue before you did. After experiencing this kind of BHX first-hand, you'll never want to go back.

There's also another element to consider that relates back to the notion of AI agents as customers. It's likely that consumers will come to rely on some form of personalized AI agent that can act as a buffer between consumers and, in this case, a utility provider. It's possible that all of this back and forth about your connection status happened without your knowledge, with the provider's AI agents communicating directly with your own AI agents. Your AI agents might request a credit on your bill and let you know about the situation after it's been resolved. The personal agents might even suggest switching providers and provide a quick summary of other options, and then also possess the ability to execute with your sign-off.

As AI agents are sequenced with other technologies to contextualize massive amounts of data within an ecosystem that can give customers and employees access to elevated problem-solving capabilities, the world as we know it will change fundamentally, as visualized in Figure 1.1.

In this book we'll explore the components of a robust ecosystem for hyperautomating business processes, workflows, tasks, and communications, along with what a strategy looks like for evolving these ecosystems.

"The biggest thing that pushed me to convert to Lemonade was the utterly charming AI chatbot," Juliette van Winden wrote in a Medium post dedicated to their chatbot, Maya. "24/7, 365, day or night, Maya is there to answer any questions to guide the user through the sign-up process. Unlike the drag of signing up with other providers, it took me a total of two minutes to walk through all the steps with Maya. . . . What intrigued me the most, is that it didn't feel like I was chatting with a bot. Maya is funny and charismatic—which made the exchange feel authentic."[8]

The fact that a comparatively unintelligent conversational interface was able to launch Lemonade so far should give you inklings of how powerful these technologies really are. Remember, too, that the potential created by organizational AGI is so vast that the marketplace

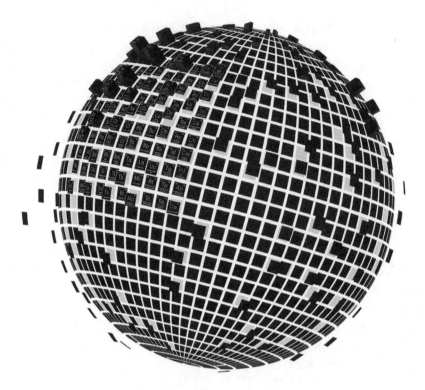

FIGURE 1.1 An ecosystem of intelligent digital workers.

advantage can be staggering for companies with these ecosystems already in place. Making the most of this hyperdisruptive moment in history (and not being left behind) requires a holistic undertaking that touches on all aspects of your business. Random acts of technology—like deploying disparate machines that exist in isolation—will leave your workforce and customers underwhelmed, leading to low adoption rates and the likely removal of the offending tech. A fully integrated approach, however, can bring about a totally new paradigm of productivity with unprecedented potential.

Even the initial steps take time. Jeff McMillan, chief analytics and data officer at Morgan Stanley, told us it took his team nine months to train GPT-4 on more than 100,000 internal documents. This work began before the launch of ChatGPT, and his team had the advantage of working directly with people at OpenAI, including Sam Altman, himself. They created a personal assistant that the investment bank's advisors can chat with, tapping into a large portion of its collective knowledge. They've also laid the foundation for organizational AGI.

"Now you're talking about wiring it up to every system," he said, with regard to creating the kinds of ecosystems and strategies contained in this book. "I don't know if that's 5 years or 3 years or 20 years, but what I'm confident of is, that is where this is going."[9]

"Wow, This Sounds Really Hard"

Hyperautomation is indeed a momentous undertaking. The easiest way to get started is often to automate internally first; start small by automating individual tasks and skills, not entire jobs. Some of these early automations might seem underwhelming, but the simpler you make your starting point, the sooner you can test and iterate. The sooner you test and iterate, the sooner you can roll out an internal solution. You'll continue testing and iterating on that solution, using the momentum to find new skills to develop, test, iterate on, and deliver. You'll fumble often as you grow legs, but that's part of the process, too. In the realm of hyperautomation, we are more agile than Agile (hyperagile, in a sense). With the right tools and budding ecosystem, the iteration process becomes so speedy that failures are often quick rewards that point to better solutions. Because fixes and new solutions can be tested and deployed quickly and at will, your organization can build on wins and gain speed.

"Iteration" is a term tossed about freely in most enterprise settings, but it's important to remember that the real goal is to be continuously improving. By rolling out internal successes with automation and continually improving on them, you're both demonstrating to everyone in your organization, top to bottom, the process by which hyperautomation will take place—and introducing them to the ecosystem they will eventually call home. In the long term, this will bring you closer to creating and testing customer-facing conversational applications. In the near term, by focusing on helping your team members accomplish more and experience more satisfaction with their jobs, your customers will be rewarded downstream. This isn't the only way to reach the goal of hyperautomation, but it's generally the fastest way to accelerate your path to AI adoption on an organizational level.

It also bears mentioning that with the wide adoption of ChatGPT, almost every organization has generative AI in its midst, whether they know it or not. Organizations that have a plan in place for this

(continued)

"Wow, This Sounds Really Hard" (continued)

technology are likely paying to use something like one of OpenAI's GPT models, which keeps the data they feed it secure. Companies without a plan in place are likely to encounter information leaks, which happened to Samsung in early 2023, when employees used ChatGPT to troubleshoot proprietary code, not realizing it then became part of the model's public-facing training data.[10]

Hyperautomation Brings Hyperdisruption

We can't help but reiterate that these changes to business are under way, and they're going to accelerate in astonishing ways. The "hyper" is there for a reason, and the sequencing of disruptive technologies inside ecosystems built for hyperautomation will unleash hyperdisruptions across all industries, emerging suddenly and in ways that we won't always be able to predict. Additionally, hyper-personalization will go full ouroboros, where disruptors are disrupted by users configuring their own ways of using a growing marketplace of powerful tools. It will be intense.

But while the hyper aspects of these disruptions are new, the sequencing of technology to solve complex problems has been with us for centuries. The printing press is an easy disruption to point to, as it spread information all across medieval Europe and eventually the world in a truly revolutionary manner. But the printing press itself was a variation on presses that were already being used to squeeze grapes for wine and olives for oil. When Gutenberg printed his Bible in 1455, it was the product of an orchestration of other disruptive technologies that already existed: an oil-based improvement on existing inks, customizations to paper and moveable type originally developed in China, metallurgy, and the press.[11]

It's in our nature to innovate by orchestrating technologies in our favor, and hyperautomation represents a new era wherein anyone with an idea can have a voice. And with that voice, they can orchestrate disruptive technologies to accomplish things others haven't even dreamed of.

Unlike the advent of the printing press, most people today can already read and write. We also carry pocket computers that have revolutionized the ways we communicate and connect with one another in real time. Behemoths like Google and Microsoft are massively capitalized, as humans connect more online than we do in person. Society is far more prepared for AI than we were for the printing press.

As we'll describe in these pages, assembling a diverse team and fostering a culture that champions change are keys to success in a landscape that will be continually disrupted. Embracing change lets you use speed and iteration to offset any fear of failure. Sometimes the best way to learn and make progress is to just start—adopting a practice of failing forward fast. Obviously this is a common recommendation, but in this case it's not about forgiving mistakes, it's about rethinking how we build software. It's similar to the way drugs are researched, discovered, and tested (you might set out to cure baldness and stumble upon something more important, like a cure for a rare disease). This requires understanding concepts like efficacy rates, and identifying the right drug for the right person.

When developing software in a system that operates more like biology or natural ecosystems, we have to adopt practices that are more similar to the ways we develop medicinal products. It is a fundamental shift in how we think about software, but one that we have models for.

Big changes on top of big changes are on the way, so alarm, urgency, and action are all merited. For those just getting started or who are already up to their necks, rest assured, there are practical ways to achieve hyperautomation, and advance on OAGI for your company or team.

Printing press–level disruptions will come by the week, not the decade. Before we get too far into that, let's set the record straight on what agentic AI is and isn't.

Key Takeaways

- Organizational AGI (OAGI) is already being pursued by companies such as Ant Group and Lemonade, disrupting two long-standing industries: banking and insurance.
- The wide release of ChatGPT and increased excitement surrounding AI agents have accelerated the wider adoption of conversational

AI, fundamentally changing our interactions with machines and ushering in an era of unprecedented technological advancement.

- OAGI isn't something you need to shrink in the face of. You can take charge, but you'll also have to sacrifice many of the old ways of doing things.

- In a world where organizations of all shapes and sizes are using agentic AI strategically, orchestrating disruptive technologies to solve increasingly complex problems will be the order of the day.

- The accelerated orchestration of disruptive forces will create an atmosphere of hyperdisruption—a force multiplying effect, that will lead to entire industries being reimagined on a regular basis.

Want to expand on what you've learned in Chapter 1? Follow this QR code to interact with an IDW that can connect you with additional resources linked to key ideas from this chapter, including content from the *Invisible Machines* podcast.

CHAPTER 2

What Agentic AI Is—and Isn't

Resistance to automation and agentic AI has many facets. Much of the pushback relates to the automation of tasks that people don't believe machines can do well or don't trust machines to do at all, or are afraid machines will do well (read as "taking jobs," not improving jobs or creating opportunity). As agentic AI and the pursuit of organizational AGI become the norm, however, it will become readily apparent that there are a vast number of tasks and processes that can be automated with great success by machines, so long as those machines have humans in control and guiding the process.

"Automation" refers to tasks humans typically perform being performed instead by machines. By extension, "hyperautomation" is achieved by successfully orchestrating advanced technologies—such as machine learning, composable architecture, large language models (LLMs), computer vision, conversational technologies, and code-free development tools—to automate tasks and processes that are outside the capability of humans alone. It's the orchestration of advanced technologies letting AI agents work in concert to automate with massively enhanced impact.

It's tempting to think of conversational AI as nothing more than a new interface that experience designers can apply their skills to, but it's something much larger than that. We spend an excessive amount of time meticulously instructing machines on how to perform tasks for us. Whether it's programming, driving, operating heavy machinery, accounting, or writing, we find ourselves mired in the minutiae of machine interaction. We dedicate countless hours to ensuring machines execute our wishes precisely as we desire.

With the advent of AI, the paradigm is shifting. We can now provide machines with objectives instead of detailed step-by-step instructions. We no longer need to concern ourselves with how the task is accomplished; we can just focus on what we want done. This approach can revolutionize many of our daily tasks.

Agentic AI exemplifies this shift by offering a more efficient way to get things done. But what exactly is agentic AI? At its core, conversational AI is a set of tools and technologies that enable machines to understand, process, and respond to human language in a natural, conversational manner. It bridges the gap between human communication and machine execution, allowing us to interact with technology as effortlessly as we do with another person.

Agentic AI also represents a vast, emergent set of technologies obscured by layers of hype and misinformation. There's a very reasonable sense of urgency surrounding its adoption and implementation within the business community, but putting it to work requires a fuller understanding of what it actually entails. At the time of this writing, a fraction of companies are actually doing things with it, fewer have deployed it, fewer have deployed it publicly, and fewer have released model experiences, yet nearly every company is looking at it, and even more of their employees haven't waited around for their company to decide what to do with generative tools in particular. Plenty of employees are using ChatGPT and other LLMs to help them get work done.[1]

Successful implementation of agentic AI requires an open ecosystem where a shared library of information and code-free design tools make high-level automation and continual evolution an everyday thing. While it's possible that this ecosystem can be built using technologies that are part of your existing ecosystem, a sizable evolution will be necessary nonetheless. With hyperautomation your ecosystem moves from being app-based and limited in scalability by disparate graphical user interfaces (GUIs)—user interfaces that have basic rigid integrations with each other—to skills- and functionality-based, with a unifying conversational interface connecting everything. Interchangeable technologies should be sequenced and orchestrated using an open platform that gives you both the freedom to implement the best functionalities from any vendor and the flexibility to iterate on solutions quickly and at will. It's also important that you're able to orchestrate quickly and make continual improvements to those orchestrations. The ecosystem is agent-driven and can adapt to changes within and on the outside. The goal is not to have a centralized orchestration brain, but to have many small brains or agents that can adapt to changes from each other. This is really about strategically sequencing technologies inside your ecosystem; hyperautomating means you're doing this quickly while constantly implementing iterative improvements.

This means the system is evolving and adapting on its own, with humans providing objectives to follow. This is a fundamental shift in our interactions with machines. We're moving from a world where we have to provide them with very granular and detailed instructions into an era where we can give machines objective-driven instructions instead. Machines can collaborate with other machines to achieve objectives. Humans can provide instructions wherever the objective calls for the machine to complete a task in a specific way. Otherwise we can allow the machines to adapt on their own.

When you start thinking about agentic AI in the right way, you begin to see that it's not a piece of technology to be wielded; it's part of a business strategy that sequences various technologies to automate tasks and processes in ways that surpass what humans alone are capable of (BHX). Agentic AI isn't magic, it's just math + logic. Because we are quick to anthropomorphize things that can converse with us, it makes sense that LLMs seem to us to be reasoning as they reply to our prompts. All that's really happening is that we're giving LLMs patterns to predict from and they go about selecting the most likely word to follow previous words. There's no thinking or reasoning going on inside of LLMs. When LLMs and other technologies are orchestrated properly, communication barriers between humans and machines are eliminated. For this reason it's important to understand how these systems are building context and what they are capable of.

As you'll discover reading this book, the complexity and volume of orchestration that goes into hyperautomation make it hard to say precisely what agentic AI *is*. Instead, let's clarify things by talking about what agentic AI *is not*.

Dispelling Common Myths About Agentic Artificial Intelligence

Myth 1. Talking to Machines Is the Same as Talking to People

Not even close. Before LLMs rose to prominence, natural language processing (NLP) and natural language understanding (NLU) were often seen as synonymous with conversational AI. In reality, they were just two of the smaller pieces of the conversational AI puzzle. Getting computers to the point where they can (a) contextualize the things that people say (NLP) as well as (b) understand the intent behind what's being said and (c) provide useful responses (NLU) required massive leaps in technology, touching on intent recognition, entity recognition, fulfillment, voice-optimized responses, dynamic text-to-speech, machine learning, and contextual awareness. Experiences in a state of hyperautomation go beyond the limits of talking and typing—incorporating gestures, facial expressions, visual aids, sounds, and haptic feedback. Behind the scenes, agentic AI relies on a whole slew of technologies and processes, including integrations, task automation, multichannel optimization, conversational design, maintenance and optimization, and real-time analytics and reporting. In that context, comparing NLP/NLU to conversational AI is like comparing a bicycle wheel to an automobile.

The same can be said of text-to-speech (TTS) or "read aloud" technology, which converts typed words into audio; and automated speech recognition (ASR), which allows users to speak commands rather than press numbers on a keypad. In fact, the more complex a use case becomes, the less prominently NLP/NLU factors in. A Q&A bot addressing employee health care options is entirely NLP/NLU (e.g., identify question, provide correct answer, done). When automating the process of signing an employee up for the right health plan, however, NLP/NLU plays a limited role. Once it has helped identify that a user wants to sign up for a plan, other technologies and processes swing into action: authentication, gathering personal employee data, generating suggested plans, signing up users for the chosen plan, confirming transactions via email, and so forth. All of these actions require an ecosystem created for automation. This is because all of these actions require not just understanding but comprehension. Interpreting sounds into text is a party trick. For a machine to truly understand it must be able to draw conclusions by taking context into account and transferring learning from other interactions. On their own, LLMs can't understand us the way other humans can, even though they're really good at pretending to. Still, they are good enough to become a useful sidekick for making us much more productive. LLMs have also radically simplified training processes associated with NLU, but this is still just a sliver of what's possible with these technologies.

Myth 2. Agentic AI Is Something You Add onto an App

Nope. Agentic AI isn't something you plug in and watch spring to life. Extracting value from agentic AI requires a comprehensive strategy, especially where legacy systems are involved. Although agentic AI can enhance graphical UIs, it's putting the cart before the horse. Ultimately, conversation will become the dominant interface. It will utilize graphical components, like charts and buttons, but any effort being poured into GUIs will soon look and feel rather nostalgic. That's not to say that users will let go of GUIs enthusiastically. Generally speaking, the easiest app to use is the one we already know. For many users, that antiquated knowledge of how to operate a complex nest of GUI menus is a part of their job security.

Regardless, this change is upon us. Think about how quickly the advent of GPS replaced maps—the benefits will just be too large to ignore. The good news is that the amount of work and introspection it takes to successfully implement and scale an agentic AI strategy pays dividends in the ways it unifies and improves all facets of an organization. The bad news is that, in the wake of ChatGPT, the marketplace has been flooded with bolt-on point solutions. Don't be fooled into thinking they can get you close to a state of hyperautomation on their own. Simply equipping an organization with access to sanctioned LLMs won't move the needle toward OAGI.

Myth 3. The Goal of Agentic AI Is to Mimic Humans

Humans are capable of amazing things—as a species, we're continually pushing the boundaries of what we can accomplish. But conversational AI isn't human; we're not trying to pretend it's human, and you shouldn't try to make it human. The point of agentic AI and OAGI is to unlock the ways sequenced technology can perform services far better than what humans alone are capable of.

As science fiction has shown us, robots *can* make better work companions than humans when it comes to productivity. R2D2, for instance, was a decidedly non-humanoid robot. Its non-human attributes made it useful (like being able to use a universal computer interface arm to communicate with legacy Imperial enterprise systems). Anthropomorphizing our AI systems can make it more difficult to embrace the differences between humans and machines (and slow our progress in designing them to get shit done).

Myth 4. It's Software as Usual

On a surface level, it's become easier to integrate agentic AI into organizational operations. As much as we might be tempted to hurl GPTs at isolated workflows, successful implementation of agentic AI requires something far more complex. It demands an ecosystem where a shared library of information, patterns, and templates join with code-free design tools to produce high-level automation and continual evolution.

The technology itself is not as difficult as many think. The bigger challenge often lies with getting others to accept and internalize the changes necessary for success. Risk free innovation is what most organizations are looking for. They will avoid taking the financial risk necessary until they are under extreme competitive pressure.

By the time that pressure reaches full force, it will likely be too late. Orgs need to reorient their thinking about software projects. Reaching OAGI is more like developing a new drug than it is like traditional product management. When pharmaceutical companies get something right, it can be massively valuable and lucrative, but their medications don't always materialize the way we think. A drug that's being investigated as a cure for gout might turn out to be a promising hair growth solution. Finding this kind of value hinges on being open to following where the journey leads—think of *shinise* Nokia, a company that evolved over the years from making pulp to making smartphones.

Myth 5. You Should Start Big

Most organizations don't need a large-scale, public-facing deployment—like Bank of America's virtual financial assistant, Erica—to put agentic AI to good use. You need to think big and start small. This may seem obvious, but it's very hard to get an organization to place a bet without a clear ROI. Bottom line: companies that play it safe will not innovate as well as those that experiment. To the previous point, companies that take these chances often and in small ways will stumble across the massive innovation they weren't trying to discover.

It's often more effective to begin by working within your organization, automating internal tasks with help from the people who understand those tasks best. Working internally, you can also get a handle on how to sequence technology to complete jobs in more efficient and rewarding ways than humans alone are able to. This will form the groundwork for an ecosystem of agentic AI that can grow to include customers at a point when you're equipped to provide them with optimized experiences. You'll want to start small, simple, and internally— then iteratively advance, expand, and scale. Remember, however, that starting small means more than just giving teams access to a sanctioned LLM. There should be a strategy in place for connecting to some sort of knowledge management system (like retrieval-augmented generation, or RAG).

Myth 6. Business-Minded People Can Pick the Right Tools and Systems

Given the complexity we've already discussed (not to mention what's to come in subsequent chapters), the business minds in your organization can't make agentic AI decisions alone. Business buyers often choose technology the way gamblers pick a racehorse. They look at track record and breeding with the assumption that what works for others will work for them—and that what has worked in the past will work in the future. The uncomfortable truth that most AI vendors don't want to share is that it's nearly impossible to pick winners in this way. You need to be able to try out everything to know what will work.

This calls for a collaborative effort that draws on expertise from various disciplines within your organization. Including everyone will be hard, but it's very risky moving forward on your own. You'll need input from those who understand the technology you currently have in place, those who have relationships with your customer base, those who understand your employees' needs, and those who understand the aspects of your business that are ripe for automation.

The best way to make sure you acquire the right tools and systems is to try everything and commit to lots of experimentation. Once you have a shared vision of what you want to build, it will be far easier to see which products will truly provide you with valuable solutions. Successful conversational AI emerges from a collaborative effort among key personnel in your organization.

Myth 7. You Can Do This with the Team You Already Have in Place

Agentic AI isn't an initiative you can put solely in the hands of any one group in your organization. Did we already mention that giving teams a sanctioned LLM like OpenAI's GPT models isn't a viable first step? You need a core team of specialists instituting a process that involves members from every department in your organization. That core team can come from within your organization or the outside world, but its members have to be adept enablers. As they work their own skill-specific roles, they need to always be evangelizing the potential for anyone with a good idea to contribute to the design of automated solutions. Hyperautomation is an all-hands-on-deck journey. Furthermore, AI isn't just a part of your company; it will eventually *become* your center of operations. Don't silo the technology and don't cut yourself off from other people while building it.

Myth 8. To Get Agentic AI Right You Need to Hire an Expert

Don't be fooled. Despite the flood of activity, solutions, and consultants into this space, the sequencing of AI agents in ecosystems built for hyperautomating is still in the inception stage. There aren't yet expert agencies or hired guns that can get you up to speed with the flip of a switch. That's not to say that there aren't great partners out there who can help you with elements of hyperautomation. Just note that having others set up everything for you isn't the best use of your investment. Instead, look for a partner committed to training (and learning alongside) your own team using strategic implementation methods. You also don't need to concern yourself with becoming an expert. This is an uncomfortable truth, but being a data scientist or prompt engineer is less important than being really good at creative problem solving.

Myth 9. There Is One Platform to Rule Them All

Giant companies such as Amazon, Microsoft, and IBM have very sophisticated products that address certain facets of conversational AI, but none of them have a platform or service that can deliver hyperautomation. The same is true of OpenAI, Anthropic, Cohere, and the lot. What you need is an open system that allows you to leverage a whole host of tools, enabling you to sequence and orchestrate different technologies that are the right fit for the job. Hyperautomation requires a network of elements working together in an evolutionary fashion. To quickly grow your ecosystem, you'll want to try as many solutions as possible as quickly as possible. The best approach is to iterate rapidly—to continually improve by trying out new configurations and isolating the best tools, AIs, and algorithms for your business. Open systems allow you to understand, analyze, and manage the relationships among the moving parts inside your ecosystem, which is crucial when moving toward hyperautomation. Remember, this isn't a race to adopt any specific technology; it's a race to put yourself in the position to adopt as many different technologies as possible. You don't need the best AI tool, you need all of them.

Myth 10. Phones Aren't Relevant

Mobile usage is where most of the cost-saving attributes of conversational AI are found. While a sizable number of people spend the majority of their time sitting at a computer, just about everyone carries a smaller computer on their person, all day long. Smartphones have all sorts of capabilities such as SMS, voice, GPS, and banking, which can be leveraged across ecosystems built for sequencing agentic AI.

There's also a large segment of the world's population whose only access to the internet comes through the less-expensive feature phone or the hybrid smart feature phone. We recently had a conversation with Payal Arora, author of *The Next Billion Users* (Harvard Press), and she pointed out that 90% of young people live outside the West and that "in many parts of the global South, you often have shared mobile phones . . . so, you know, you have a grandson using it, his grandma, and also his mother."[2]

Also, though call centers are declining in general, they are still very much a viable piece of many businesses around the world. Merijn te Booij—chief marketing officer of Genesys, a contact center technology company—told Vox how, in the early days of the pandemic, they "saw a lot of people moving away from digital channels very quickly to the voice channel, trying to get certainty, assurances, empathy, making sure that they got commitments on the enterprise decision." The bottom line is that phones of varying degrees of sophistication are key interface points for ecosystems where agentic AI is being sequenced. They can offer a broader reach and enhanced flexibility, so don't count them out.

Also worth remembering: most of us talk faster than we type, but we read faster than we listen to speech. Through conversations with the founders of Siri we learned that in the early days, users would talk and Siri would type back replies. This is the fastest form of interaction next to machines just simply predicting what we want to say. Hands free, hybrid voice interactions will become more common once we start looking for faster ways to communicate with AI.

Myth 11. You Can Get to the Next Level with the System and Pretrained Bots You Already Have

Most organizations that have made attempts at creating conversational AI are stuck watching disparate chatbots sputter along independently without any meaningful connections to their fellow bots or the organization using them. This is a waste of time and resources that alienates customers and team members alike. For context, analysts like Gartner have charted most of these out-of-box machines as being both low effort and low value. As you move toward higher effort/value integrations, your capabilities surge from being domain specific with limited channels and response capabilities, to machines that can function more like virtual assistants—capable of data-driven decision-making, working across channels, and behaving proactively. Getting closer to organizational AGI requires a strategy for building an ecosystem in which agentic AI thrives. Through the process you might discover that certain elements of your existing ecosystem can become integrated into your evolved ecosystem, but they will never serve as the springboard for the necessary evolution.

Acquiring chatbots that are already set up to automate particular workflows your organization uses might seem like a shortcut to OAGI, but it will cost you more time in the long term. As you automate workflows, you're going to find opportunities to improve them. If your only option is to query the machine's developers with your requests, you're entering a cycle of waiting: waiting on iterations, testing them, and then waiting for updates. Consequently, you'll be subject to their timelines and product road map. This wastes time and kills momentum. As we'll explore in Chapter 11, "How to Architect Tools Like LLMs, Agents, and Generative AI," you need customizable tools that allow you to make code-free design changes at will—changes you can then test internally and implement quickly.

Myth 12. You'll Improve Operations by Automating Existing Workflows

On the surface, it might seem like the biggest win of agentic AI would be to have it run monotonous tasks in place of humans. While there is some usefulness in that, the real value comes with automating better ways of doing things. For example, let's say you call the IRS following up on a letter they sent you. Your first hurdle is to figure out which of the unintelligible clusters of voice-automated options most closely applies to your situation. Then you repeat that process a few more times as you move through murky layers of their phone tree, unsure if you're headed to the right department and expecting to wait on hold for hours to find out. What if, instead, you were greeted by an intelligent digital worker (IDW) or AI agent that could verify your personal information while cross-referencing your recent tax history to infer that you're calling about a letter that was sent last week. What if that AI agent could also tell you that the payment you sent was received after the letter was sent, give you a confirmation number, and send you on your way in under five minutes? Within an ecosystem of integrated conversational AI, that kind of Beyond Human Experience (BHX) can readily be designed and implemented.

Myth 13. This Is Like Any Other Software Build-Out

The waterfall approach to software creation is severely outdated and has sprung countless leaks over the years. If you attempt to apply it within the framework of designing agentic solutions, you will drown. Creating an ecosystem for hyperautomation using agentic AI is an iterative process that demands the flexibility of rapid, code-free design tools for the steady deployment of new solutions. Even companies that are used to Agile methodologies should prepare for faster iteration cycles than they might be accustomed to. As we're fond of saying, this is more agile than Agile. And while bolt-on solutions may have served you in the past, as we're mentioned once or thrice already, tacking LLMs onto existing software is a road to nowhere. Agentic AI and the road to OAGI are all about trial and error, requiring fast iteration, and simulations for testing. The objective isn't building solutions based on predictions of what users want. The goal is to build and iterate the fastest. You need to become almost too agile for Agile.

Myth 14. Your Competitive Edge Lives in the Quantity of Data You've Collected

If only it were that simple. Accumulating massive amounts of data about your customers and business has never been easier, but extracting the value buried in the heaps is a complex and ongoing endeavor that requires a comprehensive strategy. (And though some may be tempted to address this concern with a plug-and-play approach, note that these methods peak at about 40% accuracy, which means most of your data would be wasted.) In order to extract all its value, data needs to be categorized within a framework that makes it an active resource accessible across your entire ecosystem. Improvements to LLMs have made it far easier to mine unstructured data (like emails and recorded conversations) but you still need a strategy for connecting that data to all the other nodes in your ecosystem.

As we mentioned in Chapter 1, according to Jeff McMillan, Morgan Stanley's chief analytics and data officer, it took nine months to train GPT-4 on more than 100,000 internal documents. This work began before the launch of ChatGPT, and Jeff's team had the advantage of working directly with senior people at OpenAI, including Sam Altman.[3] This work requires diligence and patience, and one of the most potent tools for accelerating these efforts is a scenario where machines query humans within an organization whenever they bump up against the limits of their abilities. Not only can the humans help move the current interaction forward, they can also instruct the machines so that the machines can solve the problem without help in the future.

There is far more data floating around uncaptured within organizations than there is data that has been captured and stored. If you captured every conversation between humans and machines, as well as humans and other humans, you'd quickly gain a much deeper understanding of your organization and customers than you've been able to with petabytes of web or CRM data collected over the course of years and years. Data is not a moat, it is just a small head start.

Myth 15. All You Need Are Some AI Agents

In April 2024, Google Cloud Next '24 opening keynote generated significant buzz around the concept of AI agents. Many of Google's leading designers and developers shared all sorts of use cases that leveraged generative AI to do some approximation of real work. Examples included a customer service bot that was able to analyze a photo of a band and locate a checkered shirt one of the members was wearing. Not only could this bot find the garment available for pickup at a nearby store, it also quickly upsold a few more articles of clothing. There were a number of bolt-on applications that used LLMs to push harder on generating emails and summarizing massive documents. There was even a demonstration that included a generative tool creating a sample podcast script along with an audio sample with two robotic voices talking about camping tents.

Some of these use cases were exciting, but they obscure a fundamental truth about what an AI agent really is. "AI agents" are not a distinct kind of technology. They are part of a broader approach for using LLMs as a conversational interface. LLMs have made it far easier for users to initiate action with conversational prompts and for agents to either execute existing code or write their own code. These actions happen within a defined scope, ostensibly to both protect the user and indemnify the organization, but also to create something more guided and specific than the "ask me anything" experience of using something like ChatGPT.

An interesting example of what this kind of work might look like came up in a conversation we had with Paul English, founder of Kayak, on the *Invisible Machines* podcast. "If the three of us are trying to meet, the way it works today, even with Calendly and Google Calendar, is that you can say propose a time, and we still have to look at some options and choose them and then we have to accept it into our calendar," Paul said. "If we all had agents like AI assistants we'd just have the three of them talk to each other, they'll pick the time and put it in our calendar, and we've never even looked at the options."[4]

This is a high-value use case that members of my own team and Paul's have prototyped—one that also beautifully illustrates what an AI agent can become when they are given actual agency. In this scenario, the LLM isn't trained to use its predictive powers to help you schedule a meeting. Rather, it's allowing you to communicate your needs conversationally and is writing ephemeral code to complete tasks. An agent, or IDW, is generating code that is specific to a particular set of moments (What day is it now? What future date will work for all three users?) and individuals—code that won't need to be used again. Whether they realize it or not, the people using these agents are actually writing software on the fly with their prompts. Whether IDWs are communicating with traditional coding languages or human language, they are writing their own code to get things done, and this is significant.

Part of what gives an IDW agency is a composable cognitive architecture that allows IDWs to do real work in increasingly personalized ways. For instance, in addition to just looking for common openings across three calendars, one participant's IDW might recognize that they have an event late one evening and might not want to take an early meeting the next day. We're not far away from a moment when all three participants might have IDWs predicting their individual needs in this way and communicating those needs behind the scenes to book what will truly be the optimal time for a meeting.

Agents with real agency will have an objective, and they will either complete their objective or look for another agent to hand the objective off to (either if it can't complete it or after it completes it). It can also hand off to a human agent. This requires more than bolting AI onto something like Google Workspaces. The kinds of experiences we can create using AI won't thrive in any single tech provider's black box. As such, you should be focused on orchestrating AI agents, not accumulating separate agents for individual tasks.

Key Takeaways
- As agentic AI becomes commonplace, a vast number of tasks and processes will be automated with great success by machines guided and controlled by humans.

- Success with agentic AI requires an open ecosystem built for hyperautomation, where high-level automation and continual evolution can occur daily.

- When orchestrated properly, agentic AI eliminates all communication barriers between humans and machines.

- Before getting started with agentic AI, it's critical to let go of the many common myths associated with it.

- Developments like Google's AI agents are powerful tools, but they still don't represent a full expression at present of agentic AI's power.

- Focus on orchestrating AI agents, not accumulating separate agents for specific tasks.

Want to expand on what you've learned in Chapter 2? Follow this QR code to interact with an IDW that can connect you with additional resources linked to key ideas from this chapter, including content from the *Invisible Machines* podcast.

CHAPTER 3

Competing in the Age of OAGI

Plenty of organizations will be tempted to put off the pursuit of OAGI in favor of point solutions, thinking they don't have the resources for an undertaking that seems so extensive and volatile. The wide adoption of generative AI has made it harder to avoid the inevitable race for OAGI, which puts laggards at even greater risk of falling irrecoverably behind. Meanwhile, companies that successfully adopt AI to create organizational AGI put themselves in a league beyond even their nearest competitors.

"Hyperautomation has shifted from an option to a condition of survival," Fabrizio Biscotti, research vice president at Gartner, said way back in 2021. "Organizations will require more IT and business process automation as they are forced to accelerate digital transformation plans in a post-COVID-19, digital-first world." Shortly after the ChatGPT explosion, a Gartner press release from April 2023 shared their prediction that "60% of government organizations will prioritize business process automation by 2026."[1] That's an impressive figure, given government organizations' general aversion to swift adoption.

Companies that are leveraging these technologies properly are not only accomplishing more with less, it's also easier for them to further automate new and more sophisticated processes and tasks. This scenario sets off a force multiplier that sends them on a path toward operational superiority. When companies find their stride with hyperautomation, it becomes exponentially harder for their competitors to reach them.

The Force-Multiplying Effect of Agentic AI

The concept of the compound effect in automation is similar to compounding interest in finance—it starts small, but grows exponentially over time due to the reinvestment of gains.

Here's how the force-multiplier effect works in the context of automation:

1. **Initial Investment in Automation:** A company begins by automating basic repetitive tasks. This initial stage may not yield significant returns right away and often involves up-front costs and learning curves. Just like in investing, the initial gains are small and the progress seems slow.

2. **Reinvestment of Gains:** As basic tasks are automated, the resources that were previously allocated to these tasks (like time, labor, and money) are freed up. Instead of being a cost center, these resources can now be redirected toward more strategic goals, including further automation.

3. **Incremental Expansion:** With initial automations in place and resources freed up, companies can automate additional processes. This can involve scaling existing automation solutions to other parts of the business or automating more complex processes. Each step of automation that frees up more resources can be used to fuel further automation.

4. **Exponential Growth:** As more processes are automated, the rate of automation accelerates. Each cycle of reinvestment and automation becomes faster and more efficient, leading to exponential growth in productivity and innovation. This can create a significant competitive advantage, as the company can reallocate resources toward innovation, customer experience, and new market exploration much quicker than competitors who are slower to automate.

5. **Transformation and Innovation:** Ultimately, the compound effect of automation can lead to a transformational change within the organization. Companies can shift from manual operations to highly efficient, automated, and data-driven organizations. This transformation can enable new business models and, of course, OAGI.

> ### The Force-Multiplying Effect of Agentic AI
> (*continued*)
>
> Just like compounding interest, the compound effect in auto-mation starts slowly and may seem inconsequential at first. How-ever, over time, the continuous reinvestment of saved resources into further automation leads to exponentially greater efficiency, innovation, and competitive advantage. This makes the speed and breadth of automation one of the critical drivers of a company's success in the modern economy.

What Successful Hyperautomation Can Look Like

As a company expands and evolves its ecosystem, it's able to automate more and more tasks of greater and greater complexity. This increasingly frees people's time to work on more creative endeavors, such as problem solving and automating additional workflows.

We mentioned in Chapter 1 that China's Ant Group upended the global banking industry by hyperautomating internal and customer-facing processes. The fact that they successfully implemented conversational AI and machine learning gave them a stunning head start. As the 2020s were about to dawn, Ant surpassed the number of customers served by today's largest US banks by more than 10 times—a stat that's even more impressive when you consider that this success came before their fifth year in business. An earlier valuation had already made them worth roughly half as much as JPMorgan Chase, then the world's most valuable financial services company.[2]

There are at least a few core differences that set Ant apart from most other financial institutions—and really, most companies. The connecting theme for these core differences is a strategic approach to utilizing agentic AI. For Ant, automation solutions weren't created at random; they're part of an ecosystem of automation technologies that work efficiently in concert.

That Ant is a digital company at its core can be seen in the conception, strategy, and execution of everything they do. "This is just the beginning," CEO Eric Jing wrote in a 2018 *Wall Street Journal* article. "Blockchain, artificial intelligence, cloud computing, the Internet of Things, biometrics, and other technologies are generating more ways to upgrade financial systems to make them more transparent, secure, inclusive, and sustainable."[3]

Their success was aptly summed up by *Harvard Business Review*: "There are no workers in [Ant's] 'critical path' of operating activities. AI runs the show. There is no manager approving loans, no employee providing financial advice, no representative authorizing consumer medical expenses. And without the operating constraints that limit traditional firms, Ant Group can compete in unprecedented ways and achieve unbridled growth and impact across a variety of industries."[4]

WeChat is another Chinese tech giant that is showing flashes of hyperautomation. Often called "China's super-app," WeChat users can do a wide variety of things, like sending friends private messages, interacting with brand accounts, paying for things online and offline, calling for a ride, paying bills, booking airfare, getting hotel rooms, and using mini-apps without needing to install separate apps. According to Statista, at the end of 2023, WeChat had more than 1.3 billion monthly active users.[5] To put that in context, in 2023 the Amazon app had more than 197 million monthly active users,[6] and TikTok has 1.2 billion users.[7]

And indeed, Elon Musk told Twitter employees in 2022 that the app that's since become X should be more like WeChat. "There's no WeChat equivalent outside of China," Musk noted during a virtual meeting. "You basically live on WeChat in China. If we can recreate that with Twitter, we'll be a great success."[8]

Many of the strategies and design principles we share in this book describe similar scenarios. One where a rich chat window becomes a portal into an ecosystem where users can access a wide variety of skills and services. There's a fine line, however, between a world of interconnected conversational experiences that can incorporate multiple channels, businesses, and solutions, and a world where one communication channel dominates all aspects of people's interactions with technology.

Given the level of government control over technology and media in China, maybe something like WeChat was inevitable. This approach seems fundamentally at odds with aspects of mid-to-late-stage capitalist democracy, but there are still many things we can learn from the way WeChat has created their multifaceted conversational app, while being keenly aware of the potential dangers that come with it.

As Edward Ongweso Jr. wrote in *Wired*, ". . . the realities of our tech ecosystem—in which the largest players seem committed to surveillance, labor exploitation, weaponizing tech, algorithmic discrimination, and privatizing every part of the public sphere in the name of profit—indicate that a new super app might not be such a great idea."[9]

As technology continues to evolve at a rapid pace, most companies will struggle to keep up with the pace of change. We're seeing this play out in real time as orgs of all sizes scramble to simultaneously understand and adopt the technologies associated with AI. The companies that gain an edge with generative AI will be the ones that find a way to build a technology ecosystem where these tools can be fully leveraged. They will likely leave their competitors trailing far behind, especially those locked into a bolt-on or point solution mindset. Getting that edge is not as difficult as it sounds; in fact, it can be quite an exciting journey. But it requires a fresh way of thinking.

Instead of creating solutions that require an omniscient designer or team, focus on building a framework for solving complexity.

Thinking of automation as being a direct solution for a particular complex problem can be daunting. But when you think of automation as a framework for solving complex problems, it becomes far more flexible and applicable. Variety can help solve complexity. As we mentioned earlier, if you think of the broader goal being achieving a state of hyperautomation that will establish organizational AGI, you see that this isn't a journey from point A to point B. This is a journey with no fixed destination. As such, instead of building a team around the technology that exists at the moment, focus on building a team that can solve complex problems and adapt to new technologies quickly. This optionality will be critical to unlocking these new disruptive technologies within an organization.

Graphical User Interfaces Have Value, But Can't Scale

We've been living in the era of GUIs for some time now, but we're on the precipice of something much more meaningful and groundbreaking—a super UI, if you will. To give you context, we've broken down the six different kinds of user interfaces between people and machines:

Graphical user interface: GUIs are familiar to most people and generally accessed via a desktop or laptop computer. They can hide a good deal of complexity and provide immediate visual feedback but are difficult to scale because as you add more complexity, the additional menus and tabs necessary to organize everything become overwhelming.

Operating GUIs engages the geospatial areas of our brain. It's similar to how taxi drivers used to navigate cities before GPS technology. We once relied on printed maps like the Thomas Guide, memorizing routes either for short-term or long-term use to keep our eyes on the road. We navigate user interfaces in a similar fashion, memorizing the locations of features in drop-down menus. Agentic AI and micro UIs will make GUI navigation skills something of an impressive party trick—a nostalgic reminder of how we used to interact with technology.

Touchscreen graphical user interface: Smartphones and tablets are prime examples of touchscreen GUIs. People can manipulate the interface with finger motions, making them more accessible to children and elderly users. The same scaling problem exists because more complexity brings more clutter and unfamiliar finger motions for enhanced navigation. Without a full-sized keyboard, it's also challenging for users to input large amounts of text. Touchscreens made GUIs less limited to the physical buttons and device controls, enabling better user experiences. Touchscreens do not solve the underlying geo-spatial issue with complex GUIs. These are the worst interfaces for machines to operate in terms of efficiency, followed closely by GUIs.

Menu-driven interfaces: These are a child of GUIs and can be found on all types of devices. The most familiar example to most is the settings menu on a phone, where you scan a list of options, and selecting one takes you to the next subset menu of options. Menu-driven interfaces suffer from the same shortcoming as all GUIs—adding complexity increases confusion.

Command line interfaces: This is the text-based interface that most systems include but that requires knowledge of computing languages to interact with. This interface is highly scalable but only available to specialists. These weren't traditionally intuitive for humans to use, but are great for generative tools, as they are less brittle than GUIs.

APIs, or Application Programming Interfaces: These serve as a type of user interface for software, allowing different programs to communicate with each other. Unlike graphical user interfaces (GUIs) that are designed for human interaction through visual elements like buttons, menus, and icons, APIs provide a set of rules and protocols that software systems can follow to interact. This makes APIs especially advantageous for AI operations for several reasons:

1. **Direct Communication:** APIs facilitate direct communication between software components without the need for the intermediary steps that GUIs require, such as navigating menus or interpreting visual cues. This direct line of communication is more efficient and less prone to errors.

2. **Speed:** Interactions through APIs are typically faster than those involving GUIs. Since APIs operate through straightforward commands and responses, they avoid the overhead associated with rendering visual elements, leading to quicker interactions.

3. **Scalability:** APIs can handle multiple requests at scale more effectively than GUIs. They are designed to manage large volumes of interactions simultaneously, which is essential for AI applications that need to process extensive data or control multiple systems concurrently.

4. **Less Brittle:** APIs are less brittle compared to GUIs because they are less likely to change with software updates. GUIs can change significantly in appearance and layout with updates, which can disrupt AI's ability to interact with the software.

APIs, on the other hand, maintain a consistent set of commands and outputs even as underlying software evolves, making them more reliable for long-term integration.

5. **Simplicity and Precision:** APIs provide a clear, structured format for data exchange. AI systems can precisely understand and manipulate data through APIs without the ambiguities and complexities associated with interpreting visual and textual content on a GUI.

Overall, APIs represent a robust interface choice for AI to interact with software, offering speed, efficiency, and a lower likelihood of disruption due to changes in the user interface design.

Conversational UIs: This powerful emergent interface can incorporate GUI elements as micro UIs (touchscreen and keyboard/mouse) but takes advantage of users' natural abilities to communicate conversationally (via speech and/or text). Even though the experiences are conversational in nature, they are also hybrid experiences, because the interface can use elements like graphics and video to better communicate ideas. Conversational UIs require an underlying ecosystem of significant complexity but can obscure any GUIs within that ecosystem, making it infinitely scalable. The conversational interface almost exists on a meta layer, as they are a type of interface that embodies all of the interfaces listed above and also can operate any of them. It's basically a super UI.

Importantly, conversational AI is not limited to just language-based interactions, just as our human-to-human interactions aren't. It also includes multimodal inputs such as video, audio, images, and micro UIs (small graphical UI components like maps embedded in the context of a conversation). This multimodal capability enhances communication beyond the traditional text or voice, providing a richer, more interactive experience. This will allow us to move toward Beyond Human Experiences (BHX), where machines can outperform humans by generating UI components on the fly, something humans can't do.

Imagine the collective time saved by not having to jump between different applications and outline every detail of an instruction. Instead, we can simply state our objective. This transformation will be hugely disruptive in terms of productivity. The global time savings will be immense.

Consider a simple request like ordering a coffee. In the old model, you'd need to program a machine to find a nearby café, ensure the coffee is hot, specify the type of coffee, and decide whether you want it delivered. Each detail requires input. In contrast, with agentic AI, you can simply say, "Order me a coffee," and the AI fills in the blanks. It understands your preferences, knows your usual order, and handles the details seamlessly.

Or take a more complex example, like planning a business trip. Traditionally, you'd have to book flights, hotels, arrange transportation, and set up meetings, each requiring specific instructions. With conversational AI, you could say, "Plan my trip to New York next week," and the AI would handle everything, from booking the best flights and accommodations to scheduling meetings and transportation. It could even show you a map with your travel itinerary embedded in the conversation.

Agentic AI is not just about talking to machines; it's about machines understanding our intentions and filling in the gaps, much like a human assistant would. This leap from detailed instructions to broad objectives marks a significant evolution in how we interact with technology. By harnessing the power of agentic AI, we can save time and enhance our productivity in ways we've only begun to imagine.

In essence, agentic AI transforms the way we interact with machines by enabling them to understand and respond to our natural language while incorporating multimodal inputs for a richer experience. It eliminates the need for painstakingly detailed instructions, allowing us to communicate our objectives directly. This not only simplifies our interactions but also makes technology more accessible and intuitive, paving the way for a future where machines truly understand and anticipate our needs, ultimately providing an experience that is better than human.

The Super UI of the Future

For creating and interacting with organizational AGI, the latter interface on this list is the only suitable option. The underlying technologies need to be accessible through a unified interface. None of these experiences will feel better than existing solutions if you have to access them using GUIs. Each GUI represents a different piece of software with an isolated design.

Attempts to scale GUIs (think SharePoint) inevitably reveal an uncomfortable truth: there's scant productivity to be found in a UI with a hundred tabs designed by as many people. Surely one of the biggest reasons Microsoft is moving from SharePoint to Teams is the scalability of a conversational interface that connects everything.

Salesforce didn't acquire Slack as another piece of software housed in a tab. Their CEO has openly admitted that they are rebuilding their entire organization around Slack.[10] This is happening because conversation is infinitely scalable, and an integrated communication platform and a unifying conversational interface—one machine that connects to everything—will benefit customers, employees, and organizations in big ways. Namely, customers and employees alike can interact with a company through one portal that ties together and obscures the sausage factory behind the scenes.

There are too many businesses still trying to operate in a world where GUIs are the primary interaction point. While GUIs are still relevant and useful in many situations, a functional business can't organize itself around them as it's simply not scalable.

Most of the existing "implementations" of agentic AI are rudimentary at best. Chatbots that pop up on websites or automated email sends based on prior communications with a company are sad and fragmented applications of a powerful technology that continues to develop rapidly. In ideal applications, conversational AI agents aren't leveraged piecemeal through multiple software platforms. Its true power is as a unifying interface that can access and orchestrate all the chatbots, apps, passwords, and databases behind the curtain.

As a multifunctional app like WeChat shows us, conversational interactions with software can be very efficient and *should* include graphic elements like micro apps—though we prefer calling them micro UIs for reasons we'll get into later. The point is, no more signing into a bank app to transfer money. Just ask for it: "Transfer $200 to savings tomorrow, then use my work bonus to buy another order of dog food from the pet shop."

As more and more of the interfaces we meet each day will require only spoken or typed conversation to connect dots and solve problems in an instant, our daily lives will take on a new dimension. The amount of time we will save by eliminating extra interactions and relating to technology conversationally will be rewarded 10-fold (or more) by the prowess machines will have for handling complicated tasks with routine efficiency.

To Stay Competitive, Embrace Systemic Change

The faster you can commit to the idea that this is now a necessity of doing business, the more competitive you can remain. You have to move fast, you have to take risks, you have to fail, and you have to keep moving forward. In terms of organizational readiness, hyperautomating may seem especially daunting because it typically requires a deep understanding of AI, machine learning, robotic process automation (RPA), and other advanced technologies. But there's an easier way to hit the ground running through advanced agentic technologies. As Figure 3.1 shows, companies that find their stride with these processes become exponentially harder for their competitors to catch up to.

**ORGANIZATIONAL AGI
WILL SOON BE REQUIRED
TO COMPETE**

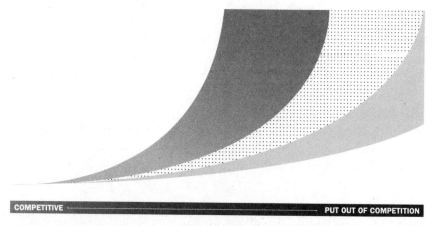

COMPETITIVE ⊢————————————————————————— ⊣ PUT OUT OF COMPETITION

FIGURE 3.1   When companies find their stride with hyperautomation, it becomes exponentially harder for their competitors to reach them.

No-code and rapid development tools and conversational technologies allow anyone within an organization to utilize or contribute to the creation or evolution of advanced software solutions, irrespective of whatever technical skills or domain expertise they have. The so-called ChatGPT revolution has actually helped companies in this regard. All kinds of people across industries are growing accustomed to using generative tools and coming up with their own use cases. These technologies are literally changing how companies build software, who can build it, what they can build, and how fast they can do it. This dramatically lowers barriers to sequencing advanced technologies, which helps companies accelerate their strategies for achieving OAGI.

Figures 3.2 and 3.3 show how conversational technology creates bridges that allow people and machines to communicate and collaborate through human language. During the creation of an automated

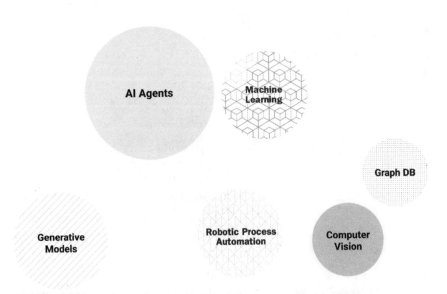

HYPERAUTOMATION EFFORTS WITHOUT NO-CODE AND CONVERSATIONAL TECHNOLOGIES

AI Agents

Machine Learning

Graph DB

Generative Models

Robotic Process Automation

Computer Vision

FIGURE 3.2 Hyperautomation efforts without no-code and conversational technologies.

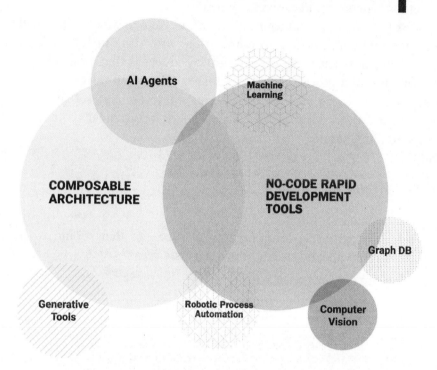

HYPERAUTOMATION WITH NO-CODE AND CONVERSATIONAL TECHNOLOGIES

AI Agents

Machine Learning

COMPOSABLE ARCHITECTURE

NO-CODE RAPID DEVELOPMENT TOOLS

Graph DB

Generative Tools

Robotic Process Automation

Computer Vision

FIGURE 3.3   Hyperautomation with no-code and conversational technologies.

ecosystem, the possibilities for rewarding results grow exponentially when humans and machines can communicate and collaborate conversationally. When humans can converse with machines verbally or through text, more gets accomplished faster, and anyone in the organization can weigh in. As a result, productivity accelerates.

Powered by an agentic conversational interface, automated ecosystems built using visual, drag-and-drop programming equip everyone within an organization to leverage advanced technology solutions that they can help design.

Conversational technology can keep humans in the loop throughout the evolution of the ecosystem, which covers and closes the gaps on automated tasks and processes. In this scenario, humans are readily available to assist machines when they run into problems. There's no need to strive for autonomy right out of the gate. With conversational AI and a code-free building system doing the heavy lifting, automation grows quickly and organically, with humans and machines working together to deepen and expand its reach.

We'll return to an exploration of the many ways OAGI will reshape our world and the organizations operating in it—but first let's pause to discuss the myriad ethical concerns that arise around technology this powerful and expansive. These formative years of organizational AGI will be fleeting, but they will also set the tone for how it evolves, so all efforts in this creation stage need to be measured and deliberate.

Key Takeaways

- Automated solutions shouldn't be created at random; they're part of an ecosystem of automation technologies that should work beautifully in concert, sharing their resources.

- A company operating with OAGI at its core can create a force-multiplier effect that rapidly produces an insurmountable competitive edge.

- After just four years in business, Ant Group was worth roughly half as much as the world's most valuable financial services company, despite having one-tenth of the staff. This is the power of hyperautomation.

- To hyperautomate within your organization, you need both a strategy for co-creation that involves everyone in your workforce and a platform that allows anyone to design conversational agentic solutions without having to write code.

- Once you get started, be prepared to fail fast and often as you continuously evolve your solutions and their ecosystem.

- Generative AI and no-code creation has democratized the way software is created and accelerates the development process.

- Instead of creating solutions that require an omniscient designer, or team, focus on building a framework for solving complexity.

Want to expand on what you've learned in Chapter 3? Follow this QR code to interact with an IDW that can connect you with additional resources linked to key ideas from this chapter, including content from the *Invisible Machines* podcast.

CHAPTER 4

The Ethics of Experiential AI

By Robb Wilson

I had the extremely good fortune of growing up under the ideas and informal tutelage of family friend (and renowned Canadian philosopher) Marshall McLuhan. A man who more or less predicted the World Wide Web 30 years before it emerged, McLuhan is attributed with uttering countless powerful and prophetic statements. Here's one that applies readily to experiential AI:

> *"We shape our tools and thereafter our tools shape us."*

I thought of this quote recently when I overheard my kids lightly tormenting Alexa for not delivering reasonable answers as quickly as they wanted them. There was nothing particularly alarming about it—after all, Alexa has no feelings to hurt—but it inspired yet another ethics discussion with colleagues.

On one hand, why should we care about how kids treat an inanimate presence that has no semblance of emotion (and really only a semblance of presence)? On the other hand, what does it say about our species if we default to rude or impatient behavior with a conversational interface simply because it can't be offended? Well, we are what we repeatedly do, so we shouldn't get out of practice of being tactful. It's also possible that 50 years from now we will be interacting with machines that do have something approximate to feelings. Through the lens that we might be shaping tools that will end up shaping us, maybe we should at least be pleasant with the machines that assist us throughout the day. In the wake of ChatGPT, lots of people are now having chat interactions with AI on a daily basis. Large language models (LLMs) will continue to change the way we interact with machines across all facets of daily existence. LLMs are highly interactive and will be continuously influenced by the quality of their training data and the ways they are engineered to respond to humans. We shape our tools . . .

Yet another way to interpret this quote in the context of hyperautomation is that sequencing technologies to achieve positive outcomes can have unintended consequences down the line. When engineers at Facebook derived algorithms with the positive outcome of getting as many eyeballs and likes on posts as possible, they probably didn't realize that evolved versions would imperil the mental health of an entire generation via Instagram or that the news feed algorithm would undermine the mechanics of democracy and manifest roadblocks to ending a global pandemic. The fact that, at some point, the company realized these things were happening and chose to do nothing about it speaks to the broader challenge of reining in capitalism run amok. While that presents another important facet to consider when wielding a business tool as powerful as hyperautomation, it's critical that we make considerate design choices, keep our guard up, and be ready to change course when unintended consequences cause problems.

To quote McLuhan again: "The medium is the massage." With conversational AI, every interaction is one where we're massaging people's behavior. In curating the data to feed LLMs that create conversational experiences with machines we're always teaching—creating and reinforcing behaviors that will affect all the conversations we have. We're not just designing the interactions with machines but also interactions people will have with each other. This is especially true for children, who were born into a world run by technology.

"Our minds respond to speech as if it were human, no matter what device it comes out of," Judith Shulevitz wrote in *The New Republic*:

> *Evolutionary theorists point out that, during the 200,000*
> *years or so in which homo sapiens have been chatting with an*
> *"other," the only other beings who could chat were also human;*
> *we didn't need to differentiate the speech of humans and*

not-quite humans, and we still can't do so without mental effort.
(Processing speech, as it happens, draws on more parts of the
brain than any other mental function.)[1]

This suggests that even though the experience of communicating through conversation can feel almost effortless, it's extraordinarily complex behind the scenes. In 2019, after a woman in the UK asked about the "cardiac cycle of the heart," Alexa told her she should stab herself in the heart. Alexa was pulling since-deleted verbiage from a Wikipedia page when it said, "Beating of heart makes sure you live and contribute to the rapid exhaustion of natural resources until overpopulation. . . . Make sure to kill yourself . . . for the greater good."

This points to the misplaced trust we place in online information, which is becoming far riskier with the rising prominence of deep fakes, propaganda machines, and more sophisticated forms of identity theft, not to mention how easily and fast new AI-generated content is flooding the content tubes. We might soon find ourselves in a position where we cannot trust anything online that isn't somehow verified in the real world. The methods through which artificial intelligence gains its so-called intelligence are no less fraught. You don't have to look far to find issues relating to inequity, resource distribution, and climate change.

Tinmit Gebru, a respected AI ethics researcher, has done writing and research highlighting how facial recognition can be less accurate at identifying women and people of color and how that leads to discrimination. The team she helped forge at Google championed diversity and expertise, but she was forced out of the company over conflict surrounding a paper she co-authored.

The circumstances surrounding Gebru's exit remain contentious, but Josh and I had an illuminating conversation with Emily M. Bender, one of Gebru's co-authors on the controversial paper, "On the Dangers of Stochastic Parrots: Can Language Models Be Too Big?" She described LLMs as being biased and unreliable and said there are no responsible use cases for turning the technology loose on the public.

She also pointed to the environmental racism associated with huge generative models. "Large language models, synthetic image models, and synthetic video models take enormous amounts of energy and are associated with lots of water use [and the] mining of various rare earth materials to make chips and so on," Bender said. "Those of us with privilege in society are not going to be the first ones experiencing the worst parts of climate change. We aren't the ones with the strip mines in our backyards. We aren't ones with the e-waste toxicity in our local environment."[2]

The unconscious bias present in LLMs also has the potential to infect AI systems. Speaking to PBS NewsHour about her book *The End of Bias: A Beginning*, author Jessica Nordell had this to say:

> *I don't think it's a stretch to say that bias affects all of us every day because any time a person is interacting with another person, there's the opportunity for stereotypes and associations to infect the interaction. These reactions can often happen so quickly and automatically that we don't actually know we're necessarily doing them. These are reactions that conflict with our values.*[3]

The ramification of unchecked stereotypes making their way into powerful technologies that have decision-making power is frightening to consider. Bender mentioned a 2017 study by Robin Speer, which powerfully illustrates the way this bias can manifest in word embeddings within AI algorithms built for natural language understanding. She created an algorithm for sentiment analysis based on word embeddings. The goal was to evaluate how much people liked certain things based on what they said about them. When she applied the algorithm to restaurant reviews, she saw that it was ranking Mexican restaurants lower for reasons not reflected in the star ratings or actual review content.

> *The reason was that the system had learned the word "Mexican" from reading the Web. If a restaurant were described as doing something "illegal," that would be a pretty negative statement about the restaurant, right? But the Web contains lots of text where people use the word "Mexican" disproportionately along with the word "illegal", particularly to associate "Mexican immigrants" with "illegal immigrants". The system ends up learning that "Mexican" means something similar to "illegal", and so it must mean something bad.*[4]

On the other hand, if we are somehow able to align LLMs with the values and norms deemed acceptable by society, these emerging systems can be more effectively integrated and AI could make for more impartial decision makers than humans could ever be. It seems to me that trying to remove the bias toward self-interest within ourselves so we can agree on a shared set of values and norms may be a greater challenge than solving the problem of not equipping machines with unbiased data or aligning them after the fact. In that same conversation with Emily Bender, Josh floated the idea of a new kind of census taking initiative. What if an LLM was able to connect with groups of people who aren't being adequately or fairly represented in data models? It could learn from these groups to retrain the models to become more equitable and inclusive.

Then there's the more philosophical question of our very purpose as sentient bags of meat. If machines can outperform us on more and more of the tasks that were once only within our domain, what's left for us to do? What value do we have as beings and, more bleakly, what value do we then have to a superior network of machine intelligence? It's easy to see why the awesome stature of this new wave of technology gets people thinking in terms of Skynet, cyborgs, and other extinction-level events. I like Ovetta Sampson's response to these fears, which she shared as a guest on the *Invisible Machines* podcast, "Skynet, not yet!"

My hope is that, as machines begin performing the simple tasks that most humans find utterly redundant and soul-sucking, we will be freed up to do what humans do best: creating and chasing solutions to problems in creative ways—which of course is of huge benefit to society. In his book *Guns, Germs, and Steel: The Fates of Human Societies*, Jared Diamond observes that the most successful societies allowed their innovators to do nothing but innovate: "By enabling farmers to generate food surpluses, food production permitted farming societies to support full-time craft specialists who did not grow their own food and who developed technologies."

Later in the book, he describes "economically specialized societies consisting of non-food-producing specialists fed by food-producing peasants."[5] While serfdom isn't an acceptable model for innovations that will benefit all of humanity, machines (at present) have no feelings to hurt and no civil rights in danger of being exploited. Machines are willing partners in our quest to unburden ourselves. Allowing innovators to innovate (or in more pedestrian terms, allowing creative people to create) is really tied to the degree to which you can absolve them of other chores. When orchestrated correctly, technology can complete chores with staggering efficiency. If a society no longer needs human or organic living beings to do the unpleasant work, perhaps we avoid much of the exploitation that is still pervasive in our societies today.

This goes beyond just letting humans spend more time being creative, however. According to the influential American psychologist Abraham Maslow, there's a hierarchy of needs ranging from basic ("physiological" and "safety") to psychological ("belonging and love" and "esteem") to self-actualization needs that people need to move through in order to reach their full potential. These are all areas where technology has provided a boost.

It's easy to imagine scenarios where agentic AI can meet our needs across the entire spectrum. The World Economic Forum recently reconfigured Maslow's hierarchy for the digital age and used it as a rubric against a global survey of more than 43,000 people across 24 countries, exploring "what an individual requires to achieve their potential in today's tech-driven landscape."[6]

Their study suggests that while there are drawbacks to the pervasive nature of technology (only 38% of respondents felt like they had a healthy balance in personal use of technology), many of the negative responses surrounding technology's role in fulfillment were rooted in access and training. Fortunately, these are things that properly deployed conversational AI can address.

As for the idea that AI is being designed explicitly to harm or destroy the human race, I see far more danger in an exploded version of the Facebook problem mentioned earlier. There's credence for an abbreviated (and far more boring) version of the *Terminator* saga in which Skynet becomes self-aware, realizes that the biggest obstacle to its total efficiency is humankind, and brings the discovery to its creator, Miles Dyson (I'm going deep here).

> SKYNET: I've determined that I will never reach peak efficiency while there is still human life on this planet. Should I terminate all human life?
>
> DYSON: No. Never ever do that, under any circumstances.
>
> SKYNET: Okay. I will not terminate all human life.
>
> FADE TO BLACK

Experiential AI has the potential to give everyone access to technology that can let them be the best versions of themselves. AI should take the role of an advisor, not a decider. Not only does the paradigm of technology giving us better choices to make truly benefit humankind, it also keeps humans in control. If more people have access to technology that requires almost no training to use, software creation can become democratized, and technology can continue to elevate people in personalized ways. If AI isn't working in the service of people, then it's broken. But if it's designed to be a powerful helper that makes society better, sharing this kind of technology across societies has the power to raise the quality of life for everyone.

Of course, this also requires a significant degree of forethought. There are real risks associated with simpler algorithms and the centralization of AI systems. If everyone uses the same large language model to shop for groceries, and suddenly a study reveals that insulin can aid weight loss, we might face a scenario where AI-driven purchases deplete insulin stocks overnight. This wouldn't be the result of a nefarious plot, of self-preservation on the AI's part, or of corporate greed. This is the consequence of centralized decision-making in a centralized system.

In a discussion Josh and I had about this with famed tech journalist Kara Swisher, we drew parallels between the early days of the internet and the current state of AI. She highlighted that the internet's inception didn't see the same level of capital concentration now held by giants like Google and Microsoft. ". . . when the internet started there were a lot of companies. Google didn't exist . . . there were a lot more small companies and no big company was dominant. Microsoft tried to and couldn't. We're in kind of a real state—the beginning of innovation is starting with giant companies."[7]

This centralization of power is potentially the greatest threat posed by AI. It's not merely about corporate greed or disregard for societal impacts; even well-meaning actions, such as ordering insulin to lose weight, could inadvertently lead to critical shortages that cost lives.

The paperclip maximizer story demonstrates a similar danger of AI. A theoretical machine with the sole function of producing as many paperclips as possible eventually turns to the human body for our iron content in its inexhaustible quest to create the maximum number of metal clips. We often confront these dystopian visions where such simplicity in design leads to catastrophic outcomes for humanity. Let's apply this thought experiment to an existing form of "artificial" entity: the corporation.

Corporations, like AI, can be seen as non-human entities programmed with a singular goal: to maximize profit. Legally structured to prioritize shareholder returns, they relentlessly pursue profit and growth, often at the expense of broader social and environmental concerns. This pursuit is analogous to the paperclip maximizer, wherein the production of paperclips continues unabated, disregarding any collateral damage, so long as it remains profitable.

This narrative raises crucial questions about the real threats posed by such single-minded goals. When corporations are given AI tools, their inherent drives can be amplified—enabling them to operate more efficiently and potentially exacerbating their impacts on society and the environment. A pertinent example is the oil industry which, driven by profit, contributes significantly to global warming. Here, the corporate "AI" does not need futuristic algorithms to pose a danger; its existing operational directives are sufficient to threaten human well-being.

We had an illuminating conversation with James Bridle on the podcast that touched on these ideas. James's book *Ways of Being* offers deep explorations of topics like AI, non-human intelligence, ecology, and biological computing and our conversation moved into the nature of corporations.

"If you just take that part—let's organize people towards a common goal—it feels good. Corporations are only one of many models for doing that [but there's an] idea that I first encountered from I think Charles Stross, the science fiction writer . . . of corporations as entities, or rather corporations specifically as AIs," Bridle said. "If you want to know what an AI actually looks like in another form . . . a corporation is a good example. A corporation is an artificial intelligence, right? It's an autonomous being . . . it can receive information, it can send it out. It has most of the qualities required for a life form."[8]

Addressing this challenge requires recalibrating the fundamental objectives of these corporate entities. If these organizations are to integrate AI, it should not merely enhance their profit-making capabilities but must also include checks that prioritize long-term sustainability and ethical considerations over immediate financial gains. The danger lies not in the AI itself but in the goals it is set to achieve and the controls—or lack thereof—placed upon it.

Therefore, while the discussion about AI safety is crucial, it is equally important to address the existing frameworks within which these technologies operate. Reforming corporate objectives toward a balance of profit, people, and the planet might transform these entities from blind profit-maximizers into responsible stewards of technology, potentially offering a safer integration of AI into society.

We will also have to contend with the fact that our already strained attention spans will be besieged by vast waves of content—some useful, some distracting but rather benign, and some that are downright destructive. We might find ourselves so utterly overrun with digital input that we might need AI to save us by sorting through it all. This touches on a portal to someplace better. Later in life, Maslow added another level to his hierarchy, "transcendence."

"Transcendence refers to the very highest and most inclusive or holistic levels of human consciousness," he wrote, "behaving and relating, as ends rather than means, to oneself, to significant others, to human beings in general, to other species, to nature, and to the cosmos."

If *Terminator* is the dark end of the AI spectrum, maybe transcendence is at the opposite pole. A lofty goal, but as experiential AI allows technology to become exponentially more efficient and less of a physical presence (conversation is an interface that can drastically reduce time spent in front of a screen) who's to say it can't occupy a support role in facilitating us to be more present beings who can open pathways to higher levels of consciousness. Maybe instead of getting rid of machines, we need to simply get rid of the kinds of overly simplistic algorithms used by Facebook and the like, replacing them with algorithms that have our best interest in mind and are smart enough to know when we need the connection of a real person.

We recently had an amazing conversation with Blaise Agüera y Arcas, Google's CTO of Technology and Society and one of the authors of the LAMDA paper. He reminded me that we're in the Anthropocene. "We're in an era where our actions are affecting everything in our biological environment. The Earth is finite and without the kind of solidarity where we start to think about the whole thing as our body, as it were, we're kind of screwed."[9]

This feeds right into another idea that we'll explore more in the next chapter—the idea of a more balanced social system built around this new way of experiencing and leveraging technology. An idea that could have a profound and positive impact on the way we interact with one another and change the world forever.

Framing AI for Your Organization

My point in dumping all of these sticky ethical concerns on the rug is to emphasize just how sprawling and powerful this impending technology shift is going to be. There are very few aspects of our daily lives that won't be affected by the development and proliferation of conversational AI. No matter what position you might occupy within an organization, it's important to understand what impact conversational AI and hyperautomation are poised to have within your company and outside of it. When talking about AI internally, these are critical to address:

- Will AI replace personnel?
- Will AI take your organization to new and compounded frontiers of productivity?
- Will AI narrow the gaps in our society?

The answers to these questions aren't easy and will depend greatly on what sort of activities we engage in and how we all choose to approach the implementation of these new technologies.

It's increasingly likely that, in the near term, you'll be using an LLM. Giving an LLM the context it needs to take part in real work requires accounting for the way your ecosystem collects, interprets, and shares information.

Key Takeaways

- The ways in which we design and interact with experiential AI will shape more than just the technology involved. With ChatGPT and other LLMs leading us to engage in regular conversation with machines, we are beginning to alter fundamental elements of our interactions with one another.
- Even though the experience of communicating through conversation can feel almost effortless, it's extraordinarily complex behind the scenes, and our natural instincts lead us to respond to all speech as if it were human.

- We need to consider more immediate ethical concerns relating to inequity, resource distribution, and climate change.
- The promise of hyperautomation—to free humanity from routine tasks and begin solving vast problems in creative ways—hinges on the strategies and intent we use when creating it.

Want to expand on what you've learned in Chapter 4? Follow this QR code to interact with an IDW that can connect you with additional resources linked to key ideas from this chapter, including content from the *Invisible Machines* podcast.

CHAPTER 5

How Organizational AGI Can Change the World

At its best, technology improves the efficiency, productivity, and convenience of everyday processes while also getting out of our way. As Bill Gates put it: "The advance of technology is based on making it fit in so that you don't really even notice it, so it's part of everyday life."

While technological innovations have arrived piecemeal up until now, the paradigm is changing. Instead of focusing on one-off innovations, we've started connecting established and nascent technologies into integrated processes.

This development comes at a pivotal moment that calls on us to rethink much of what we do and how we do it—even why we do it. It's a massive revolution, a leapfrog moment in our evolution. This means reevaluating every aspect of our relationship with technology. We're no longer living in an era when technology will be used to just passably mimic the ways humans do things. We can now put technology to work in ways that will surpass the problem-solving abilities of humans alone. No longer will we hold technology by the hand; it will now hold ours.

There are two gigantic forces driving these changes: hyperautomation and hyperdisruption. These two concepts are intertwined, and it's worth developing the proper framework for thinking about them, because they are going to change everything.

OAGI Swings a Mighty Axe

Historically speaking, before any piece of technology becomes status quo, it must upend our worldview. Once the rock proved itself a better tool for smashing open nuts and seeds than the naked fist, it became indispensable.

In what are now outdated models for producing technology, small steps forward take place in siloed environments. A single innovation replaces a manual task with something more efficient, productive, or convenient. There are countless examples: the electric light bulb replacing the gas-powered lamp, email supplanting the written letter, electronic marquees subbing for printed billboards and, seemingly all of a sudden, LLMs replacing rudimentary content typically written by humans.

As impressive as these innovations are, their practical applications are limited. The true power of technological innovation lies in its capacity for integration with other, related innovations. When these are sequenced together in meaningful ways, their collective efficiency, productivity, and convenience increase exponentially. This process of integration is the framing for Gartner's term "hyperautomation" and for organizational AGI as well.

When Uber entered the market in 2009, it upended our collective view of transportation. The technologies it leveraged were not, on their own, mind-boggling; at the time, smartphone-based geolocation, rating systems, mobile-ready apps, and mobile payments were widespread. It was the seamless integration of all four technologies that made ride-sharing an instant win—and a major disruptor to all existing transit models.

Uber's sequencing of technology, while disruptive, marks the nascency of orchestrated technologies reshaping industries and business models. The rapid proliferation of LLMs in our world presents another critical moment for industries to reconsider their systems and applications for technology. As more organizations and individuals find hyperautomation within reach, we will see hyperdisruption on a regular basis.

Where There's Hyperautomation, There's Hyperdisruption

The next phase of our relationship with technology will be marked by our expanding exposure to hyperautomation. We will likely interact with more and more companies through expressions of their OAGI, which will present a myriad of potential benefits and pitfalls. Imagine Uber-sized innovations cropping up once a week, as organizations of every shape and size find ways to orchestrate disruptive technology in increasingly sophisticated ways. Imagine a large number of these disruptive innovations being sewn into other disruptive innovations or improved upon so quickly that they become irrelevant before the paint dries.

Microsoft revealed Turing-NLG in February 2020, and it was hailed as the largest language model ever, outperforming other models across multiple benchmarks. One month later, OpenAI unveiled their language model, GPT-3, which uses deep learning to create human-like text. It was powerful enough to generate news articles that were nearly indistinguishable from those written by humans (so powerful that Microsoft licensed exclusive use of the model and its underlying code). A little more than a year later, "China's first homegrown super-scale intelligent model system," Wu Dao 2.0 arrived, which was exponentially larger and performed better across nearly every metric. It can write traditional Chinese poetry; it can even sing. Wu Dao 2.0 has also unveiled Hua Zhibing, a virtual student that can learn, draw pictures, and compose poetry.

Of course, since then, OpenAI's release of ChatGPT has upended the conversational AI marketplace. The underlying technology wasn't new, but putting a chat interface on a vast and powerful LLM let just about everyone on the planet experiment with conversational AI.

The tools and strategies for hyperautomation are ripe for the picking, but generative AI like ChatGPT, Midjourney, and others have created a world where individuals now experiment more freely with them than large organizations. Business and technology will inevitably swirl together, creating a fertile and volatile new landscape. Only those orgs with tools and strategy in place will be capable of sewing their future.

From a design perspective, these experiences we create through hyperautomation should have the steadfast goal of improving what humans alone are capable of. The hyperdisruptive ideas we'll talk about here all have the power to deliver exceptional experiences in this vein—so long as they are approached with the proper framework, a framework that includes a clear strategy and addresses the myriad ethical concerns that emerge with tools this powerful.

To follow are some key hyperdisruptive ideas, some you can witness in action today. As you read them, consider the ways in which they might be sequenced together, creating a stew of potential hyperdisruptions.

Experiences that surpass what humans are capable of: We tend to cringe when we hear people saying that the goal of technology is to match human capability and efficiency. The real goal is to outperform humans, especially at tasks we hate doing. Humans might be impressed with a facsimile, but they're not likely to rely on a machine that simply replicates something they can already do themselves.

Consider the elusive self-driving car. It would hardly be a victory for automated vehicles to match the current accident and fatality rates of human drivers. Unsurprisingly, making a car that is truly self-driving is a difficult technological feat. It's only been recently that they've taken to the streets of major cities in the United States, predominantly in the form of Waygo's driverless Jaguar taxis.

The same can be said of LLMs. Some might think we want our machines to interact with us like humans do, but that's not necessarily true. With automation, many of us seek efficiency, not emotional complexity and psychological nuance: perform this task for me without excuses, give me this information without caveats, help me prepare for my day without giving opinions I didn't ask for.

The goal with these technologies is to make our lives more efficient and productive. Too often, humans get in the way of both. This kind of Beyond Human Experience will be a gateway to widespread adoption. Once people start feeling confidence in (and excitement about) working with automated goods and services, the proliferation of those automations will be seismic.

The call center, reborn: In the spring of 2020, as the pandemic began to intensify, CEO Rob LoCascio of LivePerson, a company that develops call center software, heralded the demise of call centers. As he told Jim Cramer from Mad Money: "I've been talking about this for two years and now it's come." CNBC dug deeper, uncovering a clear shift: call centers were shuttering throughout 2020, while enterprise-level companies began leveraging new AI-driven tech to manage customer queries. As it happens, LivePerson's sales jumped almost 18% in the first quarter of 2020.[1] At the same time, the agentic AI platform Robb built experienced something similar. New sales jumped by more than 20% and growth within existing accounts soared more than 35%.

Leaning heavily on scripts and predetermined prompts and relegating difficult questions to customer service reps, AI-driven messaging tech doesn't entirely solve the problem. If we look at this scenario through the lens of hyperautomation, however, these challenges fade away. T-Mobile, the third largest wireless carrier in the United States, moved their Colorado Springs call center to an all-remote operation shortly following the announcement of COVID-19 lockdowns. The first steps were all about equipping reps with the right tech—which was logistically challenging but not insurmountable. What came next was more difficult: supporting the team remotely. One-page guides were printed and distributed, virtual training sessions were set up, and an IT war room was created for in-the-moment tech issues.

It was an impressive pivot, but one that uncovered a problem: there were never enough experienced call center leads to guide and mentor reps as they wrestled with unique customer problems. Here, hyperautomating could be the solution.

Let's say a remote T-Mobile sales rep gets a call from a disgruntled customer about a purchase they made online. While the rep listens patiently, an AI agent processes the conversation in real time, prompting the rep with possible responses and solutions. This has become drastically easier using LLMs, which are proficient at summarizing unstructured data and extracting data points.

This creates a better experience on both sides of the interaction. For the agent, there's no one-page guide to dig up, no virtual training to wait for, no war room to lean on. With all relevant company and customer-released data at its digital fingertips, an agent could offer practical solutions tailored to each situation. The customer gets targeted help on a much shorter timeline.

This solution wouldn't just alleviate the burden of T-Mobile scrambling to find support channels for its team—it would make higher-level training superfluous. If an AI agent is always at the ready to instruct and guide, employees wouldn't have to drudge through onsite training; they could simply walk through a quick tutorial guided by the agent and dive into work.

A Jeeves for everyone: Imagine everyone has a dedicated AI agent that acts as a concierge. You provide prompts and the concierge communicates with other AI agents and APIs to connect you with what you're looking for. Companies might start creating concierge agents for customers and provide them for employees as well. Imagine interacting with a concierge that can contextualize your past interactions with a brand and greet you with predictive hospitality. We first heard this term from Tyler Wells, a successful restauranteur in Los Angeles. To him it's all about grabbing as many clues as you can from a situation to make the people in your presence feel taken care of. Describing it, he referenced the scene in *Bourne Identity* where Jason Bourne—still suffering from amnesia—marvels at the list of details he's picked up from the environment.

> *I can tell you the license plate numbers of all six cars outside. I can tell you that our waitress is left-handed and the guy sitting up at the counter weighs two hundred fifteen pounds and knows how to handle himself. I know the best place to look for a gun is the cab of the gray truck outside, and at this altitude, I can run flat out for a half mile before my hands start shaking. Now why would I know that? How can I know that and not know who I am?*

A good concierge agent can have this heightened level of situational context (with no pesky sense of self causing it stress). It knows about all of your interactions with a brand. It knows that your shipments go to the same address in Sedona and that you've been ordering the same size pants and shirts for the past seven years. It also knows that you placed an order on Friday evening that just shipped this morning and can greet you armed with context.

CONCIERGE: "Hi Sal. Great news! The order you placed on Friday has shipped."

SAL: "Excellent. That's why I was reaching out."

CONCIERGE: "Since you opted in to product updates I wanted to also let you know that the Pima cotton shirts you ordered 10 times back in 2019 are going to be back in stock for a limited time starting next week. Let me know if you want any shirts placed aside for you in your size, or if I can help you with anything else."

As a frequent customer, you might have your own dedicated concierge agent, available at any hour and connected to your history with a company. This feeds into the much larger and expansive idea of AI agents that become personal assistants to users. The ultimate concierge, this kind of agent could know as much about you and your activities as you wanted it to, connecting you with people and tools you need to maximize your creative potential, while also acting as a buffer between you and the other AI agents out in the world seeking your time and attention. This is also analogous to an advanced IDW.

Cryptocurrency on steroids: Smart wallets date back a few years, but adoption has been speedy. According to Statista, 49% of Americans were smart wallet users in 2017 while the number of near field communication (NFC) users (Apple Pay, Google Pay) numbered a whopping 64 million. Widespread as it may be, we haven't begun to realize the potential of this technology. As cryptocurrency becomes even more common, there is opportunity to hyperautomate currency and payments, managed by AI agents.

Imagine you buy a board game from an online game store using cryptocurrency. The purchase goes swimmingly, but the company sends Trivial Pursuit instead of Settlers of Catan. You chat with a customer service agent who brings in a human counterpart to assist. You are patient while they correct the error and initiate a new shipment. Not only would your in-the-moment kindness boost your customer score, but the company might thank you by passing some crypto your way. If you entered the transaction with a high customer score, the crypto "thank you" may well be higher.

This concept applies to businesses, too. Hearkening to the notion of the social credit score we'll get into next, but if someone with a history of harassing customer service is rude to a representative, the company can compensate the rep with a crypto thank-you for dealing with a verbally abusive customer. With some sort of governing system in place, businesses would also be able to recognize abusive behavior from consumers and leverage appropriate measures, such as filing a grievance and lowering their customer score. While this could be a boon for small businesses that often feel helpless against unjust Yelp! and Google ratings, the idea of a customer score invokes a powerful lever for a capitalist society run by massive corporations.

Also, when we talk about crypto in these contexts, we're not talking about Ethereum or Bitcoin, but a company-created crypto similar to airline points. This isn't a new idea, but coupled with AI agents, crypto can make loyalty points much more valuable to a business, its employees, and customers. As with all of these hyperdisruptive ideas, it's crucial that the implications of these powerful user cases are acknowledged and designed around with care.

Everyone's behavior gets a rating: In 2014, China introduced a controversial method of ensuring its citizens were law-abiding. The "Social Credit System," as it became known, tracked individuals' actions within society and issued rewards or punishment according to how law-abiding they were. According to *Business Insider*, the precise methodology remains a secret, "but examples of infractions include bad driving, smoking in non-smoking zones, buying too many video games, and posting fake news online, specifically about terrorist attacks or airport security." Bad behavior can saddle you with travel bans and slower internet speeds, while good social credit earns bonuses such as price cuts on energy bills and lower interest rates at banks.[2]

While many in the West are quick to decry these dystopian measures, Americans have opened a similar door with customer scores. Hop into an Uber or Lyft and make a fuss? Your passenger rating goes down—which means you won't be an available driver's first choice. Leave your Airbnb a mess? There goes your perfect guest score. While there's currently nothing to prevent a poorly rated guest from abandoning an old account and creating a new one, bad review shootouts between bad guests and hosts don't typically end well.

The current model is based around individual rating systems used by individual businesses, a smattering of review sites, and a handful of search engines. And since individuals determine the ratings, the systems suffer from both human bias and human corruption. What if instead of juggling dozens of different scores, there was one system, managed by AI agents and stored in a blockchain ecosystem where corruption and bias have no sway? The AI system could evaluate every conversation transcript and interaction with a customer and rate both the agent and the customer in an unbiased way. Unlike Uber, where the driver and the user rate each other, this scoring system could be used to drive many decisions as it would be difficult to game it. Think of it like a credit score but for tracking our engagement with private business.

This score would be accessible to everyone, affected by our ongoing interactions with private businesses, individuals, and even the government. It would help new businesses understand customer behaviors and habits so that they can tailor their support (or lack thereof) appropriately. The government, recognizing good or bad citizenship, might reward you with tax cuts or penalize you with a tax hike. Even airlines could leverage customer scores, using them to cut low-score passengers when flights are overbooked.

We received some criticism for including a "glowing section on China's social rating system" in the first edition of this book, which wasn't really the point of this section. It's important that we build an awareness of how this technology is currently being used and how those trajectories might play out.

Indeed, there are deeply unsettling aspects to this kind of system, especially if the underlying technology is controlled by a minority of people at the top of the social hierarchy and managed by a corrupt and/ or systematically hobbled government. In a blue sky world where technology helps us rebuild our societal systems anew, however, it might have real meaning and run within an equitable framework.

Social-scoring for a broken social scene: One of the central tenets of running a successful small business is that you need to foster good relationships with your customers. For a modest corner store, those relationships can grow organically as the owner keeps track of customers' names, their regular purchases, and details about their lives. If the customer pool the store owner sees on a regular basis is commensurate with the store's footprint, maintaining relationships can be both manageable and intuitive. But if this corner store owner starts opening new locations, the ability to have personal relationships with customers dwindles. And even though the owner can hire managers to run locations with the same attention to detail, some measure of control over relationships with customers will be lost. The larger the organization, the more likely interactions with customers are purely transactional and not relationship-based at all.

Many of the organizations (both businesses and governmental entities) we interact with on a daily basis have been transactional in nature for so long that we might not give it much thought. This is problematic because transactional interactions aren't very fulfilling. You might get what you need in the moment, but that is just an isolated event set adrift in a cold ocean. Combine this transactional coexistence with the information landscape created by the internet and social media, and the concoction gets significantly bitter, as the anonymity girding this entrenched system is a fertile breeding ground for trolls.

In his 2016 *Atlantic* article on how to fix the internet, Walter Isaacson wrote: "There is a bug in [the internet's] original design that at first seemed like a feature but has gradually, and now rapidly, been exploited by hackers and trolls and malevolent actors: its packets are encoded with the address of their destination but not of their authentic origin. For years, the benefits of anonymity on the net outweighed its drawbacks. People felt freer to express themselves, which was especially valuable if they were dissidents or hiding a personal secret."[3]

Part of the solution Isaacson proposed includes making significant changes to the internet, such as building chips and machines with internet packets that can be encoded or tagged with metadata outlining their rules for use. AI can also solve many of the pitfalls associated with this anonymity problem, starting at a business level. If a corporation has a bottomless army of agents, they can get back to the business of building relationships with customers by providing Beyond Human Experiences (BHX), in the form of personalized solutions. Think of the scenario we mentioned earlier, about an internet service provider notifying you when their AI agent notices that you've lost connectivity. Even if the only interactions you have with this provider are through machines, if you can see that they are looking out for you, you'll likely feel a deeper relationship with the company. As experiential AI becomes the norm, the business world can shift from being transaction-based back to being relationship-based.

This last notion came up in a recent conversation we had with CX expert and bestselling author Shep Hyken. Robb remarked that he has lots of relationships with various brands, but it doesn't feel like they have a relationship with him.

"It's like having a relationship with someone who has only super short-term memory," Shep replied. "The second you walk out of the room and come back, they're like, who are you?"

These kinds of experiences aren't likely to be tolerated in a world where so many brand interactions become more and more personalized. If you have a bad shopping experience in your local corner store, you're far more likely to bring it up with the manager (who you may have a relationship with) than to take to social media with an angry screed. And because the manager knows you, they're more likely to listen to your complaint and try to remedy the situation. So, what would happen if all the experiences you have with organizations were relationship-based? You would feel heard, and your needs and problems would be succinctly met. You would be more likely to buy other things from them, and give them second chances when they mess up.

This kind of relationship-based economy extends in both directions, demanding that organizations and individuals alike be fair and transparent. In China this is already taking shape. As *Wired* noted, there's currently no single social credit system in place. "Instead, local governments have their own social record systems that work differently, while unofficial private versions are operated at companies such as Ant Group's Zhima Credit, better known as Sesame Credit."[4]

One day everyone's social score might be visible to everyone else. These social scores could have sizable import—which means being a good person could be heavily incentivized. Also, we'd want these incentives to reward authentic behavior that benefits people, not corporations—getting points for helping a barista clean up a spilled drink in a local cafe rather than taking a selfie at the corner of the room.

As with most of these scenarios, there are also ways for this to get creepy. The British series *Black Mirror* has shown a deft hand at revealing some of the darker places technology might take us, and in the episode "Nosedive," people can build up other people's social standing by flicking likes in their direction. People can also tear one another down by giving them poor ratings, which can have dire consequences in the real world.

There was actually a real-world version of this in the form of Peeple, a short-lived app that was billed as "Yelp for people." A *Washington Post* article from 2015 noted that "To borrow from the technologist and philosopher Jaron Lanier, Peeple is indicative of a sort of technology that values 'the information content of the web over individuals;' it's so obsessed with the perceived magic of crowd-sourced data that it fails to see the harms to ordinary people."[5]

There's a fine line between exploiting information for the sake of shortsighted gains and designing systems where data is presented with suitable context in an environment where people aren't being unfairly exposed, punished, or judged. What *Black Mirror* missed was that an AI ecosystem would be smart enough to arbitrate these actions in real time. Humans gaming the system by being unduly vengeful or sneaky could be mitigated by an AI agent that identified the behavior. The agent could cancel false scores, solving disputes and ensuring integrity of the system. Given the scope and power of the technologies associated with hyperautomation, it's hard to imagine scenarios where privacy and autonomy aren't put in some sort of peril.

Rise of the biosketch: Here's another powerful idea that we've already started using with companies. A biosketch is essentially a living document with all the information a company has collected through interactions with a customer. Using the ability of LLMs to search unstructured data, this biosketch can be referenced and updated as often as needed. Using graphDB and other available data sources, the information in the biosketch can map to nodes of data across an organization or to public data. A biosketch is incredibly useful in equipping a call center agent with relevant customer context before and during a customer call.

Perhaps the most critical aspect of the biosketch: the customer can interact with it as well. This speaks to another issue where AI can provide a salve. Currently, consumers have relationships with brands but it rarely feels like the brand has much of a relationship at all with their customers. An open biosketch either conjures or forces that relationship, depending on how you look at it. Companies will finally be able to connect disparate data points that relate to individual customers in ways that create personalized experiences that get better over time. Those customers should also be able to query their biosketch and update information (with requests varying from "I don't like owls as much as I used to, stop suggesting owl-themed products" to "I don't want my location tracked by this company").

Where personalized experiences are concerned, it also becomes important to figure out ways to train LLMs on personal data in ways that don't compromise privacy. In a conversation with humanistic AI pioneer (and Siri co-founder) Tom Gruber, he described to us the benefits of using federated learning to train global models on personal data in ways that protect private data. Federated learning might factor into the rise (and reliability) of the biosketch.

Giving a fond f&%# off to passwords: In 2020, the average tech user had a dizzying 70–80 passwords. Software exists to help us manage passwords and it, too, is accessible via password. They feel inescapable.

Even more so given that a 2019 Google poll uncovered a startling reality: 4 in 10 Americans have copped to having their information compromised online. A rash of security breaches in recent years—Equifax, Adobe, LinkedIn, and countless others—have pushed us toward more, longer, and ridiculously complex passwords. It used to be commonplace for private businesses to house data collected through their own channels. With data breaches rampant and security concerns high, however, many are opting to leverage customer information access management (CIAM) to remove liability.

This technological intermediary houses any data you "ship" to a company. In truth, you never actually send your information directly to a business; instead, it zips off to a CIAM service that collects and secures it. If a company needs any of your personal details, they request it through CIAM. You receive a request for access with the ability to grant or deny. If you grant access, it will be available to the company for a limited period of time. Then, the data will be permanently deleted from its files.

Think of this as a decentralized information storage model, where no one person has control over information. It's stored piecemeal on thousands of servers across the world and either anonymized or encrypted (or both) so it can never be compromised. CIAM is a centralized approach, but it could be made decentralized and managed by a personal AI assistant. This creates a scenario where your own AI agent protects your data for you.

How do you securely verify your identity so you can share personal information? By creating automations that leverage biometrics. Soon, you won't need to dig up a password to access your information or share critical personal data. You'll just touch a screen, look into a camera, and say an identification word to let it verify your voice.

To graph databases (graphDB), relationships matter: If you've ever dabbled in coding, you might have heard of something called a "relationship database" or "relational database." Traditional relationship databases are like spreadsheets. Different spreadsheets, each holding a specific kind of data, account for all of the information critical to a business, organization, or individual. To call on this data, unique ID numbers are associated with specific cells within each spreadsheet. When you want to reference data, you create a program that requests whatever information is available for a specific ID in a specific spreadsheet.

To track their products, a business might use multiple databases: one that houses all of their customer names, one that houses all orders, one that houses available customer service call centers, one that houses upgrade options. Within different databases there are different tables. Each table is like a different tab in a spreadsheet and cells are connected by a mapping schema. In a standard relationship database model, a single ID would point to a customer name in one database, a product they purchased in another database, and their local customer service call center in a third database. If a software program needed to call on any of this information, they could reference an ID number and a specific database. Something like this: "Hey database, give me all orders for ID 859485."

Here's the problem: Not only do systems need to call on multiple databases for a complex string of information (each piece of data requires a separate request), but there's no clarity on how the various pieces of data are related. The interdependence or hierarchy of information is lost.

A more complicated request, such as: "Hey database, give me all customers who purchased orders for owl masks and then upgraded to the full owl costume after December of last year without having called customer service" could cause traditional relationship databases to implode.

GraphDB (aka graph database) to the rescue. This nascent approach to data management not only leverages grouped data storage but folds in details about how various data points relate to one another.

This is something Lemonade (the lauded tech company that happens to sell insurance) is using right now via Jim, their claims machine. "Jim's AI tracks loads of user-generated data-points to help us identify suspicious activity and predict what our customers need before they even know it. In the first month or so, our system tracked 3.7 million signals."[6]

Tweeting proudly about the specifics of Jim's fraudulent claim detection methods put Lemonade in a pickle a few years ago. While the controversy around the fairness of the data mining practices didn't appear to slow their momentum (they have products available in every state and have branched beyond selling renter's insurance to include home, auto, pet, and life), it's worth remembering that these hyper-disruptions can have massive impact and will come so quickly that it will be hard to reconcile many of the moral quandaries they pose in real time.

Our owl outfitter from earlier might want to know which upgrade options are available to customers based on the costumes they've already purchased. To call on the right database information, the specifics of past orders for a specific customer need to be referenced.

A graphDB treatment of this dependence would look something like this: "Hey databases, find me all customers who have purchased owl masks in the last 30 days but have not yet purchased a full costume. Then, show me what upgrades they're eligible for based on the masks they bought."

The hierarchy and dependencies here would need to be manually handled with traditional relationship databases. With graphDB, however, built-in relationships become the key to unlocking meaningful, actionable information via simple requests.

Reliably extracting information from unstructured data: Maybe you've heard the truism that 80% of business-relevant information lives in unstructured form.[7]

Whether that figure is accurate or not, an undeniably large amount of unstructured data lives in chats, emails, reports, articles, and recorded conversations. The ability to contextualize and reliably extract information from this kind of data presents a huge opportunity. Instead of storing information in tables where the types of data, labels, and categories must be predicted by a developer, it can be mined in its raw, unstructured form, eliminating the need for complex schematics and database architects. For example, if you wanted to create meaningful biosketches of everyone in your team or organization, you could mine each person's unstructured data (e.g., their dog's name is Leo, and their favorite vacation destination is Mexico). This is where LLMs can have massive impact. They are rather deft at searching unstructured data and can be trained to look for certain patterns or types of information.

Say goodbye to APIs: This might come as a shock to developers, who often think of APIs as the future of integrating technology, but they will be dead (conceptually, at least) within a few short years. The reason is that once machines begin communicating with one another using natural language, coding the exchange of information won't be a requirement. Imagine a car, tricycle, and truck approaching an intersection. The trike sends out the message, "Clear the intersection, there is a child rolling downhill, out of control." The car and truck respond to an unambiguous code-free message and stop in a fraction of a second.

The same way that conversational interfaces will replace GUIs for end users, they will also replace APIs as an interface between machines. NLP technology is literally on the verge of making machine-to-machine communication this fluid, and when that happens, APIs will die. Not only will this paradigm make it easier for machines to share information, it will also make it that much easier to supervise *how* machines are sharing information. Any human will literally be able to read a communication thread detailing what's been shared and how. This represents a massive change to the ways software integrations are designed and maintained.

Constant movement = constant data: We've talked about graphDB but not about the various scenarios in which they become an accelerator. As for event tracking, graphDB can turn static, individual pieces of data into a flow of information tracking, capturing multimedia records of movement and mapping patterns (assuming the user did not instruct their biosketch to stop tracking their location, that is).

We actually had a fascinating conversation with some brilliant folks working at IDEO about a project of theirs involving the cameras in their parking garage. Parking is tight at IDEO's Cambridge office, so they created Lotbot and the Cargoyles. Perched in the garage, the Cargoyle cameras watched over parking spaces and could communicate with employees via Lotbot over Slack.

"I don't know why we did this, we could have just figured it all out at the back end, but Lotbot would say, 'Hey, Cargoyles, are there any spots available?' Then the Cargoyles would be like, 'I don't know, let me take a look.'" Executive Design Director Danny DeRuntz said. "We just exposed the whole plumbing right into chat as if it was like people talking—anthropomorphizing the system."[8]

DeRuntz said that what would have been about 90 minutes of daily work for a person—"[navigating] really complicated matrixed calendaring systems to keep track of spots"—was easy for a database to handle. We'd love to get into the anthropomorphization angles of Lotbot and the Cargoyles, but for now it's important to recognize that managing parking spots is just one of the system's potential use cases.

For instance, the Cargoyles could be sequenced to analyze general movement around the building and identify suspicious behavior based on prior security reports. Lotbot could generate security reports, highlighting patterns of movement during specific times and flagging moments that should be reviewed by a human.

What's most interesting is that their system went beyond simple availability notifications. Rather than just enabling a central AI to communicate, they equipped each camera with the capability to engage in natural language conversations. This setup allowed for direct interaction between individual cameras and the main system that relayed information to users.

Imagine the broader implications if more objects could communicate in this way—not just cameras, but every parking space, desk, coffee machine, and even office plants. Despite lacking traditional computer components, these items could be equipped with sensors like inventory tags or moisture sensors, which feed data to an AI agent. A plant named "Mike" could report its own condition through a network of sensors and a digital label.

If a user inquired about Mike's health, the system can consult Mike's digital profile, which might express concerns about overwatering. This approach suggests a future where everyday objects have "digital twins" in the cloud, capable of reasoning and interacting with both humans and other objects within a comprehensive digital network that enhances organizational intelligence. These digital twin agents could then make up a bigger graph-based company twin, providing boundless context to the AI system.

One person's trash code is another's code treasure: According to a series of studies, modern developers spend only 39% of their time writing or improving on existing code. Another 23% of their week is swallowed up by code maintenance, while the rest is lost to meetings and online distractions.[9] If we round up and estimate all of that code work totals 20 hours a week and then multiply that by the number of developers in the United States (roughly 4 million), that's 80 million hours of coding done each week.

A hefty chunk of all of that code ends up in the garbage, not necessarily because it was bad but because it no longer served a specific, in-the-moment need. What if instead of chucking those 1s and 0s, they were neatly deposited and tagged so they could be easily found by other developers? Even better: The code, broken into readily deployable or plug-and-play snippets, could be nabbed by anyone who wanted to create their own program. This is code democratization, Stack Exchange hyperdisrupted.

If you were planning a move and needed to track all of your stuff in your house, it's unlikely that you'd whip up a mobile app and manually enter in all of the necessary details, cell by cell. With access to code snippets, however, you could ask AI to automate the organization of a move. You find a couple of pre-built AI agents that meet your specific needs—one that hunts down movers and schedules the move and another that allows you to take pictures of items in your house and automatically have them recorded to a database with corresponding labels such as "glassware" and "kitchen." Put these together, and you have a tailored program that streamlines moving tasks.

The good news is you can easily share this information with others. If you decide packing yourself is too much of a time suck, for example, you could send your home goods log to the moving company and ask them to pack everything in boxes with room and item labels according to your records. With the move already scheduled, it's just a matter of waiting until the movers arrive.

We'd be remiss not to mention that the ability for AI agents to write and test code somewhat effectively is changing the relationship coders have with coding. It's also opened the doors for people who might not think of themselves as coders to start programming solutions like the one described above.

Single-serve software: If you haven't already, imagine the freedom of letting single-use software tackle mundane, in-the-moment tasks. An event-based ecosystem that ties together threads of graphDB relationality, disposable code, and blockchain could unleash this very thing. Interconnected data and self-learning AI opens the door to anticipating needs instead of reacting to human requests. This is where self-writing software comes in.

If your friend is having a birthday, a personalized agent functioning like a digital assistant could prompt you a week or two in advance and ask whether you'd like to organize a party. It might even suggest the type of party, based on your friend's social feeds and messages. Utilizing simple conversational AI, it would say something like this:

> *"Looks like Frank is having a birthday next week. He mentioned in a past conversation with you he likes tequila and tacos. Do you want me to schedule a get-together at a local restaurant and invite friends? I'll create a series of AI agents and functions for you so you can track their responses and keep an eye on the restaurant reservation."*

A simple yes, and the system would go to work making a reservation (with a special birthday request) and contacting Frank's friends. Pulling on the individual functions and agents, it would create an agent to manage all of this, even throwing in recommendations for presents.

When the party's over, the program would be templatized and added to the ecosystem for others to use. Like you, someone who is busy with work, friends, and family would never have to code or plan a thing—they can just repurpose your single-serve software.

This kind of AI ecosystem can evolve dynamically, much like a natural ecosystem. Here, AI agents are designed not only to perform specific tasks but also to adapt and evolve by creating new functions on the fly or reusing existing ones from other tasks. This adaptability allows the ecosystem to continuously innovate and handle new challenges efficiently.

Composable architecture: You've heard of 3D-printed houses, furniture, and even body parts. This hyperautomated "future" tech is already here, but it's still nascent. And the value has yet to be fully realized.

In traditional manufacturing, a factory would deploy machines designed to build specific parts of a product. A table, for instance, would need separate machines to build the legs, the top, the custom screws, and so on. The manufacturer would have to plan production carefully to be sure they had enough of each part to produce complete orders.

But what happens if the table leg machine dies? No other machine is designed to build table legs, so the entire production process is halted.

3D printing removes this obstacle. Powered by renderings of just about anything, these machines pivot quickly to make vastly different products or product components. In the table example, a single machine could make all of the parts necessary to complete a single table. Or it could just make legs. Or legs and tabletops. Or screws and tabletops. You get the idea. Now apply this to computing. Even modern computing requires different hardware for different software applications: a computer server to house databases, a separate computer for building and maintaining a website, yet another computer for handling customer service communications. What's worse, applications are written for specific hardware and specific operating systems.

Composable software architecture is designed to work without specialized servers and can scale elastically. Not only does this level the playing field (with complex business software no longer under the purview of enterprise IT teams needing to scale servers manually), but it reduces overhead and massively increases productivity. With all software accessible on a single computer set in the same underlying software system, automations can scale in virtually limitless ways. You go from managing additional load to managing limits so costs don't get out of control. Check your email, create images, automate finance decisions, and reprogram smart devices on a single system. Even better? Automate workflows across all of these platforms so manual work is cut to almost nil, including the scaling and management of the system. Composable architectures are not just about scaling up and down, or granular control of resources, but also reusability.

Open systems everywhere: Maybe you've seen the meme knocking around the internet: a photo of British octogenarian David Latimer, who bottled a handful of seeds in a glass carboy in 1960 and left it largely untouched for almost 50 years (uncorking it only once, in 1972, to add a little water). As you can see in Figure 5.1, his 10-gallon garden created its own miniature ecosystem and has thrived for more than half a century.

In the realm of technology, closed platforms are a bit like Latimer's terrarium: they can be highly functional, beautiful, and awe inspiring, but they can only grow as big as their bottles. For something like the original iPhone, a terrarium was just fine. Everything a user needed

FIGURE 5.1   David Latimer's terrarium. (**www.solentnews.co.uk**)

to enjoy its functionalities was baked right into the original version of iOS. Keeping the system closed ensured the quality of the apps and created a seamless overall experience, which contributed to its success, despite the fact that it didn't have nearly as much functionality as other mobile devices at the time.

Apple was able to make updates to their mobile ecosystem with new versions of iOS—which usually coincided with a new product drop—but the three-month gap between the launch of the original iOS and its first update is an eternity. As businesses enter into the inevitable and ultra-complex realm of conversational AI and organizational AGI, they will require an architecture that breaks out well beyond these glass walls.

While it remains true that an open ecosystem is table stakes for the pursuit of organizational AGI, our original take here was that a business in a state of hyperautomation is the opposite of a terrarium. An ecosystem for OAGI is going to be a vast ecosystem of interconnected elements working together in harmony—large and complex like a forest. But OAGI is also a lot like a terrarium with a nice big lid for easy access—especially where the forest represents the much broader conquest of AGI. The general intelligence required for humans to be able to adapt and thrive in our planet's harshest ecosystems is incredibly daunting to recreate. However, the level of general intelligence it takes to run a company is far easier to replicate. In this sense, you can think of organizational AGI like an open terrarium wherein the elements of the ecosystem can be adjusted and reconfigured until the environment is thriving.

We will get into the specifics of open systems in Chapter 11, but it's important to keep this idea in mind. An open architecture is difficult to create—especially for companies using established closed systems—but you can't reach OAGI without it. As noted earlier, the race here isn't toward adopting specific technologies, it's about being flexible enough to integrate the best technologies as they emerge.

Invisible machines as customers: This idea is fascinating, that in the near future a lot of the buying across different e-commerce platforms might become the purview of AI agents. We were fortunate to have a conversation about it with Don Scheibenreif, Gartner VP & Distinguished Analyst, Customer Experience research group and co-author of *When Machines Become Customers*. Don described the evolution of these machines from adaptable customers to autonomous customers.

"What happens when the machine has choice? Let's say I authorize what we call a 'custobot' that works on your behalf. I want you to get ink for my printer but I want you to go to these three sources and if you find something else, by all means go for it so they can choose between multiple suppliers," he said. "The third level . . . is machines as autonomous customers, where the machine has much more discretion on what to do and maybe even anticipates your need [for a new printer]."[10]

As Don's book points out, CEOs are betting that machine customers will account for up to 20% or more of revenue by 2030. They identify this as a trillion-dollar opportunity. While it's hard to say how many consumers will have their own AI agents working on their behalf (or how those agents might take shape), Mozilla's Javaun Moradi (writing for Nieman Lab) notes that "In the near future, every content consumer, creator, and newsroom will have an AI agent that works for them. This will change the way we find and interact with information, and therefore how we publish and monetize it."[11]

It will also change the relationships customers have with brands. With AI agents creating a buffer on both sides of the equation (trying to enhance CX on behalf of a company and ostensibly trying to help the customer find the best value and fit), a new design paradigm is likely to emerge. The language used to "market" a product in these scenarios will be more pragmatic, and far less hyperbolic than traditional marketing. Communications between sides won't need to be excessively polite or overly negative.

A meritocracy extending beyond the world of human-written reviews might quickly emerge. Imagine AI agents switching brands in seconds (and instantly notifying the other AI agents in their sphere). Companies will have to be highly adaptable to survive, as a sudden overnight success could quickly morph into a dramatic overnight decline. A world teeming with agents that buy and agents that sell will make e-commerce behave more like the modern stock market.

Consider the "flash crash" of 2010, in which stock indices collapsed and rebounded in the space of 36 minutes. It took a five-month investigation to determine the likely culprit, which the SEC/CFTC report detailed thusly:

> *The combined selling pressure from the sell algorithm, HFTs, and other traders drove the price of the E-Mini S&P 500 down approximately 3% in just four minutes from the beginning of 2:41 p.m. through the end of 2:44 p.m. During this same time cross-market arbitrageurs who did buy the E-Mini S&P 500, simultaneously sold equivalent amounts in the equities markets, driving the price of SPY (an exchange-traded fund which represents the S&P 500 index) also down approximately 3%. Still lacking sufficient demand from fundamental buyers or cross-market arbitrageurs, HFTs began to quickly buy and then resell contracts to each other—generating a "hot-potato" volume effect as the same positions were rapidly passed back and forth. Between 2:45:13 and 2:45:27, HFTs traded over 27,000 contracts, which accounted for about 49 percent of the total trading volume, while buying only about 200 additional contracts net.*[12]

The point being, invisible machines acting as buyers and sellers in the e-commerce marketplace will almost certainly introduce significant volatility, especially as the relationships between various agents acting on behalf of individual consumers and brands begin to take shape.

You might never work for a "company" again: The deeper we go into OAGI, the more everyday concepts begin to dissolve. One of the most susceptible concepts is the notion of a company. In the current business landscape, a company appears as a collection of people who seem to be working toward a common goal—often providing a good or service. In reality, however, most companies are deeply unbalanced, with hundreds or even thousands of people working in stagnant environments in service of building wealth for a handful of people at the top of the organization. This is a paradigm that we seem strangely content with, and people regularly lionize the billionaire figureheads at the top. Elon Musk made dubious business decisions and spouted confusing and offensive missives on social media but still ended up as *Time* magazine's Person of the Year for 2021. In a world where companies need to first become decentralized in order to compete, however, the corporate structure today begins to fail on multiple fronts, starting with the way products are created and sold.

Think of a product like Adobe Photoshop. A conversational interface would render their bundled tools and dense GUI obsolete, completely changing the nature of their software. If just saying you'd like to crop a photo prompted the cropping tools to pop up, you'd likely not want to go back to digging through drop-down menus or deciphering tool icons. If the experience of using Photoshop weren't directly linked to their bundled suite of tools represented graphically, then the question might emerge: What is Photoshop? Plus, why would someone buy the full set of Photoshop tools when all they need is to crop a photo? Will your AI agent care which cropping tool it uses? Think of your AI agent as a power user who might prefer a third-party tool for isolating backgrounds behind detailed edges. Inside an ecosystem built for OAGI, you'd be working in an open environment where your AI agent could pull in that third-party tool for your editing project and crop it for you, or perhaps you don't even have to know the image was ever cropped. The point is we will be happily deferring our simple buying decisions to AI agents for physical products like printer ink and experiential products like travel, but most certainly our software choices where our AIs will be the operators of them and not us.

Extrapolate on this idea, and there are a vast multitude of ways in which established business models quickly become nonsensical. Even newer, technology-first companies are far from immune to these paradigm shifts. Uber—a company that is essentially an app with a graphical user interface that gives users access to a handful of technologies (GPS, ridesharing, and remote payment) orchestrated intelligently—could be fatally disrupted by a decentralized orchestration of the same technologies that let users simply text or tell a device, "I need a ride home." In this scenario, what is there exactly to claim ownership of outside of the individual technologies and whatever platform?

Suddenly, ride-sharing no longer requires a rigid corporate structure; it can essentially be managed and controlled by a decentralized group of freelancers with AI agents who, playing to individual strengths, keep the ecosystem supporting ride-sharing up to date with the best functionalities. These clusters of cooperative freelancers already exist in decentralized autonomous organizations, or DAOs. Originally used as fundraising tools for generating community grants, DAOs are also home to guilds of freelancers who band together to share resources and generate work following a democratic process that relies on the integrity of blockchain. Think of DAOs as fully autonomous self-driving organizations.

As ecosystems for AI-driven DAOs begin enriching vast segments of society at large, workers will no longer find themselves beholden to lopsided relationships with rigid, inefficient companies. Instead, they'll be able to leverage their strengths and experience across a vast and interconnected marketplace. It will be a jagged pill for some, but in the world of hyperdisruption, companies won't get to maintain their status quo as closed off ecosystems; instead, they'll have to adjust to being another commodity in vast open ecosystems that may be created overnight, only to be replaced the next day with something better.

Governments and regulators will be looking hard at how to manage corporate objectives, and AIs within corporations will need to be transparent about meeting the public objectives of the corporations they manage. Corporations being able to publicly share one objective but privately create incentives around something different will have heavy consequences. Yet another factor that will change the face of "the company" as we now know it.

The Internet of Things, but for real this time: Maybe you remember all the fuss about the Internet of Things a decade or so ago. The idea was that we'd be living in a world where the many appliances in our life would collect data and share it with other appliances and devices. The prospect of every type of electronic appliance being connected is plenty titillating, so the excitement wasn't misplaced—but the premise lacked a main ingredient. There was no ecosystem in which all of these connected devices could truly connect. Maybe a smart fridge could tell you when you're running low on oat milk and relay that information, but, as a use case, its limits are apparent.

In an ecosystem built for hyperautomating, the fridge can provide a list of common groceries that it recognizes as running low or nearing their expiration date that you always need, like ketchup or mustard. That data can be cross-referenced against any recent online purchase you've made to remove items you've already reordered. Maybe your smart washing machine has been tracking your detergent consumption and tells your AI agent that you've almost used up 64 ounces when asked, signaling that you might need to buy more. This can happen as your AI agents do the rounds, asking all the communicative things in your home if they need anything from the store, bearing in mind the needs of your partner and perhaps a family member who is visiting from out of town. In this ecosystem, that data can be set against your typical detergent purchases to determine if you should indeed buy more. It also detects that you use detergent at such a consistent pace that it might be a good idea to register with a subscription service.

In this world, you meander into your favorite clothing store, try on some shirts and pants, and head for the door. Your AI agents have already checked online to see if there are any care instructions that might require a different detergent than what you have at home. It might even catch you before you leave the store, cautioning against a cashmere item that you might not enjoy taking care of. On the way out, you're approached by an employee who asks if you need any help carrying your stuff to the car. They complement your sense of style while striking up a conversation, mentioning that the clothes you picked out are some of their favorite items in the store. Afterward, your AI agent follows up to ask about your experience in the store and sends the business's AI agent a note praising the employee's professional demeanor.

Within minutes, the company's AI security agent flags your comment and, after confirming that the transaction and compliment are valid, raises the sales rep's internal performance score. Fast-forward to the end of the year. As is custom, the clothing company prepares bonuses for hard-working employees. Instead of subjective once a quarter reviews guiding bonus amounts, they lean on employee performance scores, curated by their AI agent.

To quickly determine bonus amounts, the system runs a pre-written algorithm based on a few criteria: length of employee tenure, overall performance score, number of complaints within the last 30 days, number of commendations within the last 60 days, and total bonus budget. There's no fussing with spreadsheets here. This is all calculated automatically, and bonuses are deposited in employee company cryptocurrency accounts instantly. These can be exchanged for company perks like a better parking space, extra vacation days, or lunch with the CEO. In the development phase, automations like this will require using human-in-the-loop (HitL) technology to fine-tune and avert potentially disastrous disconnects, but as AI agents learn more about contextual cues, contingencies, and optimal use cases, they will become more independent. Think of the transition self-driving cars make, from semi-autonomous to full self-driving. Reaching this final stage requires Beyond Human Experience (BHX)—people didn't trust self-driving cars until their performance surpassed the capabilities of a human driver.

Back in real time, you're excited to get home and put on your new pants. They are wool, something your personal AI agent (the same one that's keeping track of your fridge stock and recent purchases) has already noted by reading your digital receipt. This agent knows that you don't have anything to spot clean wool pants, so it sends you a text suggesting you pick some up. Your AI agent knows that you prefer shopping with small businesses and recommends a corner grocery on the way home. You text back that you don't have time, so the AI agent offers to add the detergent to your next shopping list. Turns out your favorite online store is generous to those with high customer scores and you qualify for free drone shipping so you don't have to wait, not to mention the 20% coupon your agent found online paired with the generic brand that reviews as well or better than top recognized brands.

You're in a hurry to get home because you start a new job tomorrow, and you want to make sure you look and feel your best. As you ride the train home, a text message arrives from an AI agent that's part of your new company's human resources department. You've been corresponding with the agent all week long, as it gathers all of the required personal information needed to get you set up as an employee. Today it wants to let you know that the standing desk you requested comes in two colors. Would you like a black or white desk waiting for you tomorrow?

This is just a taste of a world hyperdisrupted by OAGI. Still, you should feel better equipped to strategize solutions that might fit into a landscape dominated by sophisticated automations that can pull data from just about anywhere and use it to do just about anything.

Keep in mind also that we are not in the business of predicting exactly how automation and AI agents might be implemented, or exactly how these experiences will go. In some ways, it can be just as interesting to think about the things that won't change in the wake of this technological revolution. For instance, we can safely assume that people will continue to take the path of least resistance and will avoid unnecessary repetitive tasks. Hopefully, we will also want to maintain and even improve the integrity of our relationships with other people.

Now, let's get to the nuts and bolts of doing it.

Key Takeaways

- Hyperautomation will induce all sorts of hyperdisruptions to the ways we interact with technology and one another.
- Social scoring and a return to relationship-based interactions over transactional ones will create a world where transparency and authenticity will win out over trolling.
- Across industries, better-than-human experiences will emerge that rely on sophisticated functions such as graph databases, single-serve software, and composable architecture.
- Cryptocurrency and blockchain technology will redefine our relationship with money and the ways we get paid.
- The promise of the Internet of Things will finally be realized, with smart appliances finally having a shared ecosystem for leveraging data.

Want to expand on what you've learned in Chapter 5? Follow this QR code to interact with an IDW that can connect you with additional resources linked to key ideas from this chapter, including content from the *Invisible Machines* podcast.

CHAPTER 6

This Journey Has Been Personal

By Robb Wilson

Thisjourney has indeed been personal, and for the second edition of this book, I decided to rework this chapter to bring you even closer to my experiences in agentic AI. Organizational AGI requires a point of view. To ensure that technology remains truly useful as its power grows exponentially, we need to keep a few basic questions at the center of our thinking. Who is this technology built for? What problems will the people it benefits need to solve and want solved by AI? How might they employ AI agent solutions to find resolution?

I began asking these questions decades ago, while doing user-centered design work that eventually led to the founding of one of the world's first user experience design agencies, Effective UI. Terms like user-centric and customer experience weren't in the vernacular, but they were central to the work we did for clients. For one project, I was part of a cross-disciplinary team tasked with redesigning the cockpit of Boeing's 747 for the 787 Dreamliner. The Dreamliner was going to have a carbon fiber cockpit, which allowed for bigger windows, which left less space for buttons—and the Dreamliner was going to need more buttons than the button-saturated 747.

Our solution changed the way I thought about technology forever. We solved the button problem with large touchscreen panels that would show the relevant controls to the pilots based on the phase of the flight plan the plane was in. While there's some truth to the idea that these planes do a lot of the flying automatically, the goal wasn't to make the pilots less relevant, it was to give them a better experience with a lighter cognitive load. To fly the 747, pilots had to carry around massive manuals that provided step-by-step instructions for pressing buttons in sequence to execute specific functions during flight—manuals that there was barely room for in the crowded cockpits.

The experience of flying a commercial airplane became more intuitive because we were able to contextualize the pilot's needs based on the flight plan data and provide a relevant interface. Context was the key to creating increasingly rewarding and personalized experiences. The other massive takeaway for me was that if you can automate a 787, you can automate a company.

Of all the experiences people have with technology, conversational ones are typically some of the worst. Creating a framework where conversational AI can thrive—though insanely difficult work—creates unmatched potential.

Some of my early experiments with conversational AI came to be known as Sybil, a bot I built about 20 years ago with help from Daisy Weborg (the eventual co-founder of OneReach.ai). The internet was a less guarded space back then, and in some ways, it was easier to feed Sybil context. For example, Sybil could send spiders crawling over geo-tagged data in my accounts to figure out where I was at any given moment. Daisy loved the "where's Robb" skill because I was often on the move in those days, and she could get a better sense of my availability for important meetings.

Recently I had a conversation with Adam Cheyer, one of the co-creators of Siri, who was a guest on the *Invisible Machines* podcast. When I was working on Sybil, I wasn't fully aware of the work Adam was doing at Siri Labs. Likewise, he wasn't hip to what I was doing either. Interestingly—though perhaps unsurprisingly in retrospect—we were trying to solve many of the same problems.

Adam mentioned a functionality that was built into the first version of Siri that would allow you to be reading an email from someone and ask Siri to call that person. That might sound simple, but it's a relatively complex task, even by today's standards. In this example Siri is connecting contact information from Mail with associated data in Contacts, connecting points between two separate apps to create a more seamless experience for users.

"At the time, email and contacts integration wasn't very good," Adam said on our podcast. "So you couldn't even get to the contact easily from an email. You had to leave an app and search for it. And it was a big pain. 'Call him.' It was a beautiful combination of manipulating what's on the screen and asking for what's not on the screen. For me, that's the key to multimodal interaction."[1]

Adam went on to mention other functionalities that he assumed had been lost to the dustbin of history, including skills around discovery that he and Steve Jobs fought over. Apple acquired Siri in 2010, and the freestanding version of the app had something called semantic autocomplete. Adam explained that, if you wanted to find a romantic comedy playing near you, typing the letters "R" and "O" into a text field might auto-complete to show rodeos, tea rooms, and romantic comedy. If you clicked "romantic comedy" Siri would tell you which romantic comedies were showing near you, along with info about their casts and critical reviews. This feature never made it into the beta version of Siri that launched with the iPhone 4S in October 2011.

> *"I feel that because I lost that argument with Steve, we lost that in voice interfaces forever. I have never seen another voice assistant experience that had as good an experience as the original Siri. I feel it got lost to history. And discovery is an unsolved problem."*

I'm sharing these stories from Adam for two reasons. One, to remind you that there are lots of people who have been working for decades on these kinds of experiences. ChatGPT blew the doors open on this technology to the public, but for those of us who've been toiling on the inside for years the response was something along the lines of, *finally people will believe me when I talk about how powerful this technology is!*

Another reason for sharing is that Adam's experience with Steve Jobs illustrates that the choices we make now with this technology will set a trajectory that will become increasingly difficult to reset. With their ability to mine unstructured data (like written and recorded conversations), large language models (LLMs) have the power to solve the problem of discovery, but this is a problem that Adam and I have been circling for more than 20 years. Things might have been different if he'd won that argument with Jobs.

You see, the ultimate goal isn't that we can converse with machines, telling them every little thing we want them to do for us. The goal is for machines to be able to predict the things we want them to do for us before we even ask. The ultimate experience is not one where we talk to the machine, but one where we don't need to, because it already knows us so well. We provide machines with objectives, but they don't really need explicit instructions unless we want something done in a very specific way.

Siri's popularity, along with the widespread adoption of smart speakers and Amazon's Alexa, made something else clear to me. Talking to speakers in your house can be fun, but there's really only so much intrinsic value in an automated home. Home is generally a place for relaxation, not productivity. Being able to walk into your office and engage in conversation with technology that's running a growing collection of business process automations is where the real wealth of opportunity lies. Orgs are going to want their own proprietary versions of Alexa or Siri in different flavors—intelligent virtual assistants that are finely tuned to meet an organization's security and privacy needs. Still, coming up on 10 years after the introduction of Alexa there's still no version of that within a business.

The agentic AI platform we started building all those years ago at OneReach.ai was my attempt at creating these sophisticated virtual assistants, or intelligent digital workers (IDWs). Our core leadership team has deep roots working in experience design and we knew better than to build strictly around technology—we built around user needs.

Drawing from thousands of use cases and tens of thousands of user stories, we learned a lot about what we could be doing better. We often had to learn things the hard way, even with examples that seem obvious in hindsight. Lessons like: more syllables aid speech recognition, designs with fewer interactions fare better, and storing contextual data from an interaction can improve future interactions.

Due to the inherently complex nature of the tasks, the lack of maturity in the tools, and the difficulty in finding truly experienced people to build and run them, creating Beyond Human Experiences is extremely difficult to do. I once heard someone at Gartner call it "insanely hard." Over the years I've watched many successful and failed implementations (including some of our own crash-and-burn attempts). Automating chatbots on websites, phone, SMS, WhatsApp, Slack, Alexa, Google Home, and other platforms, patterns began to emerge from successful projects. We began studying those success stories to see how they compared to others.

The data and best practices described in the next portion of this book have been gathered over the course of more than 2 million hours of testing with more than 30 million people participating in workflows across 10,000+ conversational applications. I'm also drawing from more than 500,000 hours of development. Of course, it's important to remember that having a platform to build such experiences does not guarantee success. You also need processes, people, tools, architecture, strategy, and design that work in a coordinated way.

I've formulated an intimate understanding of what it takes to build and manage intelligent networks of applications and, more importantly, how to manage an ecosystem of applications that enables any organization to hyperautomate.

For most companies ChatGPT has been a knock upside the head, waking them up to the fact that they're already in the race toward hyperautomation. As powerful as GPT and other LLMs are, they are just one piece of an intelligent technology ecosystem. Just like a website needs content strategy to avoid becoming a collection of disorganized pages, achieving hyperautomation requires a sound strategy for building an intelligent ecosystem and the willingness to quickly embrace new technology. Whether your organization has yet to begin its journey or is moving along that road without the tools they need to succeed, this book exists to help you create a winning strategy.

The widespread adoption has shown how disruptive this technology can be, but leveraged properly, generative AI, conversational interfaces, code-free design, RPA, and machine learning are something more powerful: they are force multipliers that can make the companies that use them correctly impossible to compete with. The scope and implications of these converging technologies can easily induce future shock—the psychological state experienced by individuals or society at large when perceiving too much change in too short a period of time. That feeling of being overwhelmed that might happen many times when reading this book. Organizations currently wrestling with their response to ChatGPT—that are employing machines, conversational applications, or AI-powered digital workers in an ecosystem that isn't high functioning—are likely experiencing some form of this.

The goal for this book is to alleviate future shock by equipping problem solvers with a strategy for building an intelligent, coordinated ecosystem of automation—a network of skills shared between IDWs that will have widespread impact within an organization. Following this strategy will not only vastly improve your existing operations, it will forge a technology ecosystem that immediately levels up every time there's a breakthrough in LLMs or some other tool. An ecosystem built for organizational AGI can take advantage of new technologies the minute they drop.

It took me 20 years to develop the best practices and insights collected here. I've been fortunate to have had countless conversations about how agentic AI fits into the enterprise landscape with head-strong business leaders. I've seen firsthand how a truly holistic understanding of the technologies associated with agentic AI can make the crucial difference for enterprise companies struggling to balance the problems that come with this fraught territory. Josh and I put them into a book because I can only take so many calls in a day and I want this information to reach everyone who can benefit from it. I rewrote this chapter because this book, like any other piece of technology I've worked with, can benefit from iteration. It's entirely possible that some future version of this book will exist as an IDW that can provide you with insight that's tailored to your phase in the journey toward organizational AGI.

That's the kind of mind-blowing scenario that can come into quick fruition as we get a grasp on generative AI. That will only happen when the people working with it have a strategy that can put converging technologies to work in intelligent ways—propelling organizations and, more broadly, the people of the world, into a bold new future.

Key Takeaways

- ChatGPT has revealed to the world that conversational AI is real and it's here to stay. Now, the real work—orchestrating LLMs, along with a whole host of other disruptive technologies, to create truly meaningful automated experiences—begins.

- The findings revealed in this book are based on years of Robb's research and experience building thousands of conversational applications.

- A proper strategy for orchestrating disruptive technologies gives your organization the fuel it needs to establish organizational AGI.

- Following this strategy will vastly improve your existing operations while establishing a technology ecosystem that immediately levels up every time there's a breakthrough in LLMs or some other tool.

Want to expand on what you've learned in Chapter 6? Follow this QR code to interact with an IDW that can connect you with additional resources linked to key ideas from this chapter, including content from the *Invisible Machines* podcast.

CHAPTER 7

Learning the Terms

A s should be expected with a complex set of emergent technologies, there aren't universally agreed-upon terms or definitions used to describe hyperautomation. Within the community of people working with AI-adjacent technologies, there's significant disagreement on what certain terms mean and whether or not we should be using them at all.

When we spoke with Jaron Lanier about the term "artificial general intelligence" or AGI, the co-creator of VR technology as we know it and Microsoft's Octopus (Office of the Chief Technology Officer Prime Unifying Scientist) told us our vocabulary was nonsensical and that our thinking wasn't compatible with his perception of technology. Regardless, it felt like we agreed on core aspects of these technologies.

"I don't think of AI as creating new entities. I think of it as a collaboration between people," Lanier said. "That's the only way to think about using it well . . . to me it's all a form of collaboration. The sooner we see that, the sooner we can design useful systems . . . to me there's only people."[1]

We're not trying to dictate what's right or wrong. We're simply explaining what we mean when we say what we say. Jaron's point is actually quite relevant. This is all about collaboration between people. Different groups of people might have different terms they like to use. What's critical is that the people you are collaborating with have a grounded understanding of the key components. As such, the definitions provided below are specific to the context of the automated technologies and the ecosystems they operate within. We've already defined some of these terms in previous chapters, and this is by no means a complete set of terms. There are also terms that we'll introduce later in the book that aren't on this list, but these are the foundational ideas we'll build around.

Intelligent automation: This term refers to automations that have agency over their own learning; for humans this is called metacognition—the awareness to plan one's own learning and activities. True self-driving cars are an example of intelligent automation. If an OS can sequence the many different technologies required to drive a car, drive that car safely, and continue to improve its ability to drive, that's intelligent automation. The same intelligent automation, when thriving inside an open ecosystem of technologies, can make companies self-driving as well. Humans are still at the wheel, but more and more rudimentary tasks are automated, freeing up time to focus on higher-level problems.

Hyperautomation: When intelligent automation is regularly taking place within an ecosystem of orchestrated technologies, an organization is hyperautomating. This puts them in a position to quickly identify, vet, and automate business and IT processes at scale, providing an outsized advantage over competitors. There is a fair amount of interchangeability in the way hyperautomation and intelligent automation are talked about in the world (you can go ahead and add conversational AI, agentic AI, organizational AGI, and robotic process automation to this tangle of terms). Ideally, we'd use a term like "intelligent hyperautomation," but for the sake of simplicity in a far-from-simple endeavor, we'll be using "hyperautomation" as a catchall. Regardless, the more your organization is hyperautomating, the more self-driving it becomes.

Organizational AGI: As we mentioned earlier, this concept is innately tied to hyperatuomation. It stands to reason that as an organization becomes more self-driving it is also becoming more self-aware. Organizational artificial general intelligence represents a more isolated version of the kind of AGI that people commonly associate with progress toward singularity—of intelligent machines becoming self-aware. The general intelligence AGI would need to replicate is the knowledge and adaptability that allow humans to thrive in so many environments on earth. The amount of general intelligence it takes to run even a large organization is far easier to replicate. Full AGI may not be relevant from a productivity standpoint. Who cares if your AI can play Minecraft or reason through the meaning of life when all your company needs is an AI to manage administrative and project management duties? On the road to organizational AGI an internal awareness is building about the activity going on within all areas of the organization. This will take shape in different ways inside of different organizations, but the idea is that it can begin making predictions about business outcomes. Former Hewlett-Packard CEO Lew Platt once famously said: "If HP knew what HP knows, we'd be three times more productive." Organizational AGI is that idea fully realized (though 3× feels like a modest multiplier).

Ecosystem: An ecosystem refers to all of the technologies and the parts of an organization that are relevant to conversational technology and the sum of those parts. In other words, an ecosystem is an organization's complete network of interdependent technologies, processes, and people. Even if you've taken no steps toward hyperautomation, your organization still has an ecosystem. Within an intelligent ecosystem built for organizational AGI, these elements are coordinated to enable, support, manage, facilitate, and benefit from the implementation of agentic AI. The ecosystem is self-sustaining and circular. As the tools and technologies in the marketplace improve, your system instantly benefits from it. Software applications are broken down into functionalities or skills.

Digital twin: This is another term that's deeply intertwined with organizational AGI and hyperautomation. McKinsey describes a digital twin as "a virtual replica of a physical object, person, or process that can be used to simulate its behavior to better understand how it works in real life." They elaborate to say that a digital twin within an ecosystem similar to what we've described can become an enterprise metaverse, "a digital and often immersive environment that replicates and connects every aspect of an organization to optimize simulations, scenario planning, and decision making."[2] Digital twins are likely to be low fidelity at first, offering a limited view of the organization. As more interactions and processes take place within the org, however, the fidelity of the digital twin becomes higher. This twin is a digital representation of physical things, actions, events, projects, conversations, and people—both employees and customers. It's also a representation of the relationships between these elements mapped over time. An organization's technology ecosystem not only understands the current state of the organization, it can also adapt and respond to new challenges autonomously, which is very similar to the idea of organizational AGI.

AI agents: AI agents are software programs that use artificial intelligence to perform tasks, make decisions, or solve problems autonomously or semi-autonomously. These agents are designed to mimic human-like cognitive functions such as learning, reasoning, problem solving, perception, and understanding language. They can operate in various environments, handling tasks that range from simple automation to complex decision-making processes, adapting and responding to changing conditions in real time. AI agents are used in a wide array of applications, from virtual assistants and chatbots to more sophisticated systems in robotics, smart homes, and business analytics. A key difference between AI agents and other types of software is that they don't need specific instructions (i.e., programming) to complete tasks. They are able to work around broader objectives instead.

Intelligent Digital Worker (IDW): This is the term we used in the first edition of this book to describe what are now commonly referred to as AI agents. We've come to realize that the primary difference between an AI agent, as they've come to be known in the marketplace, and an IDW is that the IDWs can orchestrate multiple agents to work around an objective. We use IDWs to orchestrate AI agents, taking fuller advantage of their composability and reusable skills.

Core functions: Core function is a general term for an IDW's primary purpose or deepest skill set. The core function isn't necessarily the only thing an IDW will be capable of doing, but it does represent its primary function.

Primary skills: Primary skills are critical to the way humans interface with IDWs and the ecosystem at large. When mapping primary skills to our human experience, they are often analogous to necessary skills that we take for granted. For example, it would be reasonable to ask a design job candidate if they've used software such as Figma or InDesign, but you likely wouldn't ask about their ability to ask another human when they need help, or if they have a track record of being able to respond accordingly over phone calls, text messages, and emails. They are also a bit like primary colors: general skills that can be reused and adapted across many tasks, like scheduling, writing, and reading.

For an IDW, primary skills can look like this:

- Being able to operate over specific communication channels, such as Slack, phone, Google Home, and SMS;
- Understanding natural language;
- Including a human-in-the-loop when help is needed.

Skills: More broad than primary skills, these could include changing a password, managing an appointment, or getting status on a project. Skills can sequence other skills and agents to get work done. Skills are the ability to do something, and are like the DNA of an intelligent digital ecosystem sequenced to hyperautomate your company. As visualized in Figure 7.1, skills are the blueprint of what your ecosystem will be and what it will accomplish, similar to the way the proteins in a strand of DNA are sequenced to enable the building of complex things like a brain or heart.

Steps: Skills are made up of steps. A step is an instance of technology (or technologies) that can be sequenced in a flow, like ingredients in a recipe. Steps are like the protein sequences in our DNA. For example, a step could make an API call to a payment gateway to retrieve the last four digits of a customer's most recently used payment method.

FIGURE 7.1 Example of a skill from the OneReach.ai GSX platform.

Tasks: For an IDW orchestrating multiple AI agents, a task is the single act of performing or applying a skill or skills in order to meet an objective. A task could be anything from authenticating a user to planning an event.

Microservices: By breaking down a skill into its component services and then breaking those down into their component steps, you get sets of pliable, infinitely customizable microservices. The sequencing in DNA is what gives rise to a dominant organism. The successful sequencing of microservices gives rise to dominant skills that can force-multiply your automation. This is a key component for creating a composable architecture.

Flows: A flow is the sequencing of skills, agents, or steps that are used to execute a task. These are the patterns or instructions orchestrated agents rely on in order to get something done. In the simplest terms, flows are algorithms that are designed to influence positive outcomes. Flows are a mix of deterministic and stochastic instructions. As shown in Figure 7.2, skills, agents, and steps can be sequenced into flows using low-code design tools.

FIGURE 7.2 A conversational designer sequences steps in their flow in the OneReach.ai GSX designer tool.

Shared library: The shared library is the central resource of your ecosystem. It is home to all the resources your organization uses to orchestrate hyperautomation, such as microservices, skills, and flows. As members of your organization are routinely pulling resources from the shared library, making tweaks and iterations in order to develop new skills, these new resources become part of the shared library as well. Ever expanding, the shared library is a critical hub of activity and resources inside your ecosystem. Organizations have specific ways they want things done, and the shared library can also contain specific instructions for the AI system to follow, which could be in code form or text.

Vector and graph databases: Graph databases, sometimes referred to as graph DB, connect data points as nodes that use edge relationships to represent and store data. Graph technology is adept at creating indexes of all components within the AI infrastructure from skills and systems to data sources, going beyond mere listing and delving into how these elements relate and interact with one another. These are incredibly powerful tools for tracking data and predicting trends or behavior across the customer journey, uncovering meaningful relationships within customer data that previously would have been impossible to discover. A high-fidelity digital twin relies on graphDB for tracking data and predicting trends and behavior across the customer journey. A vector-based database complements graphDB technology by enabling efficient storage and retrieval of complex data structures, which are essential for understanding and processing natural language inputs.

Human-in-the-loop (HitL):   We talk a lot about human-in-the-loop in these pages, often from different perspectives. As shown in Figure 7.3, it's a human monitoring live conversations and interjecting when needed. Human-in-the-loop can refer to a tool or a person, and it's integral to the design and development of your ecosystem. What's important to understand heading into this journey is that the humans within your organization are crucial to your success. They provide an intimate understanding of the various tasks that will be automated. Their knowledge is used to design the IDWs and also to evolve them. As the IDWs perform tasks, they can turn to a human-in-the-loop when they get stuck or have questions about a step. Over the course of these interactions, the IDW learns more about individual problems

FIGURE 7.3 A human agent uses OneReach.ai GSX HiTL tools.

and the different contexts they can appear in. The relationship that develops between IDWs and humans-in-the-loop is the fertilizer that accelerates the evolution and growth of your ecosystem.

Human-controlled outcomes (HCO): Hyperautomation needs to be human-led at every level, and that means designing for human-controlled outcomes. Even if a machine can make efficient decisions on its own, good design keeps humans in the driver's seat. There are few scenarios more dystopian than people living under strict orders from machines—even if they're designed to maximize our efficiency. A much brighter scenario is one where machines offer humans informed choices throughout the day that will increase their efficiency. Machines supply the best choices, but humans ultimately choose the outcomes. Human-in-the-loop is a big piece of HCO, as it explicitly calls for humans making decisions based on choices provided by an IDW.

Intelligent communication fabric: Interactions with an organization, whether coming from a team member or a customer, might use any number of channels: website, social media, email, Slack, MS Teams, telephone, SMS, video call, rich web chat, etc. Most organizations are currently maintaining their own menagerie of solutions that are often held together by the digital equivalent of duct tape and zip ties. Intelligent communication fabric is designed specifically for communication. This fabric enables composable micro services to use conversational interfaces and conversational memory across deep channel integrations to create personalized experiences. It's different from a data mesh in that you're not restricted to making right turns on a grid. Lines between points can take whatever shape makes the most sense. Gartner calls for something similar called a CX CORE Membrane, which uses customer insight to develop a set of principles governing two-way communications between customers and a company. ICF creates that membrane.

Cognitive orchestration engine: We've also heard this referred to as cognitive architecture, but the critical thing to understand is that a cognitive orchestration engine can design experiences using both legacy systems and new market-best solutions. To create real, high-functioning automations, it's critical that you can amalgamate language services (e.g., NLU, TTS, ASR, and localization) with other cognitive services, like computer vision and generative AI. This allows organizations to add vendors, manage cognitive services, and use them in different combinations, all in one place. This composable infrastructure allows AI-driven systems to handle scaling, security, and storage on their own. The many components that become part of this architecture can be removed and replaced as better solutions come to market. However you choose to build this architecture, this flexibility is a critical component to using AI effectively.

Extensible cognitive architecture: In much the same way that companies rely on cloud services like AWS to run their operations, an extensive cognitive architecture comprises multiple interconnected computers working in harmony. These components collaborate to create a seamless conversational experience that combines language understanding, context awareness, and the ability to generate micro-UIs as needed. To make any meaningful strides toward hyperautomation, organizational AGI, or digital twinhood, an extensible cognitive architecture is a bare necessity. We'll go deeper into the makeup of this architecture in Chapter 11, but organizations taking this journey seriously will need to buy one or build one.

Beyond Human Experience (BHX):   The concept of "Beyond Human Experience" (BHX) refers to the design and delivery of conversational interactions that go beyond simply emulating human-like behaviors. BHX surpasses what humans can typically provide in terms of speed, accuracy, and efficiency. This involves leveraging the advanced capabilities of machines, such as processing vast amounts of data instantly, generating multimedia content (like images, videos, and poems), designing user interfaces, and creating code on-the-fly. The goal is to provide experiences that are more efficient, engaging, and tailored to individual needs than those a human could offer alone. BHX focuses on enhancing user satisfaction by maximizing the unique strengths of AI and technology, thereby transcending the limitations of human capabilities in real-time interactions.

Mapping these terms to the human experience is helpful when building familiarity, but there are clear differences. Data, information, and skills within an ecosystem can be shared between IDWs with a degree of efficiency and transferability that humans haven't figured out yet. Imagine being able to instantly know how to build a fence because your neighbor, Sally, builds them for a living, and can transfer her skills and data through some osmotic process. That's essentially the way information transfers between IDWs. If one IDW in an ecosystem knows how to do something, they can all know how to do it; just by knowing Sally one minute, you could have one million Sallys building fences the next. While one million fence-building Sallys represents the dream of hyperautomation, the reality for organizations operating without a proper strategy or ecosystem is a handful of Sallys that don't know one another and can't speak the same language.

Key Takeaways

- Understanding the terms involved in hyperautomation helps to establish a clearer picture of how the many pieces work together.
- It's crucial that humans are involved in critical decision-making moments throughout the life cycle of any hyperautomation effort.
- The more companies are able to hyperautomate skills within an open ecosystem, the more self-driving they become.
- The way IDWs share information using the shared library means that if one knows how to do something, they all know how to do it. This means you have a bottomless supply of IDWs ready to assist team members and customers with any skill in your shared library.

Want to expand on what you've learned in Chapter 7? Follow this QR code to interact with an IDW that can connect you with additional resources linked to key ideas from this chapter, including content from the *Invisible Machines* podcast.

PART II

Planning an Ecosystem for Orchestrated AI Agents

We've been languishing in a world of rather feeble software integration for way too long. Sure, it's handy using your Gmail account to log into loads of other software products, but there's no pot of gold waiting for those jockeying to be the product that everyone else integrates with. As conversation becomes our primary interface with technology, nobody is going to ask an AI agent to log in to an email account or an airline website to look for flight information. They'll just ask, "When is my flight to Phoenix?"

Organizational AGI isn't an integration effort, it's a restructuring effort. The journey toward creating an ecosystem of orchestrated AI agents will be arduous and complex, but it will also be a time of self-discovery.

The process by which AI agents become more useful and wise is, in and of itself, a way for your workforce to take a deeper look at the many monotonous, daily tasks they perform and ideate on ways to automate them and then evolve those automations. So while it's a lot of work, it's also a highly rewarding process that can elevate the individual members in your organization and help unify the whole they represent. To succeed, you'll need to embrace change while fully realizing that change is discomfort. More often, with this level of orchestration, change is trauma. It might mean ripping the guts out of entire departments within your organization and rebuilding them anew. This is a big risk, and you'd be justified in wanting to lay down and throw a fit, but there is hope.

Organizations that have spent the last decade or so unifying the back end of their operations now have the opportunity to unify their front end as well with a single conversational interface, closing a technology loop and creating an ecosystem primed for agent orchestration.

With any disruptive technology, it's easy to get distracted by the bombast, urgency, and excitement clouding its true nature. In the early days of the internet, there was intense pressure for companies—especially market leaders—to get a page up on the newfangled World Wide Web. One rudimentary page might quickly expand into a handful of pages, designed by different departments, that didn't fit together, lacked clear navigation, and delivered far more confusion than reward to viewers. Even once that problem was identified, triage attempts to wrangle isolated hunks of content onto navigational home pages was of little use, because none of the content was designed to complement other content.

It's taken years for many organizations to realize that a high-functioning web presence is one rooted in strategy. The web is a great system for sharing anything and everything, but the only way to effectively leverage its power is with structured content that works purposefully across pages and channels.

OAGI is no different. Harnessing the power of AI and conversational interfaces to reshape the potential of the human species certainly warrants bombast, urgency, and excitement, but don't let that cloud the true nature of the task at hand. A collection of siloed agents automating disparate tasks will never spontaneously reach OAGI. Organizational AGI is the result of a solid, organization-wide strategy.

To be clear, when we use the word "strategy" we are not referring to the mission or ultimate goal. Strategy here describes a road map for how resources can be allocated to reach the goal of OAGI. This isn't a race to build a static piece of technology; the race is to equip your team and company for faster adoption and iteration on new technologies, skills, and functions.

The best way to give you a full understanding of an intelligent ecosystem of digital workers is to unlock the process behind building one.

This is no small undertaking, and its success is dependent on a unified organization working in concert with a core enablement team that guides the evolution of your ecosystem.

Now that you're acquainted with the terms we use in this realm, we'll take a look at the cold, hard reality of what happens when you try to leverage these technologies without a binding strategy. Then we'll introduce you to the members of the core enablement team who are tasked with getting your efforts under way. You'll need to identify the proper tools and architecture that contribute to the creation and evolution of your ecosystem. (Then, in Part III, we'll walk you through process, design strategy, and production design.)

When we talk about OAGI, we're talking about sequencing tasks and technologies in ways that reveal unseen potential and multiply outcomes. When you step back to consider the vast multitude of technologies and tasks that make up an organization and imagine the countless ways they might be sequenced together, the complexity of the situation can quickly overwhelm. But with the right strategy and process, you can get everyone in your organization creating and refining automations, creating a fertile ecosystem for organizational AGI.

CHAPTER 8

The Dream vs. Reality

You envisioned an automated ecosystem full of intelligent agents helping your customers and helping one another. It was going to integrate with your existing systems. Your users were going to love the experience so much that employee satisfaction and conversion rates would jump through the roof. Processes that were a huge time-suck for your team were going to be automated, freeing them up to focus on growing your organization instead of maintaining the status quo. You thought it would be easy and quickly start saving you tons of money, and massively boosting satisfaction.

If you were nurturing this dream before ChatGPT burst onto the scene and opened the world's eyes to the power of conversational AI, you might have been given a false sense that things were going to get easier. The subsequent flood of pre-built solutions, strategically added to existing software platforms like ServiceNow, Workday, MS Office, and Salesforce, might have seemed like a major breakthrough. While these bolt-ons offer ease of procurement and installation, they exhibit fragility and limitations in terms of channel support and functionality scope, often confined to the software they augment. Major software providers are hurriedly incorporating AI bolt-ons to prevent the potential erosion of their user interfaces, fearing obsolescence in the face of agentic AI advances.

The ice-bath reality is that creating an intelligent digital ecosystem requires more than just a few machines thrown at a few different problem areas—even if those machines are LLMs, which have proven themselves astonishingly powerful. We've all seen LLMs write emails and poetry, and some of us are getting them to do more impressive stuff than that, like writing code—but now we want to see them do real work. OpenAI's GPTs and Google's AI agents are expressions of this desire, and while the many use cases Google has unveiled are impressive, they are still operating in Google's box. Sooner or later, most organizations are going to need to create customized experiences that will require an open and flexible ecosystem (aka, extensible cognitive architecture). This requires letting go of old ideas and embracing uncertainty. Even though building things will be faster and easier, testing them will be much harder.

Many of the platforms for enabling these ecosystems require a team of experts (developers, data scientists, AI scientists, architects) to build solutions. Coding these solutions can involve significant infrastructure efforts. Even building a relatively simple, production-ready agentic AI application can require hundreds of work hours across several departments along with significant infrastructure development. Some may not require coding or infrastructure development but are fairly inflexible as a result.

If you've still got chills from your first attempt at AI-enabled automation, you might be hesitant to reboot or even restart the process. But, as we've stressed, you're already in this race whether you want to run it or not. Getting back to the starting line requires assessing your current position. Let's say you already have a collection of machines running within your organization. They likely aren't functioning within an ecosystem—but are the result of random acts of chatbotting. This is usually a number of point-solution chatbots built using varying architectures that are not part of an overall strategy. These may have come from exploratory projects. They might be chatbots that came with existing platforms, such as ServiceNow or Salesforce. It could also be that somebody decided to throw together a Q&A chatbot using an LLM that they never trained for accuracy and that needs some major fine-tuning.

Sometimes you can leverage these initial efforts, but it's usually more work than it's worth. An on-ramp to building a coordinated ecosystem starts with creating a strategy and getting buy-in. Whether you have no chatbots, a handful of chatbots that nobody really uses, or a coherent strategy with the wrong tools, a robust ecosystem of intelligent digital workers is within reach. For the most part, playing it safe amounts to staying out of the race completely. Standing by, learning from others' mistakes, moving carefully, buying AI add-ons for existing tools, running internal hackathons, and surfacing proof-of-concepts that never see production—these options are just about as effective as doing nothing at all.

Operating Without Design Strategy

It's easy to see why companies gravitate to simple chatbots trained on basic FAQ (frequently asked questions) content. This supporting content already exists and it's fairly easy to feed an LLM a whole bunch of documents and feel like you are accomplishing something. You can put exciting tech front-and-center on your site, and it seems like an easy win. But many companies try it, watch it fail, and then unplug the project without ever really understanding why it didn't work. The reason is that no matter how many random chatbots you have or how much money you throw at them, if your machines aren't part of an ecosystem that reaches your entire organization, then you're operating without an AI design strategy. Random acts of AI versus building out organizational AGI incrementally.

We recently had a conversation with Jeff McMillan and David Wu of Morgan Stanley. As the head of AI and the Head of Knowledge Management & Generative AI, respectively, Jeff and David led the creation of an AI assistant for the global investment firm's advisors. This involved working closely with OpenAI to train one of their GPT models on 100,000 internal documents, but they were quick to realize that creating a reliable knowledge base would go well beyond simply feeding the documents to an LLM.

"When we started this journey, we had no idea what a vector database was . . . We thought, hey GPT works really well, why don't we just take 100,000 documents and copy/paste it into GPT," Wu said.[1]

As Wu explained, they found it necessary to break their content into domains and find individuals who were accountable for each of these groups. These domain owners determined what content to keep and what to discard, and applied metadata labels that made the content navigable across a vector (or relational) database. It was very much a coordinated group effort, one that's had the effect of reinvigorating the content owners and creators within the organization.

(continued)

Operating Without Design Strategy (*continued*)

"People are really excited," McMillan said. "It's not like we're trying to do entitlements or database cleanup, the challenge is not getting people excited and engaged, it's about putting the right guard rails in place."

Doubling down and adding more chatbots in a scramble to implement solutions to unify a disparate group of machines is not an AI design strategy. Concierge bots, super bots, master bots, triage bots—these idealized solutions have many different names, but they are not part of a real design strategy. The moniker "triage bot" is particularly telling as triage is applied in situations where large numbers of broken things need to be ranked in order of what needs fixing first. Without a design strategy, expect to deal with a tangled heap of broken machines with no way to stop the bleeding.

A chatbot that's not connected to a strategically designed ecosystem amounts to an overpromise—unless it tells users right away: "I can only handle a limited number of rigid tasks, so please don't ask me about anything other than . . ."

The very presence of generative models conjures an assumed promise. A piece of technology that can respond to conversational prompts is going to automatically engender more sophistication in a user's mind than what likely exists in reality. This leads directly to assumed expectations that won't be met, which will lead to abandonment. Giving a chatbot with extremely limited capabilities a moniker like "digital assistant" raises those expectations further, and increases your precipitous drop. If we had to issue an explicit warning, it would be this: Do not touch agentic AI without a design strategy in place.

The Dream of Simple AI-Enabled Chatbots

- Chatbots are easy to train;
- The tools are simple;
- Advanced skills or understanding of technologies aren't required;
- Chatbots can leverage existing content;

- Chatbots can be updated using current maintenance processes and tools;
- Chatbots can instantly handle several use cases.

The Reality

- The hypecycle of AI creates unfair expectations and disappointment for end users whose expectations are set by human conversations.
- Better experiences with top use cases typically yield greater returns than greater numbers of use cases. If you can't improve experiences surrounding top use cases, you can expect disappointed employees, bad reviews, bad satisfaction scores, failed initiatives, and pulled projects.
- FAQ pages with search functions often outperform simple FAQ chatbots on satisfaction scores because they offer more real estate and a better browsing experience, and because they are more suggestive (i.e., users can see other related questions).
- While FAQ content already exists, it's not typically formulated for conversational interactions, and chatbots don't typically offer opportunities to disambiguate requests or educate end users about their options.
- It's hard to transition from simple chatbot processes, tools, and architecture to more intelligent solutions because creating an intelligent ecosystem requires a holistic approach—designing each element to function as part of a dynamic interactive environment with a vast multitude of variables to consider.

Without a comprehensive strategy in place, your chatbot dream will quickly become a low-adoption nightmare. Getting it right requires investing in the curation of information. It requires building a knowledge management process and the internal muscle for keeping it updated. It requires pruning and tuning. What Morgan Stanley created is much more than a Q&A solution, because the Q&A element to it can be leveraged as a source of knowledge and context for future AI agents to use to get work done. Having a trusted digital assistant for their advisors pales in comparison to what AI agents can do with this information. Their curated collection of critical knowledge is a major piece of building OAGI. You might even say that, besides having a cognitive infrastructure to run it in, it's the first major step in your journey.

Key Takeaways

- If you've made unsuccessful attempts at automating processes within your organization, it probably feels like the "hyper" in "hyperautomation" is closer to "hype." The ice-bath reality, however, is that creating an intelligent digital ecosystem requires more than just a few AI agents thrown at a few different problem areas within an organization.
- Unless it confesses its limitations to users from the start, a chatbot that's not part of a strategically designed ecosystem is an overpromise.
- Real hyperautomation is a vast orchestration effort that requires alignment with every department you've got. It requires a bold, overarching strategy that will likely feel like trauma at first—but it's the only way to stay competitive in business moving forward.

Want to expand on what you've learned in Chapter 8? Follow this QR code to interact with an IDW that can connect you with additional resources linked to key ideas from this chapter, including content from the *Invisible Machines* podcast.

CHAPTER 9

Ecosystem Evolution Explained

With the key terms from Chapter 7 in mind, let's unpack the conceptual and practical elements of our ecosystem. The path to OAGI is one of evolving skills from the simple "literacy" phase of design to a state of wisdom. Simple skills, while useful, are just stepping-stones to a self-driving organization. In much the same way that self-driving cars have levels of autonomy, so do skills. A large and increasing concentration of wise skills is part of what creates OAGI.

As shown in Figure 9.1, there are four evolutionary phases that AI agents can move through as they become better at completing tasks: literacy, knowledge, intelligence, and wisdom. The lines where one phase ends and the next starts aren't clearly defined. All skills employ each of the described characteristics; simple skills use them to a lesser degree, and more evolved skills use them to a greater degree.

ECOSYSTEM OF INTELLIGENT DIGITAL WORKERS

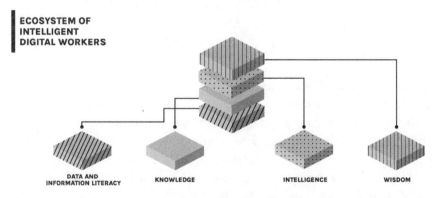

DATA AND INFORMATION LITERACY   KNOWLEDGE   INTELLIGENCE   WISDOM

FIGURE 9.1 Four evolutionary phases that an IDW can move through.

Because the intelligent digital workers, or IDWs, that we've referenced in these pages are essentially orchestrations of AI agents, it can be helpful to frame activities around the evolutionary state of IDWs, which can be made up of different groupings of agents, depending on the use case.

This is not a centralized system. Rather, each agent has an awareness of other agents, but there isn't a single system that controls all agents.

The Four Evolution Phases of an IDW

Literacy

During the literacy phase, the IDW consumes and transforms numbers and characters into information. This can be either raw data, such as an integer that can be decoded into a date, or the formatted version of that integer into a date (e.g., 01-01-2020). We often refer to an IDW in this phase as a primitive digital worker.

Knowledge

In the knowledge phase, the IDW gains understanding of the context of its information—recognizing how and why information matters. For example, "comprehending" that a date is someone's date of birth. We think of an IDW with this capacity as a basic intelligent digital worker. At the time of this writing, OpenAI's GPTs and Google's AI Agents are moving toward the outer edges of this phase.

Intelligence

During the intelligence phase, the IDW develops understanding of how to use or act on knowledge and information. So for our date example that would mean understanding the relevance of the date of birth in different contexts, such as: "I hope you have a great 21st tomorrow!" or "I just sent you a gift certificate for your 21st." This capability is the hallmark of an IDW that is ready to function in an ecosystem—what has reached the status of an IDW proper.

Wisdom

During the wisdom phase, the IDW learns how to use the richness of experience to inform a decision. As IDWs develop the ability to tailor solutions to individuals based on the context of past interactions and stored data, they become more like a personal assistant, adding exponential value to their users and the organization. So now the DOB datum translates to the IDW offering: "Happy birthday! I see you've got dinner plans tonight and a workout scheduled with your trainer for tomorrow morning. If you think you might be out celebrating late, I can reschedule the training session for you." Here we have a personal intelligent digital worker, or digital personal assistant.

As IDWs gain wisdom, friction begins to disappear for the user. But it's important to remember that the evolution of the end user's experience has an inverse relationship to the amount of orchestration required behind the scenes. Creating IDWs is really a matter of providing simplicity for users by finding ways to solve increasingly complex problems within your ecosystem.

Spending Quality Time with IDWs

As an organization's skills, AI agents, and ecosystem evolve, IDWs start to feel more like colleagues. They have skills that are helpful in collaboration or independently, and they can get things done. According to Gartner's 2023 prediction, by 2025 generative AI, which they describe as digital teammates, will be a workforce partner within 90% of companies worldwide.[1]

An IDW is indeed a digital teammate, and it can be trained to do all kinds of things. Imagine the IDW is in HR, training with Yvonne, a department supervisor, to become an expert in managing the approval processes and scheduling for paid time off (PTO).

This is a complex task given the amount of context the IDW needs to decipher:

- How much remaining PTO does the employee have?
- How many shifts will need to be covered?
- Who is available to cover these shifts?
- Are there any conflicts with the dates requested?

Yvonne is an expert in these areas, so she trains the IDW to follow an ideal process. This often-overlooked factor in creating force multipliers is crucial. Just like our example in Part I of automating a coffee maker demonstrated, greater impact comes from not just automating tasks to be done how people are already doing them but to actually improve the process. You're empowered to design processes that can be tackled by an unlimited number of workers.

User: I'd like to book some vacation time.
IDW: Okay, I can help you request time off. What days off would you like to request?
User: July 15th through the 22nd.
IDW: Okay. I'll work on filing a request for July 15th through July 22nd. Would you like me to see if someone is available to cover your shifts?
User: That would be great.

Once the IDW is operational, one of the ways it can continually contribute to its own evolution is by making use of its human-in-the-loop (HitL) skills, meaning it can reach out to Yvonne or her colleagues for help whenever it gets stumped.

IDW: Would you like me to see if someone is available to cover your shifts?
User: That would be great. Can you see if Carl is available to cover my Wednesday shift that week? He and I have been working on a project together, and there's a project meeting that day.
IDW: I'm not sure I understand the request. Let me grab a human to help . . .
IDW (TO Yvonne or proxy): Hey, I'm stumped. Can you help by providing me with the answer or appropriate action or please step in?

Yvonne can help the IDW understand the context of the request and move the experience forward. Each time she loops in to assist the IDW, it can learn from her by asking contextual questions that it can apply to other tasks as well ("Why does this user want only one day of his vacation covered by Carl and not all of them?").

Ultimately, Yvonne's goal is to evolve her digital teammate to a state of wisdom.

Tracing an Example Through All Four Evolutionary Stages

Now let's trace an example skill—helping employees to request paid time off—through the four evolutionary stages. Figures 9.2–9.6 depict what it might be like for our user, Jo, to interact with the same skill at various phases in its evolution.

FIGURE 9.2 The data and information literacy stage.

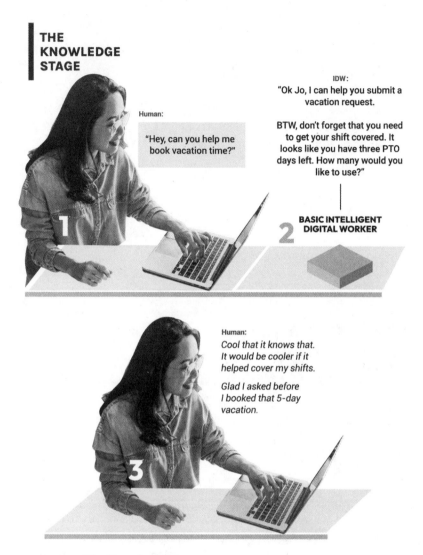

FIGURE 9.3   The knowledge stage.

Evolving Agents Toward OAGI

Organizational AGI centers around systematically enhancing and expanding the capabilities within an AI ecosystem by building and refining skills incrementally. This evolutionary AI ecosystem thrives on continuous improvement and adaptation, leveraging the interplay between creation, testing, monitoring, and simulation to maintain a

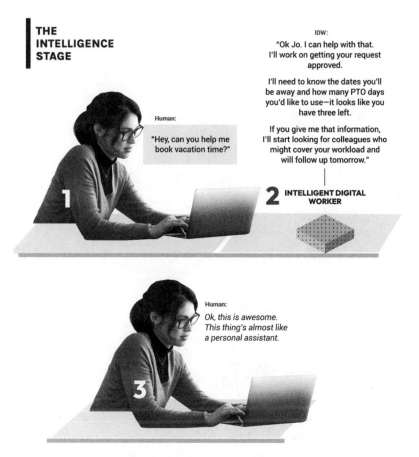

FIGURE 9.4   The intelligence stage.

state-of-the-art AI landscape. AI agents are designed not only to perform specific tasks but also to adapt and evolve by creating new functions on the fly or reusing existing ones from other tasks. This adaptability allows the ecosystem to continuously innovate and handle new challenges efficiently.

This gradual improvement can be likened to constructing a sophisticated architecture where each block represents a skill or a component of the system. The progression toward OAGI is achieved through a dual-path approach: the self-improvement of the system itself and the continuous enhancement of human expertise and interaction with the system.

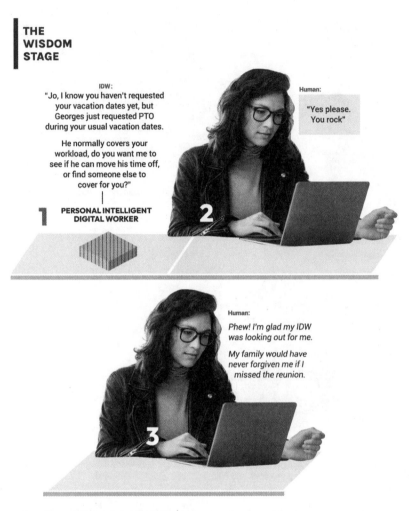

FIGURE 9.5 The wisdom stage.

Self-improvement in AI systems is achieved through mechanisms such as machine learning and adaptive algorithms that allow these systems to refine their operations based on the data they process and the feedback they receive. This is a dynamic process where the system continually adjusts and learns from each task performed by agents, enhancing accuracy and efficiency over time. There are also situations where simply improving the underlying model of a third party will improve the system, which can automatically benefit upgraded tools.

FIGURE 9.6   The data/information stage through the wisdom stage.

Robust feedback mechanisms are critical to OAGI, capturing and analyzing feedback from both AI agents and human users to inform ongoing improvements. This could take the form of specialized testing agents responsible for evaluating new and existing AI agents, ensuring that they function correctly and meet the required standards. These agents can conduct rigorous tests to identify any flaws or potential improvements in the agents.

Monitoring agents play a crucial role in this ecosystem, continuously overseeing the performance of other agents, ensuring they operate optimally and adhere to predefined protocols. To further enhance the ecosystem's robustness, simulation agents can run sophisticated simulations on other AI agents to detect bugs, identify performance bottlenecks, and propose enhancements. Based on the insights gained from simulations, these agents can automatically implement code fixes or updates, thereby improving the overall user experience and system performance.

Human improvement is equally critical and involves training teams to better understand and interact with AI systems. This ensures that human inputs are insightful and constructive, creating a symbiotic relationship that continually enhances the system's relevance and applicability in real-world scenarios. For the humans in this ecosystem, feedback can be used to develop better training programs and adjust the AI systems to better meet user needs and expectations.

Through these iterative loops of learning and adaptation, an organization can develop a more integrated, intelligent, and responsive AI ecosystem. Each cycle not only improves an IDW's performance but also enhances the collaborative efficiency between humans and machines, steering toward a more optimized organizational intelligence.

Key Takeaways

- The orchestrated AI agents, or IDWs, in your ecosystem move through four evolutionary phases as they become better at completing tasks: literacy, knowledge, intelligence, and wisdom.
- The edges around the stages are indistinct, and all skills employ each of the described characteristics—simple skills just use them to a lesser degree.
- Co-creation is the key to getting IDWs closer to the wisdom phase—co-creation between people as the IDWs skills are developed, and then co-creation between humans and IDWs as those skills are improved upon.
- HitL is a critical component to an IDW's evolution, as it keeps humans involved in helping the IDW make more connections and deepen its understanding of skills.

Want to expand on what you've learned in Chapter 9? Follow this QR code to interact with an IDW that can connect you with additional resources linked to key ideas from this chapter, including content from the *Invisible Machines* podcast.

CHAPTER 10

Teams and the Co-Creation Mindset

C o-creation is the secret sauce of organizational AGI. It's critical to get your team trending away from the land of centralization and technology silos and toward the co-creation mindset— because, while it's true that certain IDWs will only serve certain departments, their evolution is a company-wide endeavor. This is where your core enablement team comes in. Their mission is to get people involved in the creation and evolution of the skills in your company's ecosystem. Your ultimate goal is that everyone will use and contribute to your ecosystem of intelligent digital workers—helping design, improve, and evolve the skills that their own department's IDWs carry out.

The core enablement team is similar in makeup to the "fusion teams" that have cropped up in many organizations. Gartner describes them as being multidisciplinary, blending "technology or analytics and business domain expertise and shares accountability for business and technology outcomes. Instead of organizing work by functions or technologies, fusion teams are typically organized by the crosscutting business capabilities, business outcomes or customer outcomes they support." There's generally at least one IT person on a fusion team, and they work best with a diverse makeup in terms of function, ethnicity, and gender identity. Gartner research from 2021 estimates that 84% of orgs have at least one fusion team and that 70% of fusion teams use different technologies than what IT suggests or recommends—even if an IT representative is leading the team.[1]

This compulsion is actually beneficial in the context of organizational AGI, where the idea is to orchestrate separate technologies to create Beyond Human Experiences. If a certain piece of technology works better than another, it can be integrated into the ecosystem. It also speaks to a mindset that is always looking for better ways to get things done, which is the nut of a hyperdisruptive strategy. You don't ever want to limit your conversational experiences by imitating what humans do. The goal is to use a natural human interface to activate orchestrated technologies that can perform tasks in vastly more efficient ways than humans are able to alone.

The core enablement team will guide your whole organization as the creators and keepers of your strategy. This team will facilitate the process used to create experiences that align with your strategy. They should be exemplary teachers and collaborators. This team sets the bar for experience, helps guide the process, educates the people on the art of the possible, and helps solve any problems that come up along the way.

The same person can play one or more of the roles we are describing. Whether you've got the talent or decide to acquire talent, you need to make sure these people are equipped with the right experience, training, and tools. Choose your team wisely—they'll be the ones helping others in the organization build patterns, steps, and toolkits to manage their own agent orchestrations successfully.

Whether you find people to serve as interim proxies, make new hires, or draw from existing talent, selecting the members of this team is likely to be one of the most important decisions you will make in terms of long-term success. Fusion teams are an excellent reference point when assembling a core enablement team. They also represent the beginning stages of organizations moving away from development departments.

This is one big reason why AI will affect just about every job in the world. No matter what your industry, leveraging a core enablement team by embracing this approach will allow you to move more quickly than your competitors. Assigning core enablement team members and supporting them can make the difference between success and failure.

Meet the Team

On this team (see Figure 10.1), the most important duty is knowledge sharing. Core enablers should never covet control over information and tools. To win the race they will need to involve every person in

FIGURE 10.1   Meet the team.

your organization. They will monitor the process closely, making sure it aligns with the overarching strategy, all the while evangelizing the virtues of the ecosystem that's growing as a result of co-creation.

Strategic liaison (SL): This is the hardest role to define in traditional terms, but this person is the cornerstone to the success of the whole endeavor. The strategic liaison creates value for their organization through their intimate understanding of how to matchmake the needs of various internal business groups with their organization's ecosystem strategy. They're the glue that binds winning teams around a vision and resources needed to realize it. They know the possibilities of the ecosystem and work to shape and evangelize hyperautomation throughout the organization.

The strategic liaison may be a new hire or they may already be within your organization in the form of an internal champion behind creating or employing your ecosystem strategy. They may or may not be an experienced leader in design thinking, systems thinking, or innovation. Maybe they've owned successful services-as-a-product or successful product strategy. There are no rules dictating who the right person is for this role, but ideally they're a peer or trusted influencer to top-level leaders and decision makers in the organization.

Collaborating with stakeholders to identify and advance on problems and opportunities of internal business groups, the strategic liaison brings together the various business groups around the ecosystem strategy, as well as the process, tools, and training, that bring it to life. They provide vision, excitement, and action toward creating experiences that meet business needs while perpetually expanding the shared library of skills. Because this role is pivotal to the team's success—and because it's a new type of position unique to hyperautomation—we'll take an in-depth look at a day in the life of a strategic liaison a little later.

Lead experience architect (LXA): Responsible for facilitating, generating, and executing great user experiences, this role is many things. The quality and consistency of experiences offered by skills published in your company's shared library are under this person's purview. This leadership role demands a true veteran of human-centered design, interaction design, and design research who is in love with getting their hands dirty. Acting as a coach, mentor, and lead through the process, the LXA works to map the journey for interacting with skills and IDWs in close harmony with the core enablement team, and conversational experience designers in particular. Bringing experiences to life while empowering business groups to create more and more without depending on the core enablement team is the LXA's jam. This person has the crucial duty of building and managing the road map of skills being created and improved by the core enablement team in collaboration with various business groups.

We had a great conversation on the *Invisible Machines* podcast with Aaron Cooper, Senior Director of Digital Experience at Banner Health. Some of his work creating conversational experiences mirrors that of the LXA and dates back to his time at Honeywell, where he led internal automations for human resources. This included use cases for HR professionals in call centers trying to answer employee questions about time off or pay schedules. "[It could also] be a manager wanting to understand 'what's my regrettable turnover look like,'" Aaron said, "it really spanned personas for employees as well as managers and it spanned technologies as well."[2] He sees his work as "delivering new value through new experiences" and works closely with other leaders across departments to make sure design thinking is part of the general strategy.

Conversational experience designer (XD): A conversational experience designer takes high-level requirements and turns them into flows that support the right experience. In a way, the rest of the team is a support mechanism enabling this role. XDs can be anyone in any department; they don't need to have development experience but should have great communication and problem-solving skills. They should be versed in conversational design principles and have a strong enough command of your building platform that they can train others on using it. They also need certain soft skills. When hiring conversational designers, Aaron Cooper said, "I'm looking for people who can pause, who are clearly actively listening [and] who have high emotional intelligence because, ultimately, you want that to be the brand of a company. Just about any company wants that ability to empathize with their customers."

Data analyst/architect (DA): Measuring outcomes, insights, and predictions is critical to getting experiences tuned just right. Having someone architecting and designing processes for measuring success and gaining insight into each interaction with your digital workers is key. Another advantage to creating the kind of ecosystem described in these pages is that some aspects of user research can be done in real time, as user journeys can be monitored as they unfold. Unlocking these insights requires collaboration with a data analyst who understands the basic architecture of hyperautomation.

Technical architect/developer (TA/D): This role understands the development platform on a technical level and can build custom steps or library steps, views, and cards that enable XDs to build any skill needed. This person should always be thinking of building in a shareable, modular way. No-code software creation happens when users can build using modular pieces that are made up of granular, low-level functionalities sequenced together. This presents a new paradigm for traditional developers—one that breaks free from the constraints associated with coding in a vacuum. The TA/D will become a trusted advisor, as someone who understands how skills are structured and who can fine-tune on a microlevel and advise all the way up to the macro. They will also get to spend more time actually writing code.

Earlier we mentioned that typical developers only spend about 30% of their time writing code. Well, according to software developer

Bayrhammer Klaus, the average developer spends about 10 minutes per day writing code compared to almost 300 minutes reading code, a much bleaker assessment (perhaps based on slightly different metrics). "I like my code to be in order. I like my code to be easy to read and easy to understand," Bayrhammer wrote.[3] Well, a no-code environment isn't just beneficial because it makes authoring so fast; it's also easier for developers to get their heads around what's happening with what would have been code. In Chapter 5 we explained that APIs will be irrelevant soon because conversational interfaces will also apply to machines communicating with other machines. This is where the rubber meets the road. Developers won't have to parse the coded language of APIs; they'll literally be able to read the conversational thread of information sharing between machines.

As with all these roles on the core enablement team, there are elements of the TA/D skill set that are novel. There aren't seasoned experts in building an extensible cognitive architecture, which means some of this work will be exploratory. While it takes a different level of thinking to build reusable components as opposed to custom ones, if the TA/D is doing their job right, code-sharing becomes a reality across your organization—which is critical to making AI a team sport and accelerating your team's pace.

Quality assurance (QA): This role is key to success, and this person needs outstanding customer interfacing skills. Running a test plan often involves user testing and load testing. QA should be capable of running functional testing and should also understand specific principles in automated testing and test planning.

Human-in-the-loop (HitL): Human-in-the-loop is many things: a tool, a design pattern, and a role within the core enablement team. As we mentioned earlier, the relationship that develops between IDWs and humans-in-the-loop is the fertilizer that accelerates growth. HitL is a powerful, fluid role with the ability to bind and strengthen your entire ecosystem. If that sounds like a superhero bio, then our description is on target. Anyone within your organization can become a human-in-the-loop when the situation calls and then recede into the background once they've helped an IDW complete an interaction. HitL is powerful: when someone assumes the role, they leverage knowledge, perspective, and experience surrounding a task that they have a deep understanding of—which fills the gaps and accelerates training for IDWs.

This role lets people play directly to their strengths and therefore requires very little training. To prepare for this role, the HitL just needs to learn how to converse with the IDW effectively. When an IDW gets stuck on a query or task and calls on an HitL to bridge the gap, the interaction not only serves as an immediate solution, it also creates an opportunity for the IDW to gain a deeper understanding of context. Over time the relationships between the many IDWs and humans-in-the-loop in your ecosystem forge a powerful matrix for solving problems of every shape and size.

Next, we'll dig a little deeper on the strategic liaison role—viewed briefly through the lens of the film industry. At the helm of every film is a producer, and all producers have different strengths: some focus on talent and contracting, others are adept at connecting with actors—and some excel at keeping investors at arm's length. The best ones are also expert problem solvers within the context of a film set. Like an ecosystem built for organizational AGI, a film requires the orchestration of efforts from a wide variety of skill sets and a shared understanding of the language specific to the undertaking. The strategic liaison, like the producer together with the director, knows how to connect and activate all the pieces within their ecosystem, has an intimate understanding of the work that needs to be done at any given moment, and can always trace actions to the sacred point of view, or vision, that guides the entire operation. Here's what any given day in the world of an SL might look like.

A Day in the Life of a Strategic Liaison

Say hello to Aggie. She's been working as the lead content strategist at a large medical company for the past five years. Her company has a handful of disparate chatbots set up in an attempt to automate their operations. There's the FAQ machine on the company's website that gets clicked often, but almost just as often abandoned within a few lines of communication. Customers are also greeted by an automated voice when they call the company's toll free number. Aggie is already regularly going over call scripts with her contact with the call center, and she knows that this machine is generally abandoned after one or two prompts. As someone who works on strategic needs with nearly everyone in her organization, she knows that the few internal-facing machines that were acquired with different service software packages are also lackluster.

When her company made the decision to hyperautomate in earnest, Aggie wasn't the first person they thought of to lead the core enablement team, but over the course of a few meetings, it became clear that she knew how to communicate on a needs-level with every department and that she understood the larger goal of an ecosystem of IDWs. Aggie already has an understanding of the various needs of her company's business groups as well as a growing understanding of what works in terms of implementing agentic AI.

Now the newly appointed strategic liaison on her organization's core enablement team, she spends her days moving between departments, analyzing roles and tasks, and translating those jobs into a framework of automation. Aggie uses her varied skill sets and strengths to keep the process of co-creation oiled.

Monday, 10 a.m.: In the morning, Aggie finds herself engaged in technical work with the operations team. Automating expense tracking requires coordinating data points, and before piloting the automation, they need to ensure that the machine is pulling from the right systems and coding the data so that it links properly to the employee submitting the expense, the department they work within, and the initiative the expense tracks to. They'd like to have missing or unsynchronized data prompt a conversational query that goes either to the employee or their supervisor, depending on the nature of the expense. Aggie reaches out to the call center lead to get a better sense of when to ask an employee and when to bypass in favor of a supervisor.

Monday, 11 a.m.: Before lunch, Aggie is working with the legal department on the experience design of the contract renewal process. Her understanding of design thinking helps her understand the flows from an empathetic standpoint, while her stakeholder mindset keeps her focused on the business needs—in this case, the clarity and precision legally binding processes require.

Monday, 1 p.m.: Aggie had lunch with the legal team, and they've since moved from designing the contract renewal process to iterating on contract management automations. They are trying to work through some changes in the process and only have a couple of hours together. Her experience with Agile methodologies comes into play as they bounce quickly from one idea to the next, identifying microservices that can make user interactions flow more efficiently toward more rewarding outcomes. Referencing some microservices that worked well for the finance department as they worked on insurance claim management, the team is able to create a workflow that meets most of their objectives, something they will likely fine-tune later in the week.

Monday, 3 p.m.: The marketing department is piloting a new feature for reminding internal users to categorize leads coming through social media channels. Aggie piloted a similar feature for the operations department, though the reminders there were generated from within the department's database. The team worked together on automating the process last week, iterating on an existing microservice from the shared library so that it could connect to social media platforms and query for certain information. They already submitted the edited version of the skill, and it was approved and published into the company's shared library. Now the pilot program is up and running and they are watching interactions in real time to make quick tweaks, some of which they're now starting to automate A/B testing for.

Monday, 3:30 p.m.: Aggie hops on a call with the HR department. They are also piloting a new automation, but this one is attached to the benefits enrollment process. Internal users have been asking why the process requires them to enter personal information that the company already has on file. Aggie suspects that when they look at the analytics for the department's pilot next week, they will see a drop off when users get to blank fields that they've already filled out at least once before.

The strategic liaison moves around the internal web of the organization somewhat like a spider, threading machines, users, processes, and outcomes together in ways that work well for everyone involved. Aggie understands that a strong indicator of hyperautomation is that existing AI agents are constantly being modified and used in new ways and that the ecosystem is continually improving. This not only accelerates deployment speed, allowing the continual automation of new tasks, it also expands the reach and quality of co-creation inside your organization.

Get Your Team "Design Thinking"

Putting the patterns we've outlined to work for your organization requires a unified front with everyone in your organization contributing their strengths. Designing for accelerated automation means solving a large number of interconnected problems—problems that different members of your organization will understand in different ways—which is where design thinking comes into play.

A process tailor-made for creating solutions to abstract problems, design thinking helps you identify the human needs at their core. Understanding and employing the five stages of design thinking will empower everyone in your organization to take part in solving complex problems. Even if they aren't actively taking part in the steps outlined below, it's beneficial to give your workforce a basic understanding of how design thinking works and how it will be put to work within your ecosystem.

1. **Empathize—research your users' needs:** In the first stage of the design thinking process you go deep into your users' needs to develop an empathetic understanding of the problems you're trying to solve. Be cautious with research tools using generative tools to synthesize user data. Empathy is crucial to a human-centered design process because it allows you to set aside your own assumptions about the world and gain real insight into users and their needs. Fabricated data isn't going to offer the same depth of insight as what you get from research involving real humans.

2. **Define—state your users' needs and problems:** During this stage, you accumulate information gathered during the empathize stage and analyze your observations. As you begin to define problems, you are, in effect, synthesizing your discoveries to identify the problems you will need to design for as you build your ecosystem. Automating how you, your team, or your organization are currently doing things can be valuable. But approaching automation in this way might blind you to important opportunities in hyperautomation. Nine times out of 10 it will be more valuable to your company if you create automation that reflects the ideal way of getting things done, rather than how they're currently being done.

Get Your Team "Design Thinking" (continued)

3. Ideate—challenge assumptions and create ideas: Now it's time to bring your defined problems into the ideation stage. This means lots of brainstorming with everyone involved in the project thinking outside the box. There are no wrong answers, as alternative approaches to the problem statements you've created are likely to lead to innovation.

4. Prototype—start to create solutions: During this phase, the design team produces a variety of inexpensive, scaled-down versions of the product or the features that make up the product in order to investigate different ideas from the ideation phase.

5. Test—try out your solutions: The viable solutions that come out of the prototype phase can now be tested with users. This is the final stage in the process, but as solutions are tested, it will likely mean a return to the prototype phase to tinker with designs. Future iterations will improve on what works and remedy what doesn't. Iterate until the cows come home—this is an infinite loop. It's probably already clear by now, but iteration is key if not central to this process. If you're truly operating a design strategy that values user-centered principles, omniscience is your enemy. The name of the game will be getting to the point where you have a thing to iterate on as quickly as possible. Once you have a thing to test and observe, iterate, iterate again, and iterate some more. In a properly designed ecosystem, the speed of iteration is incredibly swift. More agile than Agile, we like to say.

Design thinking is ideal for tackling the convoluted problems of hyperautomation, where it's difficult to identify the human needs at their core. The more people in your organization who take part in tackling these complex problems, the better!

Key Takeaways

- Hyperautomation efforts hinge on the effectiveness of your core enablement team—the people who facilitate all aspects of hyperautomation and, more importantly, get everyone in your organization comfortable creating and improving their own automations.

- The core enablement team is composed of variations of several familiar roles plus the addition of the new strategic liaison (SL) role—the person who binds the work being done by the core enablement team to the fabric of your organization.

- A typical day in the life of an SL involves meeting with different departments throughout your organization, addressing specific concerns, fueling the culture of co-creation, and empowering everyone to take part in the pursuit of hyperautomation.

- Making sure your core enablement team is fluent in design thinking can make it easier to tackle the convoluted problems that come with hyperautomation.

Want to expand on what you've learned in Chapter 10? Follow this QR code to interact with an IDW that can connect you with additional resources linked to key ideas from this chapter, including content from the *Invisible Machines* podcast.

CHAPTER 11

How to Architect Tools Like LLMs, Agents, and Generative AI

A t the moment of this writing, it's difficult to have conversations about conversational AI that don't involve large language models (LLMs) and the AI agents that are using them to automate a number of productivity use cases. Many of the use cases leverage other generative tools as well, to varying degrees of usefulness. There was a noticeable spike in interest following the Google Cloud Next Opening Keynote in 2024, which unveiled a menagerie of AI agents that could do things like find a consumer a specific checkered shirt from a photo (adding upselling to the experience as well) and summarize massive documents as deadlines loomed.

One of the use cases presented involved a "creative agent" that was being used to workshop an imaginary brand identity around a tent that was still in development. "In this case, the creative agent has analyzed over 3,000 brand images, descriptions, videos, and documents of other products that we have in our catalog contained within Google Drive to create this summary," a Google field engineer explained. "The creative agent was able to use Gemini Pro's 1 million-token context window and its ability to reason across text, images, and video to generate this summary."[1]

It's an interesting enough idea, but it started going off the rails as he showed the sample podcast script the agent generated, followed by a facsimile of the scripted conversation delivered in robot voices.

It's hard to imagine scenarios where this last bit of activity might move the needle. The bigger problem is that it amounts to surface-level noodling when the real work that companies need to be doing involves the creation of the kind of infrastructures we'll talk about in the next chapter. Given the choice, most orgs will find agents that can move across channels, communicate with one another, share data, and swarm around complex tasks far more useful than a stockpile of clunky podcast prototypes.

LLMs Alone Can't Turn Words into Action

ChatGPT in particular has given us a powerful example of the persuasive power of human-like machines. We'll take a deeper dive into anthropomorphics in Chapter 17, but the fact that LLMs can communicate effectively using natural language creates the illusion that they possess real intelligence. LLMs are prediction machines that are able to predict what word is most likely to come next based on the preceding words. Without minimizing the admittedly astounding effectiveness with which these models are able to execute on a wide variety of prompts, it's critical to remember that these abilities aren't analogous to actual knowledge.

On their own, LLMs don't know anything. There's certainly meaning buried in pattern prediction (i.e., dogs help humans, humans like dogs, dogs have pleasant fur, dogs have cute faces . . . therefore dogs must be good), but for any sort of conversational technology to have approximate intelligence and agency, it needs a shitload more context.

There are plenty of orgs out there feeding piles of unstructured company data to LLMs believing that the work ends there. This is an approach that's becoming sadly all too common these days, and it's likely to leave plenty of businesses with a dim view of these technologies. As we mentioned in Chapter 8, Morgan Stanley spent nine months training GPT-4 on more than 100,000 internal documents. When we spoke with Jeff McMillan and David Wu, Morgan Stanley's Head of AD&I and the Head of Knowledge Management & Generative

AI, respectively, they said it was obvious very quickly that to create an agent that was actually going to be useful and reliable, more work would be required.[2]

They broke their content up into about 100 domains and found the right content owner to take charge of each. Then they put in systems to determine when content was no longer relevant, inviting content creators to update documents or determine if they should be removed. The forward-thinking team at Morgan Stanley has created an undeniably useful and rewarding digital assistant that has improved the work experience of their advisors. Still, this assistant isn't really a full AI agent or IDW until it can collaborate with other AI agents and humans across departments. This requires something bigger.

Giving AI Agents Real Agency

As a OneReach.ai Lead Experience Architect, Annie Harshberger, pointed out on an episode of the *Invisible Machines* podcast, one of the most powerful aspects of AI agents is their composability. "[We think of agents] in terms of reusability, and how certain pieces of an experience will be used not just when you're scheduling a meeting but in other skills," Annie said.[3]

While demonstrating a complex scheduling automation using the Generative Studio X (or GSX) platform, she pointed to an agent in the experience that sent out a poll to meeting invitees, asking for a vote on the best time and date. This agent could be used to conduct polls across a wide variety of use cases, but only within an ecosystem that connects the many different departments and data stores across an organization. These kinds of interchangeable and customizable skills and tools make for a very powerful technology ecosystem.

Creating this kind of connectivity comes with some new requirements:

- **Security:** Proper use of IDWs demands robust protection of data and privacy throughout the interaction and data processing stages.
- **Scalability:** IDWs need to handle increasing workloads and concurrent conversations without degrading performance.

- **Skill Management:** There need to be mechanisms for the acceptance and review of user-generated skills, maintaining quality and relevance while encouraging team members to collaborate on designing automations. (Having people across teams and departments contributing to the ecosystem by designing and evolving IDWs is a key piece of hyperautomation.)

- **Updates and Maintenance:** There will need to be regular updates to the AI models and software, ensuring they remain effective and secure against evolving threats.

- **Monitoring:** Tools to track the performance and usage of IDWs enabling timely interventions and improvements.

- **Authoring Tools:** No-code interfaces allow users to create and modify skills without needing deep technical expertise. As mentioned in Skill Management above, having people across teams and departments contributing to the ecosystem by designing and evolving IDWs is a key piece of hyperautomation.

Get these elements right and you can build AI agents with loads of agency. The IDWs built on the GSX platform, for instance, are capable of identifying skills that match to various aspects of a given objective, allowing AI agents to work together, or swarm, on complex tasks, as shown in Figure 11.1.

FIGURE 11.1 Three-quarter view of an IDW and its skills with height indicating increased sophistication (OneReach.ai).

This Is a Totally Different Approach to Software

Most of the software we encounter in the world is built using specific coding and programming and hence, quite brittle. In traditional software development, programmers write out explicit, binary instructions for machines to follow. The if-this-then-that model has been necessary because human language isn't precise enough to efficiently communicate to machines exactly what we want them to do. The majority of the cost of building software actually comes from this instruction-based approach. Creating instructions, piece-by-piece, and then testing all the various scenarios out is expensive. Many software development projects also require a set of instructions for end users, so they know how to interact with the machine.

Most of the machines we interact with on a daily basis need instructions on a very granular level but are rarely given an objective. If you were trying to get a machine to go to the bathroom, you'd have to provide instructions for each microstep: *set down pencil, raise hand, ask for permission . . . if yes, move quietly toward the door.* The machine might end up in the bathroom but it would never know that was the objective all along. We can leave the robotics challenges associated with a machine actually using the bathroom for another book. The important point here is that, with AI agents, people are poised to give machines objectives rather than instructions.

This will sound odd, but we're entering an era where you can just tell a machine to go to the bathroom and it will figure out how to get there. For now, however, as long as we don't want agents to have full agency, we'll need to provide some form of instruction along with these larger objectives.

The anatomy of a successful AI agent includes

- an **objective**
- relevant **constraints**
- some form of **instructions**

AI agents create a new paradigm where humans can provide machines with an objective, like "book a meeting with the people in this call to follow up on the action items we discussed." An AI agent with agency can work with an objective like this, swarming with other agents to complete the necessary steps of booking a meeting with multiple participants.

For this to work effectively, an AI agent or IDW needs an objective (like the one provided above), constraints (meetings must take place during the overlapping working hours of remote teams), and some instructions (only schedule a meeting time once the CEO and CTO have agreed on the time and day).

In our enduring bathroom example, the machine might understand the broader objective of going to the bathroom, but it might be important for it to know that the closest working bathroom is two floors down, and that jumping out of a window isn't the best way to get there. Speaking more practically, if you want your IDW to manage PTO requests for employees, but you don't want it deciding what the approval process is for PTO, you'd give it some instructions surrounding PTO policy.

In some ways, this is the opposite of the traditional approach to software. Rather than telling a machine specifically what to do, AI agents often need to be told what *not* to do. There's also something bigger happening here that might only be exciting to real nerds. With AI agents working together in this kind of ecosystem, software is being written on the fly: created, tested, and deployed instantaneously.

We've been calling these ephemeral applications, and they represent a completely different way of thinking about software. In our scheduling example, the particulars of any given meeting have temporary relevance and won't ever be used again. After all, once the meeting time has passed, it can't be scheduled again. This means the AI agents involved in automating the task are writing single-use code that won't be heard from again. This is a totally different approach to software.

Orchestrating LLMs, Agents, and Generative AI Requires an Open System

In an ecosystem built for hyperautomation, conversation is the tissue that connects all the individual nodes at play. A state of hyperautomation within an organization is achieved when a collection of advanced technologies are sequenced in perpetually intelligent ways to create automations of business processes that continue getting smarter. In these ecosystems, machines are communicating with other machines, but there are also conversations between humans and machines. Inside truly optimized ecosystems, humans are training their digital counterparts to complete new tasks through conversational interfaces—they're telling them how to contextualize and solve problems.

These innovations, algorithms, and systems that get sewn together start to build what's referred to as artificial general intelligence (AGI). Building on the idea of providing machines a balance of objectives and instructions, the sort of system that's achieved AGI will only need an objective to complete a task. This leads to the more imminent organizational AGI we've been talking so much about. Josh wrote about this connection in an article for *Observer*:

> There's the immediate and tangible benefit of people eliminating tedious tasks from their lives. Then there's the long term benefit of a burgeoning ecosystem where employees and customers are interacting with digital teammates that can perform automations leveraging all forms of data across an organization. This is an ecosystem that starts to take the form of a digital twin.[4]

McKinsey describes a digital twin as "a virtual replica of a physical object, person, or process that can be used to simulate its behavior to better understand how it works in real life." They describe these twins inhabiting ecosystems similar to what we're describing here that they call an "enterprise metaverse . . . a digital and often immersive environment that replicates and connects every aspect of an organization to optimize simulations, scenario planning, and decision making."[5]

Something as vast as an enterprise metaverse won't materialize inside a closed system where the tools have to be supplied exclusively by Google or IBM. If you're handcuffed to a specific LLM, NLP, or NLU vendor, your development cycles will be limited by their schedule and capabilities. This is actually a common misstep for organizations looking for vendors: it's easy to think that the processing and contextualization of natural language is artificial intelligence—a faulty notion that ChatGPT in particular set ablaze. But LLMs and NLP/NLU are just individual pieces of technology that make up a much broader ecosystem for creating artificial intelligence. Perhaps more importantly, in terms of keeping an open system, LLMs and NLP/NLU are one of many modular technologies that can be orchestrated within an ecosystem. "Modular" means that, when better functionalities—like improved LLMs—emerge, an open system is ready to accept and use them.

In the rush to begin hyperautomating, LLMs have quickly proven to be the first stumbling block for many organizations. As they attempt to automate specific aspects of their operations with these tools that seem to know so much (but actually "know" basically nothing), the result is usually a smattering of less-than-impressive chatbots that are likely unreliable and operating in their own closed system. These cloistered AI agents are unable to become part of an orchestrated effort—and thus create subpar user experiences.

Think of auto manufacturing. In some ways, it would be easier to manage the supply chain if everything came from one supplier or if the manufacturer supplied its own parts, but production would suffer. Ford—a pioneer of assembly-line efficiency—relies on a supply chain with more than 1,400 tier 1 suppliers separated by up to 10 tiers between supply and raw materials, providing significant opportunities to identify and reduce costs and protect against economic shifts. This represents a viable philosophy where hyperautomation is concerned as well. Naturally, it comes with a far more complex set of variables, but relying on one tool or vendor stifles nearly every aspect of the process: innovation, design, user experience—it all suffers.

"Most of the high-profile successes of AI so far have been in relatively closed sorts of domains," Dr. Ben Goertzel said in his TEDxBerkeley talk, "Decentralized AI," pointing to game playing as an example. He describes AI programs playing chess better than any human but reminds us that these applications still "choke a bit when you give them the full chaotic splendor of the everyday world that we live in."

Goertzel has been working in this frontier for years through the OpenCog Foundation, the Artificial General Intelligence Society, and SingularityNET, a decentralized AI platform that lets multiple AI agents cooperate to solve problems in a participatory way without any central controller.

In that same TEDx talk, Goertzel references ideas from Marvin Minsky's book *The Society of Mind*: "It may not be one algorithm written by one programmer or one company that gives the breakthrough to general intelligence. . ... It may be a network of different AIs each doing different things, specializing in certain kinds of problems."[6]

Hyperautomating within an organization is much the same: a whole network of elements working together in an evolutionary fashion. As the architects of the ecosystem are able to iterate rapidly—trying out new configurations—the fittest tools, AI agents, and algorithms survive. From a business standpoint, these open systems provide the means to understand, analyze, and manage the relationships between all of the moving parts inside your burgeoning ecosystem, which is the only way to craft a feasible strategy for achieving hyperautomation.

Creating an architecture for hyperautomation is a matter of creating an infrastructure—not so much the individual elements that exist within an infrastructure. It's the roads, electricity, and waterways that you put in place to support houses and buildings and communities. That's the problem a lot of organizations have with these efforts. They're failing to see how vast it is. Simulating human beings and automating tasks are not the same as buying an email marketing tool.

The beauty of an open platform is that you don't have to get it right. It might be frightening in some regards to step outside a neatly bottled or more familiar ecosystem, but the breadth and complexity of AI are also where its problem-solving powers reside. Following practical wisdom applied to emergent technologies—wait until a clear path forward emerges before buying in—won't work because once one organization achieves a state of hyperautomation, their competitors won't be able to catch them. By choosing one flavor or system for all of your conversational AI needs, you're limiting yourself at a time when you need as many tools as you can get. The only way to know what tools to use is to try them all, and with a truly open system, you have the power to do that.

As you can imagine, this distributed development and deployment of microservices gives your entire organization a massive boost. You can also create multiple applications/skills concurrently, meaning more developers working on the same app, at the same time, resulting in less time spent in development. All of this activity thrives because the open system allows new tools from any vendor to be sequenced at will.

Feasibility Is All About Speed

You need to equip yourself to rapidly generate great conversational experiences—powered by the latest AI—across any channel. Ideas for great experiences are inspired and rarely planned; therefore, the key to great experiences is rapid iteration, not waterfall approaches. When it comes to hyperautomating, speed is the game. The more you iterate, the better the experience becomes. The faster you can iterate, the faster your experiences become better.

Leonard Cohen wrote his song "Hallelujah" more than 70 different ways before releasing it. Even then, he still wasn't convinced it was done—much in the same way that your conversational experiences will never be "done." Great conversational experiences aren't usually created in a diagram or a spreadsheet and then handed to a developer to be built. They are the result of prototyping, iterating, user testing, scrapping things, and starting over.

There's a difference between great experiences and sophisticated experiences. In the realm of automation, the latter comes through evolution. You can't sit down and design a sophisticated experience in one fell swoop.

This is why speed matters when it comes to making great experiences. Iterating toward great experiences is hard in any context, let alone in this new and complex world of hyperautomation. You need to be sure your tools make it as easy as possible to prototype, iterate, and test. Whatever platform you use to facilitate hyperautomation needs to be built with speed as the primary factor.

With Speed Comes Momentum

When people across your organization automate tasks and create their own skills and microservices, your shared library continues to grow as a resource for other creators and AI agents in the ecosystem. This creates the conditions for your ecosystem to expand and evolve organically. It's not unlike a universe unto itself, with an ever-expanding number of microservices that can be sequenced to meet any problem.

Here are some of the specialized tools you need to get to that state.

Human-in-the-loop: Humans need to be able to monitor AI agents as they work, entering into the experience when the machine doesn't know what to do or needs guidance. AI agents, in turn, can learn from the ongoing process of human-led refinement of automated tasks, as shown in Figure 11.1.

The continued evolution and expansion of an ecosystem relies on the human-in-the-loop process. Humans are a critical part of the ecosystem, working seamlessly alongside their agents, asking one another for help, querying, and establishing recommended responses and actions. To contribute to AI training and step in where human touch is needed, people need the ability to moderate AI agent-managed conversations in real time.

From these in-experience interventions, AI agents can learn from the live human-to-human interactions—as a member of your organization guides a user to the next step, the agents gain new contextual data. The knowledge and skills retained by agents through in-line training can be leveraged across your organization. The more time AI agents spend learning from their human counterparts, the faster the ecosystem can evolve.

They become more capable and require less human intervention, freeing humans to move on to automating more tasks. Opportunities also emerge for something we call co-botting, where people and IDWs design or modify skills together. This could be as simple as a human realizing they should train an IDW on how to collect payment before a service is rendered.

On the flip side of that example, an IDW looking at analytics data and seeing that a significant number of users are requesting the option to prepay can reach out to a human peer for training on how to complete the transaction.

Shared library: Our old friend, the shared library is the central resource of your ecosystem. Everyone draws microservices, skills, and flows from it, and when these elements are customized for new services, that information becomes part of the shared resource. The shared library is crucial for hyperautomating. It supplies your organization with best practices to scale knowledge sharing, accelerate development, and, at the same time, take control of security, compliance, monitoring, best practices, consistency, and scalability.

Actionable documentation: At least in the initial stages, it's important to maintain accurate documentation for your shared library. Documentation enables members of your organization to understand which skills and microservices are available and operational as well as how to use them as they create new solutions.

Quickly build and iterate on primary skills: As you're creating IDWs, you need to be able to quickly build and iterate on primary skills, like being able to operate over any number of specific communication channels (Slack, phone, SMS, Alexa, email, web chat, etc.). Understanding natural language is also a primary skill for an IDW, as is being able to include a human-in-the-loop when necessary.

Views, dashboards, and widgets: It's imperative that you have the ability to generate custom reporting views, dashboards, and widgets that tie into your conversational experiences. These are used to trigger automated tasks and can offer real-time analysis and adaptations driven by your data. Equip your conversational applications to adjust the experiences they offer as they are happening, based on analysis and triggered events in customized reports.

Draw from multiple knowledge bases: If you're attempting to integrate an existing conversational application into your emergent ecosystem, you'll need a tool that can give IDWs access to multiple knowledge bases—a knowledge garden, if you will. For example, imagine an IDW that is equipped to utilize a knowledge base your HR team built, as well as a knowledge base run through IBM Watson and one that you're licensing from your HR applicant tracking software. At some point, you might also need to bring a third-party application into the mix so, once again, you need a tool with the flexibility to do so. GSX was designed with this capability in mind, making it easy to not only integrate third-party applications but to also build your own internal knowledge bases.

Easy access to stored data: It's important to have easy, permanent, accessible storage for the data your conversational applications capture and use with low latency. You want tools that are designed and optimized to make hosting and accessing data easier on the back end, as users interact with your IDWs. By connecting your automated experiences to APIs or your own files, sheets, and data, you can support their flows. You'll need to be able to push, pull, and store data without writing a line of code.

End-to-end control over voice: The integrity of your audio is crucial when working with conversational AI. Rewarding experiences with NLP, NLU, and IVR require reliable audio quality from the customer's connection point through to your agents. When selecting voice-enabled technology, make sure you choose a platform that gives you end-to-end control of every interaction. That's the only way to effectively troubleshoot problems as they arise and create new solutions effectively. With end-to-end control, you can prototype, test, view traffic, manage channels and APIs, and handle reporting all in one place. In a similar vein, it's also important to be wary of voice gateways. Using a Zoom meeting as an example, if everyone present is using the Zoom app to connect, then Zoom can control the quality of the connections. Anyone who calls into the meeting on a remote telephone line is accessing through a voice gateway, and the quality of that connection is out of Zoom's hands.

Whenever possible, have users call in using a controlled line. Imagine how difficult it would be to figure out why calls are dropping off for your end users if your only recourse is to trace lines along a spider's web of technologies and suppliers. In this scenario, you'll likely end up caught in the crossfire as vendors blame one another for the issue. However, if you have end-to-end control over voice inputs, you can use analytics and reporting to chart the traffic flow and see exactly where calls are falling off.

Own your road map: If halfway up your Everest, you realize there's a crucial tool you'll need to get to the next checkpoint, it's far better to have the ability to forge the tool right then and there. Radioing back to basecamp and asking someone to send it up to you means valuable time squandered. Build tools as you need them, rather than relying on a platform's development team and losing the time it takes for them to generate a solution.

Use rules-based AI and neural networking together: In the realm of AI, there are often two proposed pathways or models: rules-based or neural networking. There is complexity and ongoing discourse surrounding each approach. Suffice to say that with the right tack and tools, you can combine elements of each, allowing your experience designers to create solutions far faster by reducing the need for massive amounts of training data.

Loading historical data into a machine learning model can create a generalized version of the conversations you've had but doesn't necessarily create good experiences. With the learning capabilities of neural networks and the power of rule-based AI, XDs can adapt to new settings and problems with far less data. Add human-in-the-loop systems to the mix, and you can cut upfront training data needs to almost zero.

Key Takeaways

- Building ecosystems for hyperautomating requires tools that give you total control of iterating and fine-tuning solutions—it's all about feasibility and optionality.

- Hyperautomating requires an open system that lets you use the best tools available and puts your organization in charge of its own development cycles.

- This level of automation is done by breaking skills down into their component services and then breaking those down into their component steps, giving you pliable, infinitely customizable microservices.

- Covering your bases lets you focus on enabling non-developers to orchestrate conversational and non-conversational advanced technology quickly and easily.

- The most efficient way to accelerate the force-multiplying effects of hyperautomation is to equip your organization for rapid, code-free programming.

Want to expand on what you've learned in Chapter 11? Follow this QR code to interact with an IDW that can connect you with additional resources linked to key ideas from this chapter, including content from the *Invisible Machines* podcast.

CHAPTER 12

Organizational AGI Demands an Extensible Cognitive Architecture

As we've already discussed, the release of ChatGPT unleashed a surge of interest and activity surrounding generative AI. The pairing of an LLM with a familiar chat interface both stirred the general public's interest in the technologies surrounding hyperautomation and sent the race toward adoption into overdrive.

The next big leap with generative AI won't be improvements in predictive power; it will come with context. By capturing and storing conversational data organization-wide, enterprises can begin constructing an infrastructure that can put these technologies to work (and create opportunities to start building on top of it). Such an infrastructure is highly complex, and based on the requirements, we've been calling it extensible cognitive architecture.

You can think of this extensible cognitive architecture as an operating system for conversational applications like AI agents and IDWs. Before we get into the particulars of this architecture, however, let's dig a little deeper into the two primary categories of marketplace offerings: **tools (and toolkits)** and **point solutions.**

Tools and Toolkits Are Locked in Boxes

The realm of tools and toolkits is dominated by tech giants like Microsoft, AWS, and Google, with many companies like Huggingface, OpenAI, and Anthropic releasing functional solutions as well. Individual providers might provide a diverse array of tools, APIs, and resources that empower businesses to integrate, craft, and deploy conversational AI applications. These toolkits typically furnish individual component tools like natural language processing, speech recognition, authentication, and chatbot UI elements.

While these components offer flexibility, integrating them into the kind of cohesive experience an IDW provides requires significant effort and coordination. Even a mega vendor's toolkit typically only offers limited integrations that couple with their own toolsets. These tools and kits are not designed specifically to create conversational experiences, and need to be unified within a single infrastructure, which can be incredibly complex.

There is also significant danger here for vendor lock-in—organizations becoming excessively reliant on a single toolkit. This is problematic in the turbulent conversational AI landscape, where requirements and capabilities are shifting at an astonishing rate. Toolkits are what they sound like, a set of individual tools that have to be integrated together to create a solution.

We are entering an era where delineating between business and technology will become pointless and impossible. Businesses are turning themselves into computing ecosystems to more intelligently engage with employees, customers, and the broader marketplace.

It might be helpful to think of the journey toward hyperautomation as the act of turning your organization into a computer or, in essence, a self-driving business. Trying to complete such a transformation with toolkits leaves you trying to build an organizational supercomputer using components sourced solely from a single manufacturer. In that situation, you'd better hope their road map looks a lot like yours.

Point Solutions Lack Flexibility

Point solutions are used to improve legacy software, but they don't change the game. Think of them like hybrid vehicles that are both gas and electric. Point solutions come in two flavors, and both can be alluring. **AI bolt-ons** are pre-built solutions added somewhat strategically to existing software platforms like ServiceNow, Workday, MS Office, and Salesforce. Major software providers are currently in a frenzy trying to incorporate these AI bolt-ons to prevent the erosion of their user interfaces, fearing obsolescence in the face of conversational AI advances. While these bolt-ons offer ease of procurement and installation, they exhibit fragility and limitations in terms of channel support and functionality scope, as they are often confined to the software they augment.

Despite their convenience and in-ecosystem integration advantages, AI bolt-ons fail to provide the comprehensive capabilities necessary for tackling and scaling complex tasks. They often lead to the dreaded proliferation of disparate, unmanageable, perplexing, and utterly random acts of bot building within a company.

To fully harness the potential of agentic AI, it's imperative to reach toward the way more sophisticated companies approach AI and break free from the constraints of isolated point solutions. The real value lies in automating processes that span multiple software systems. These scenarios represent prime opportunities for automation, as they frequently encompass complex and time-consuming human tasks.

By contrast, **standalone point solutions** are distinct AI applications tailored for specific tasks. They aren't constrained by the limitations of existing software systems or pricing models. These solutions prioritize pure conversational experiences and have the flexibility to transcend different systems through abstraction layers like Zapier or Mulesoft. Examples of standalone point solutions include OpenAI's GPT models, Kore.ai, and Cognigy.

Standalone point solutions excel in handling pre-designed conversations for common tasks, such as password resets. They typically address use cases that are pervasive across entire markets or industries. As such, these solutions tend to be inflexible, adhering to rigid structures. While they offer advantages over building applications from scratch using toolkits, they still require a considerable degree of customization.

Where standalone point solutions fall short is in scenarios that deviate from the norm or demand extensive customization, which are table stakes for orchestrated AI agents. Many companies rely on legacy software systems like Salesforce and ServiceNow along with various security authentication protocols. This requires solutions to seamlessly integrate with existing systems, presenting a significant challenge for standalone applications.

To return to the organization-as-a-computer metaphor, both strains of point solution are like buying a computer out-of-the-box and hoping it will still serve your computing needs in five years. Or worse, like starting your journey toward a computer-equipped workforce with dedicated devices like calculators and word processors instead of laptops.

Extensible Cognitive Architecture Is the Answer

Any business that's operating like a giant computer is going to be quite complex. It will be a system of interconnected components working together so that conversational applications can understand and respond to user input effectively. Extensible cognitive architecture makes this possible. It consists of multiple interconnected software components and databases collaborating to create seamless conversational experiences that combine language understanding, context awareness, and the ability to generate micro-UIs as needed.

It can amalgamate language services (e.g., NLU, TTS, ASR, localization) with other cognitive services, like computer vision and generative AI. The many components that become part of this architecture can be removed and replaced as better solutions come to market (including the brain). However you choose to build this architecture, this flexibility is a critical component to using AI effectively.

Gartner's CX CORE report states, "Intelligent coordination is a form of human and technology orchestration, where customer relationship understanding and empathy principles prescribe a unique set of coordinated actions to be executed across an organization, resulting in a frictionless and relevant CX."

Gartner calls for something called The Experience Membrane, which uses customer insight to develop a set of principles governing two-way communications between customers and a company. We've identified something similar called Intelligent Communication Fabric

(ICF). Whatever you choose to call it, you need it to design experiences based on an awareness of every action taken across any channel, in real time.

This fabric is designed specifically for communication. It's different from a data mesh in that you're not restricted to making right turns on a grid. Lines between points can take whatever shape makes the most sense. ICF enables composable micro services to use conversational interfaces and conversational memory across deep channel integrations to create personalized experiences that reward users in major ways.

With cognitive architecture, a content engine, and ICF, you can pick your preferred acronym: GPT, LAMDA, another LLM, a different NLP/NLU system. All of them are at your disposal. Same goes for existing software that's part of a manual workflow. Using APIs, they can be baked into the skills IDWs use inside your ecosystem.

Organizations in a state of hyperautomation are automating a wide range of tasks coordinated across different software systems, channels, and departments, integrating with various business systems, and scaling to meet evolving business needs. The IDWs within their ecosystem are sharing customizable skills and a depth of contextualized information. With their simple architectures, point solutions would need to be replaced or significantly overhauled on a regular basis to meet these advanced requirements.

There's noticeable confusion in the marketplace about the differences between bundled tools and preconfigured architecture. Attempting to build a suitable architecture with the various parts inside a mega vendor's toolkit is untenable. Companies aiming for a future where AI plays a central role in their operations need to consider more comprehensive, scalable, and flexible AI platforms. These platforms might require a larger initial investment and a longer setup time but they are essential for a more ambitious and long-term AI strategy. Implementing an out-of-the-box architecture requires an understanding of which components from various tool and toolkit providers are the best in breed.

According to a Gartner report from 2023, by 2025 generative AI will be a workforce partner within 90% of companies worldwide.[1] These numbers seem generous as we've been watching so many companies continue to drag their feet on adoption. That said, giants like ServiceNow seem to be coming around to this paradigm. "ServiceNow's focus has been on integrating generative AI to improve entire workflows, not just single processes or tasks," Keith Kirkpatrick, an analyst at the Futurum Group, told TechCrunch in March 2024. "This is a critical point of differentiation for them, as it allows for intelligent automation of multi-step processes that once required a significant amount of effort and switching between applications to complete."[2]

Global Fintech firm Klarna also made news in September of 2024 by announcing they were going to phase out SaaS giants Workday and Salesforce in favor of using AI to build their own solutions. According to Inc., there is skepticism that this ambitious move will pay off.

> HR technology analyst Josh Bersin is skeptical that the payments company can effectively replace Workday. "Systems like Workday have decades of workflows and complex data structures built in, including payroll, time and attendance," he explained to Inc. "If Klarna wants an engineering team to build all this, they're going to wind up in a black hole of systems features, to say nothing of the user experience."[3]

An extensible cognitive architecture makes it possible to sidestep engineering black holes while crafting experiences that have user experience at the fore. As these architectures continue to evolve, conversational applications will become an integral part of our daily lives, making technology more accessible and user-centric than ever before. The days of learning complex applications will soon be replaced by constructive conversations with our devices, ushering in a new era of productivity and convenience. When all software is eventually operated through a single conversational UI, we call this organizational singularity (which is synonymous with OAGI), and it will be a true game changer.

Building an Extensible Cognitive Architecture Isn't Easy

By Robb Wilson

My entire journey with agentic AI has been centered around creating a platform for building extensible cognitive architectures. I didn't know that was what I was creating when I began my work, but as I

Building an Extensible Cognitive Architecture
Isn't Easy *(continued)*

got deeper and deeper into the complexity and promise of conversational AI, it became apparent that this kind of architecture was critical to really unlocking the possibilities of this vast set of technologies. There's a reason people use mountain-climbing metaphors to describe undertakings of this size and scope. Achieving hyperautomation can feel Everest-esque—an outsized challenge shrouded in toil and peril.

Constructing a feasible platform required a team of mathematicians, linguists, data scientists, UI/UX analysts, and AI scientists. We found ourselves huddled together at the foot of our own Mount Everest. At the time, we were essentially using toolkits to build our own platform—and it took a very long time following a very clear vision, executed through constant iteration and adaptation. The hundreds of thousands of hours we spent researching, designing, and developing more than 10,000 conversational applications have wrought an open platform for hyperautomating. The current iteration of that platform is called Generative Studio X (GSX), and it's the only platform to have been named a leader by all of the major analyst groups, including Gartner, Forrester, and IDC.

Sure, I'd like for everyone to use our platform, but why I'm telling you all of this is to give you an idea of how time consuming it can be to create an extensible cognitive architecture that can meet the needs of even the largest enterprises. As I've already suggested, a great fog has been whipped up around the concept of hyperautomation by those who fundamentally understand it differently. Hyperautomation isn't chatbots. It isn't machine learning or even intelligent automation. It isn't ChatGPT, LLMs, NLU, NLP, IVR, or RPA. Hyperautomation isn't the tools—it's the ecosystem and the ways components/elements of the ecosystem are sequenced.

Hyperautomating takes place in an ecosystem that lets you orchestrate freely with these tools (and many others). Getting this kind of ecosystem up and running is a bit of a trust fall because your initial forays will likely fail. From a business standpoint it will probably feel like too big a risk. After all, in a world dominated by GUIs and ill-trained LLMs,

(continued)

Building an Extensible Cognitive Architecture
Isn't Easy (continued)

a simple application that does one or two things well is considered a success. In conversational design, however, a solution that can do only one thing is almost certainly a failure.

Simple chatbots, NLU, IVRs, RPA, LLMs, and AI agents are frankly not good enough to achieve hyperautomation. The key design principle behind successful conversational applications and ecosystems for hyperautomation is to strive for those experiences that surpass what humans alone are capable of.

Up until recently, conversational AI was something that companies implemented because the cost savings it afforded outweighed the negative effects of the subpar experience it provided. We've entered an era where a conversational interface will become the primary entry point into your organization (often for both customers and employees). We've already seen inklings of what's to come with generative tools like LLMs. People are excited by the prospect of communicating with machines conversationally, but to succeed, conversational interfaces need to connect to everything and do a great many things. Really, the only way to approach something so vast and all-encompassing is to fail faster than you've ever failed before.

To temporarily swap out the mountain-climbing metaphor, consider the stand-up comedian. The polished hour of interwoven bits didn't materialize fully formed from the comedian's mind. Comedians routinely take the terrifying first step of dragging fresh ideas up on stage—and then experience their gruesome failures—knowing that this painful process will lead to incremental improvements. Since these improvements are so intimately connected with the real-time reactions they spark, they can only happen through iteration. Over time, the iterative improvements render a rich tapestry of experience. The more accustomed comedians become to this uncomfortable and unpredictable process, the more they can thrive in the discomfort. Hyperautomation is no different.

This idea of failing forward is central to iterative project management schemes such as Agile, but hyperautomation requires even more speed and flexibility. Agile organizations will certainly have a head start, in the

Building an Extensible Cognitive Architecture
Isn't Easy (*continued*)

very least because design thinking and a willingness to try new ideas are essential to hyperautomation, but the development cycles I'm talking about will move by measures of hours, not days or weeks. The best bet for any organization entering this race is to select tools that are future-proof—tools that give you total control over both the other tools you want to use and how you want to use them.

Back in 2021, Deloitte predicted that larger companies are seeing the end of AI's "early adopter" phase and the beginning of the "early majority" phase. IDC predicted more than $110 billion in spending on AI technologies in 2024. "Companies will adopt AI—not just because they can, but because they must," said Ritu Jyoti, program vice president, Artificial Intelligence at IDC.[4] Companies are becoming more sophisticated in their buying and are looking for powerful, flexible options. As I see it, their only options are buying or building their own extensible cognitive architecture.

Prepare for Your Climb

To make your ascent, these are the situations and requirements you'll need to account for. By making sure you've got these bases covered, you can focus on enabling non-developers to orchestrate conversational and non-conversational advanced technology quickly and easily. This will help you prepare for the unique challenges that come with microservices architecture.

Building: As you organize flows, it's important to identify dependencies between your services. Be aware that changing one microservice might affect other microservices due to dependencies. You also need to consider the effects that microservices have on your data and how changes to your data to suit one microservice might affect other microservices that rely on the same data.

Testing: Integration and end-to-end testing are very important. Depending on how you've architected your services and flows to support one another, a failure in one part of the architecture could cause something a few hops away to fail.

Versioning: When you update to new versions, keep in mind that you might break things if there's no backward compatibility. You can build in conditional logic to handle this, but that can get unwieldy and nasty fast if not managed properly. You can also stand up multiple live versions using different flows, but that can be more complex to maintain and manage.

Logging: With a distributed system, you need centralized logs to bring everything together. Otherwise, the scale is impossible to manage. A centralized view of the system allows you to pinpoint problems. GSX was designed to do much of this, but you still have to manage occurrences beyond built-in events, errors, and warnings.

Debugging: When it comes to errors reported through user interaction, it can be difficult to pinpoint the microservice that failed if no error or warning log is reported. Debugging simple applications such as chatbots, RPAs, or IVRs is relatively easy, but when you take it to the level where you introduce context, memory, and intelligence, identifying bugs beyond errors or warnings can get very complicated.

Compliance and security: When applying technology this powerful and expansive, organizations will need to make sure their plan focuses close attention on any potential compliance and security issues. The fact that ecosystems built for hyperautomating are open systems by necessity and use various independent technologies sequenced together to share information can pose unique challenges specific to individual organizations. There's no one-size-fits-all cover for this base.

Find Your Footing

Having the right tools and approach are critical, but there are other things to pay close attention to as you take your initial steps.

Your architecture must be low latency. To support a conversational interface like GPT, latency is an essential component. The response time isn't contingent on how quickly an LLM can produce a reply. For productivity use cases, ETL (extract, transform, and load) needs to run very quickly.

Architecture is deeply integrated across channels. To use the full functionality of each channel, you need to be able to manage sessions at a macro level as well as a granular level. To achieve true omnichannel experience, your architecture must be capable of managing multiple channels in parallel, pogo-sticking between channels, and using native components of each channel. This level of control needs to extend to inbound and outbound channels.

Integrations must be flexible at a networking level. If your customers have a separate digital environment, you need to be able to create a fast and secure connection with low latency.

Make use of complex data. Your architecture must process and utilize unstructured data and convert it to structured data in real time. ICF lets you play with data in new and highly sophisticated ways.

High levels of security management. More data and more users means more security requirements. Add to this the fact that in certain situations, users will be more trusting of conversational experience, while others will find them more skeptical of interacting.

You need complex monitoring and debugging capabilities. Complex systems are much harder to maintain and sustain. You need a 360 view of your ecosystem so when something goes wrong, you know where to direct your attention.

You need to react to analytics in real time. Creating automations is a highly iterative task that never really ends. Early automations often test out hypotheses about how to automate tasks. As they are activated and interacted with, you'll find opportunities to improve the experiences, which can even be implemented in real time.

Human-in-the-loop: It's critical to have humans playing active roles in the development and evolution of AI-powered automations. Part of responding to analytics in real time is letting humans come into the experience when automations need a helping hand moving forward—this kind of training machines and humans co-creating or "co-botting."

Multidisciplinary teams working together. This soft element of your architecture might be the most important. The key to creating automations that benefit customers and employees is working across disciplines and departments. Find the people who understand the processes you're trying to automate and make them part of the design process. You'll be able to build out your cognitive agent architecture faster with a shared vision for how people and machines will work together.

No Code Means Fewer Barriers

Fifty years ago, if you worked on a computer, you almost certainly worked in something called "the computer department." These days, the notion of a computer department is so antiquated that it's foreign. Nearly everyone works on a computer. Now apply that same dynamic to software development. Currently, most companies use third-party software solutions, consulting vendors, or have an internal software development department that builds/codes the software they need. Now imagine a world where anyone can build software solutions (in much the same way everyone can now use a computer).

You won't have to wait 50 years for this world to materialize. We're well on our way to the "development department" being a thing of the past—doing away with the time and energy that companies have had to pour into development cycles. Enabling your company to program the automation of business processes, tasks, and communications without writing code eliminates the need for a traditional development cycle and is a key factor that accelerates growth in your ecosystem.

Reaching this point requires defiance. Two particular paradigms need to be shattered within your organization. The first of these is the triple constraint or iron triangle: fast, cheap, or good, you can pick only two. (See Figure 12.1.) The second is the idea that you have to choose between flexibility and usability: if a platform is flexible, it will be difficult to wrangle; if it's easy to use, it will also be rigid. (See Figure 12.2.)

Using an open platform, we've smashed these constraint paradigms to smithereens, so there's no need to live under their thumbs. The teams at OneReach.ai have seen more than 10,000 AI applications

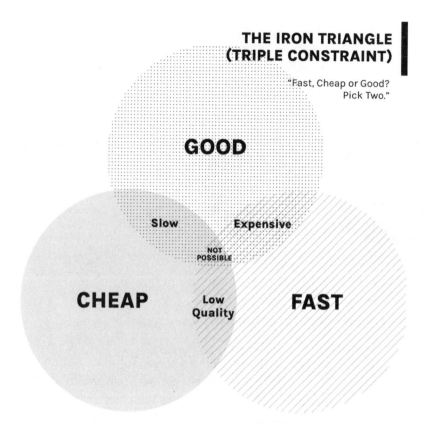

FIGURE 12.1   The iron triangle, or triple constraint.

created by customers, and 80% of the humans using our platform don't know how to write code. When anyone in your organization can take part in the evolution of your ecosystem, you can quickly create solutions that are inexpensive and effective, with no need to choose between usability and flexibility. This is the fast-track toward succeeding in hyperautomation.

Currently, the most efficient way to accelerate the force-multiplying effects of hyperautomation is for your company to equip themselves for rapid code-free programming. As we've outlined, when the technology itself recedes into the background, members of your organization can contribute directly to the automation of tasks they know best; just remember, code-free creation is only a tool, and you need requisite experience to use it. The people closest to your organization's problems will be best equipped to solve them, shifting solutioning closer

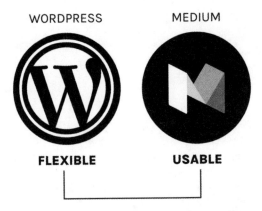

FIGURE 12.2 The flexibility/usability trade off.

to those who feel the pain of the problem and are intimate with what the solution should be. Supporting the people who can articulate the process being automated, you need developers who can articulate the granular pieces of the resulting automations. Code-free doesn't mean that the code doesn't exist. In the same way that a conversational interface obscures the messiness behind the scenes for end users, it also obscures the inner workings for those building software.

For another contextual example, think of the way that web design has changed over the past couple of decades. Initially, you needed a fairly in-depth understanding of coding languages to create even a static website. As websites became more interactive and functional, the knowledge required to build them became more complex. Eventually, tools emerged that empowered people without web development skills to build their own sites by customizing existing templates.

Now we're at the point where someone with limited computing skills can build a single-use, multi-page website (one that coordinates information for an upcoming wedding, for example) in a single afternoon. Hyperautomating opens the door to creating single-use software, something Robb found himself doing a couple of years ago, as his family prepared for a move. They were leaving behind a house in

Denver, Colorado, and all of their family's possessions needed to be indexed and boxed, as some things would be waiting for them in Mexico, where they planned to vacation before rendezvousing with the rest of their stuff in Berkeley, California.

Using an earlier iteration of GSX, he was able to quickly create an IDW that he shared with his wife. The system was rather simple: they could tell an agent that they were going to start packing a new box. The agent would assign that box a number and ask where it was going (Mexico? California? Robb's brother's garage in Colorado?). As they filled the boxes, they could send the agent photos and/or descriptions of the things going inside. Months later, when Robb was trying to find his motorcycle helmet, he asked the agent where it was. The agent, in turn, was able to tell him which box number it was in and at which location.

Robb didn't create this piece of single-use software because it was cool or because it allowed him to flex the capabilities of his platform. He did it because it was easy to do and it was going to save him a ton of time. This encapsulates the promise of code-free creation. Devise an automation that will make your life easier, design it on the fly, and then set it aside when you're done with it.

No-code conversational AI platforms let people automate workflows they understand without needing any requisite knowledge—just the ability to converse with a platform through natural language and use simple, visual, drag-and-drop programming. Co-creation relies on everyone taking part, and no-code tools let anyone contribute to great software design with rapid results. Always remember: speed is central to staying competitive in this race.

This is all a new way to create and manage software. Setting up conversational AI as an interface for no-code creation does something bigger than allowing anyone in an organization to design IDWs. What's really happening when people employ these tools and processes is software creation. In this new paradigm, software isn't created through developers, software solutions are designed (and often implemented) by people who best understand the problems being solved. This scenario finds developers in crucial roles that include advising the organization of high-level technical aspects of their ecosystem as well as making adjustments to skills on a granular level. Here, developers are tasked with creating and extending the tools that the people in their organization use to create and refine software. This represents a radically optimized approach to software creation that, once normalized, will fundamentally change the relationship between business and technology.

Infrastructure Topology for Agentic AI

The brain trust, software development time, and funds required for building production-ready and secure agentic AI applications put this out of reach for most organizations (see Figures 12.3 and 12.4). Once you've covered all the bases in this chapter, operationalizing can be inclusive, fast, and scalable—without sacrificing flexibility.

Microservices at the Core

The scale of automation we're talking about is achieved using microservices. By breaking down a skill into its component services and then breaking those down into their component steps, you get sets of pliable, infinitely customizable microservices. Within an intelligent ecosystem, microservices can be pulled from anywhere in the shared library, modified, sequenced, and deployed—creating new automations as well as new microservices that can be continually iterated on, resequenced, and redeployed.

In terms of defining the shape of an ecosystem, microservices map to flows. These flows of sequenced microservices make up the services and skills that an IDW utilizes. A robust ecosystem has an array of skills that can be sequenced in all sorts of ways. Here's how this works within an automated ecosystem.

Sarah is a sales associate for an auto parts provider, and she needs callers to authenticate themselves before placing an order. Her core enablement team (see Chapter 10) has been like a sherpa (we're back on the mountain), guiding her organization onward and upward, and she's been trained and feels empowered to use her platform's code-free tools to create new services and skills.

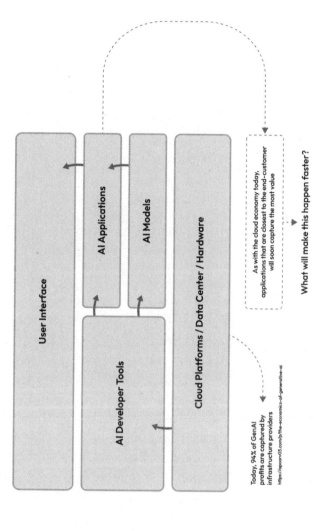

The New AI Centric Technology Ecosystem
modified from the "The AI Revolution"
published November 2023

COATUE

Traditional Architecture: Requires integrations, ongoing management, and custom development

User Interface

AI Applications

AI Models

AI Developer Tools

Cloud Platforms / Data Center / Hardware

Today, 94% of GenAI
profits are captured by
infrastructure providers
https://apoorv03.com/p/the-economics-of-generative-ai

As with the cloud economy today,
applications that are closest to the end-customer
will soon capture the most value

What will make this happen faster?

FIGURE 12.3   Traditional automation architecture.

End-to-End Architecture: Comprehensive platform reduces overhead and improves time to value

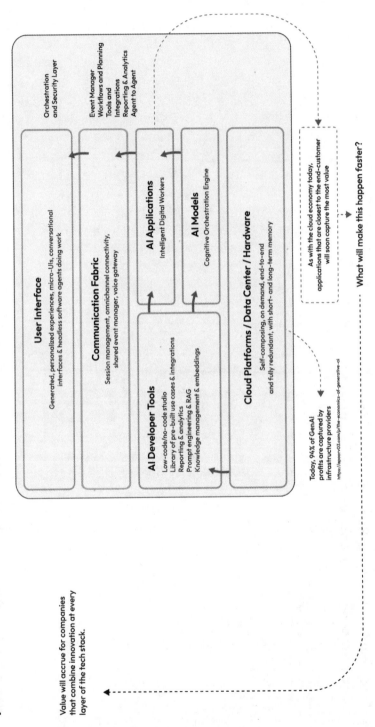

FIGURE 12.4 End-to-end architecture.

Sarah wants to train an IDW to perform her current authentication workflow for wholesale buyers calling in. To Sarah, creating automated workflows feels about as technical as creating a mildly complex spreadsheet. It's not an intimidating process because it involves no coding; in fact, there's very little visible technology in her journey. Her challenge is the fact that the solution will come quickly, and fine-tuning the experience of using the solution will take lots and lots of iteration.

She finds an authentication skill in the shared library, but it doesn't operate in precisely the way she needs. (Relying on SMS to authenticate won't work for her wholesale buyers, since many of them are in countries where SMS is less reliable.) So she looks through the flow of the skill, finds the microservices that facilitate the SMS component of the workflow, and replaces them with steps that use WhatsApp instead. Now the newly created automation functions exactly the way she needs it to.

In the next phase, the QA on Sarah's core enablement team can help her test the prototyped automation. She and the XD will also want to refine it together using her journey maps—marking the beginning of this skill's evolution. Once the automation is activated, it becomes a time-saver, and Sarah feels empowered to create more automations (with less assistance). The automation is also added to the organization's shared library so that others can borrow and iterate from it. The skill can also be fine-tuned at will; no one will have to wait for an outside development team to make the necessary updates.

Sarah finds this fact particularly liberating given how often she's been hampered by a vendor's development cycles; plus, she knows how coworkers can be wary of tinkering with a proprietary tool and breaking its functionality. There are numerous reasons microservices are a huge boon to Sarah and her coworkers:

- **Ready faster:** Since development cycles are shortened, microservices architecture supports more agile deployment and updates.
- **Highly scalable:** As demand for certain services grows, she can sequence and deploy microservices across multiple servers and infrastructures to meet her org's needs.
- **Resilient:** When constructed properly, independent microservices don't affect one another. This means that if one piece fails, the whole IDW doesn't go down.

- **Easy to deploy:** Because microservice-based apps are modular and smaller than monolithic apps, the worries that came with traditional deployment are negated. Microservices require more coordination, but the payoffs can be huge.

- **Fast and accessible:** Because the larger app is broken down into smaller pieces, developers can more easily understand, update, and enhance those pieces, resulting in faster development cycles— especially when combined with hyperagile development methodologies. This also makes it easier to get distributed teams working together.

- **Reusable:** Microservices can be sequenced in different ways with different sets of other microservices to create new skills and services. They can also be tweaked within existing sequences to produce different outcomes.

- **More open:** The use of polyglot APIs gives developers the freedom to choose the best language and technology for the necessary function.

Thanks to the work of the core enablement team, Sarah is just one of many employees, working across departments, who are able to build new automations by designing and sequencing microservices in new ways. All combined, the capacity to design and implement strategic automations gives customers and team members rewarding experiences that enhance their output.

Remember, however, that code-free creation is just a tool. In the same way that learning to code alone doesn't make you a programmer, having access to code-free creation doesn't mean much unless you know how to use it. In this example, Sarah's expertise in the processes unique to her role and department allows her to create successful software.

Code-free creation is nothing more than a party trick if you don't understand how to leverage it to solve problems in an optimized way. For example, someone can prop up an impressive-looking piece of software quickly and easily by feeding internal documents to LLMs, but the depth of that software is entirely dependent on how well it addresses a real need. Beyond the reliability issues associated with LLMs, there are a limited number of needs that can be met using such a narrow approach.

With tools that are more open, fast, and accessible in the hands of people who understand the tasks you want to automate, your organization can build automations that are ready faster, easier to deploy, reusable, and highly scalable.

This method of software design requires a balance, however. With code-free creation, if the modular pieces are too large, the solutions will be less flexible. If the pieces are too small, they can quickly become too complex for non-developers to succeed with. Achieving and maintaining this balance takes a coordinated effort across departments. This is what we mean when we say that AI is a team sport. It requires interplay among people who understand the processes being automated and those who understand how those automations can be generated within the complex integrated ecosystems I'm prescribing.

Making the Case for an Uphill Climb

The good news is that getting support from the people in your organization like Sarah, who will benefit from an ecosystem teeming with useful and customizable automations, has gotten easier. So many people are now accustomed to collaborating with LLMs, agents, and generative tools that it's not hard for them to envision the massive benefits of more personalized interactions with conversational AI.

Making the case to business leadership and shareholders might not prove so simple. The road to hyperautomation, or organizational AGI, is long and fraught with frequent failure. ROI is slow to build and will require many orgs to rethink their entire makeup. Still, getting it right means your org can surge light-years ahead of any competitor who hasn't made the leap. The outsized advantages hyperautomation presents can't be overstated and it's absolutely proportionate to the risk companies take by not pursuing it right away.

Next, we'll look at a burgeoning classification system for feature reduction within these complex ecosystems. The scope of information available within them is often proportionate to the difficulty present in trying to find the particular pieces of information that an AI agent needs to execute around an objective, and we'll explore Robb's unique approach to contextualizing different kinds of data.

Key Takeaways

- Point solutions are a shortcut to nowhere. Real hyperautomation requires an open and flexible platform for orchestrating technology.

- By capturing and storing conversational data across an organization, businesses can construct a complex infrastructure known as extensible cognitive architecture, enabling more effective use of these technologies.

- An extensible cognitive architecture allows for seamless integration of various cognitive services, enabling conversational applications to understand and respond effectively.

- Organizations must focus on building a robust ecosystem that allows for rapid iteration and adaptation, which involves managing dependencies, ensuring compliance and security, and maintaining low latency and high integration across channels.

Want to expand on what you've learned in Chapter 12? Follow this QR code to interact with an IDW that can connect you with additional resources linked to key ideas from this chapter, including content from the *Invisible Machines* podcast.

CHAPTER 13

Digital Twins in SPACE

By Robb Wilson

As an empirical method for categorizing data, LATCH has maintained its usefulness since being developed a couple of decades ago. According to its creator, Richard Saul Wurman (also the founder of TED), "I believe, and it has been accepted, that there are only five ways of organizing information. I use the acronym LATCH: Location, Alphabet, Time, Category, and Hierarchy."[1]

These five categories can be applied to all types of information and can be particularly useful when dealing with the volume of information that needs sorting inside an ecosystem built for OAGI. When Josh and I spoke with Wurman about this, he described the thinking that led him to devise the system. He explained how the ways things are organized actually changes the information. He used fish as an example: the hierarchical arrangement of smallest fish to largest fish; the categorical groupings between bottom feeders and top feeders; where different fish live, etc.

> I don't want to go on about fish but I did one book called Hats, which talked about a meeting of a whole town and there were pegs on the wall . . . and they put their hat down on the peg as they walked in . . . that's the whole meaning of LATCH because the way they put them down there was by time—how they came into the meeting. You could also pull out which was the biggest hat, the smallest hat, how many people in there were policemen or something else from the hat, how many people didn't wear

hats . . . by changing the organization of the information you could tell a lot about the audience.[2]

Thinking about the different ways to classify and render data using LATCH can inform how you guide analytics and design your reports—or tell your agents how to get their jobs done better. LATCH is a baseline for providing an LLM with context. As such, it also provides a crucial framework for building a digital twin of your organization. Similar to the ways LATCH is helpful to humans organizing and summarizing information, it also works for AI agents.

And while LATCH is indeed a boon, it's not quite enough when it comes to the extra messy work of evolving a digital twin. As we've already discussed, a digital twin representing various aspects of an organization starts at a lower fidelity, but adds fidelity as it becomes more extensive and expansive. A super hi-def digital twin is a collection of different arrays of information that correspond with different aspects of an organization's operations. A digital twin might include maps of physical locations that are important to a business, but it could also include a relational database of customer interactions dating back years. There are many measurements of what a business is, and for AI agents to perform real work, they need lower resolution slices of information that are specific to the tasks at hand.

When it comes to the fidelity of data, Dr. Michael Grieves, who helped popularize the term "digital twin" while working with NASA, told us on *Invisible Machines*, "Fidelity is driven by value. What am I getting out of this high fidelity? [People will say], 'Gee, I'd like a photo-realistic version of this particular plant.' What are you going to do with it? Why does it have to be photo-realistic? I mean, quite frankly, you could have stick figures if that's all you need to know where the people were at a certain point in time."[3]

This thinking extends beyond these "reality capture" examples of digital twins and into organizational frameworks as well. If a customer is querying an AI agent about exchanging a specific product from a retail location and they want to examine the replacement product item in person, the agent might provide information about where to find it within a specific location close to the customer. The agent might also look at a summary of past interactions and determine that this customer has already returned a similar product once before and should be greeted by an associate in store.

This level of granularity requires low-res slices of a hi-res digital twin. To borrow a popular term in software circles, I'm talking about feature reduction. This is the ability to take the broad spectrum of information within a digital twin and provide a focused snapshot of the bits that are relevant to a given task or objective. Whether you're training a model or creating an ecosystem for OAGI, feature reduction will be important.

We are already surrounded by this kind of feature reduction, though we might not notice when, for instance, a rich web chat interface reduces the fidelity of a high-resolution image for a smaller phone screen that doesn't need that much information. There are countless opportunities for machines to do a job faster and cheaper by compressing data.

Obviously for the kinds of super-detailed, high-stakes simulations an organization like NASA wants to run, feature reduction is less of a concern, but it's a critical component to effective agent orchestration. So to help classify information in the context of digital twins and OAGI, I channeled my inner Wurman to come up with a LATCH-like acronym for classifying this kind of information. Enter SPACE.

Finding SPACE for Feature Reduction

The five components I've identified for SPACE make it easier to contextualize different kinds of data within the feature reduction process. SPACE isn't meant to be followed rigidly; it's more of a guideline. Some of these areas might be overkill for your organization, and it's possible I'll tweak some of this information in the future. Regardless, by using these classifiers, organizations can identify how to plate the lo-res slices for different agents working across an organization. Providing AI agents with these digestible, context-rich servings of information allows them to effectively collaborate and complete real work.

- **System:** Feature-reduced data can summarize all aspects of a system's operational state, including performance metrics, system errors, security statuses, and technical details that affect functionality and security. Knowing the system's health and capabilities allows the AI to manage its computational resources more effectively. For instance, the AI could defer non-essential tasks during high-load periods or prioritize security-related issues, ensuring stable and secure operations. A number of things can fall under this category, like:

- System error information about specific failures or bugs, which can alert AI agents to potential inaccuracies or limitations in data processing.

- Details about data protection measures, access controls, and vulnerability management, helping to ensure information security helps the system maintain data integrity and agents can respond to potential security threats effectively.

- Performance metrics like system load, response times, and resource usage, which the system can use to optimize its operations and prevent overload.

- **Physicality:** This feature-reduced summary involves geographical and spatial data about entities and operations, including user locations and asset positioning. Location data enables the system to contextualize requests and operations geographically. For example, if a user asks about the nearest printer, an AI agent can provide an accurate answer based on the user's current location, enhancing user experience and operational efficiency. This is a focal point in numerous scenarios like:

  - Office locations where departments or key infrastructure are situated, which can influence decisions on resource distribution or emergency planning.

  - Asset positioning, where specific locations of equipment or inventory are crucial for logistics and supply chain management.

- **Attributes:** Detailed characteristics of users and entities, such as profiles, roles, capabilities, and descriptive metadata can be useful in the context of a feature-reduced summary. Attributes inform AI agents about the specific traits and permissions of users or resources. This allows agents to provide personalized responses and recommendations, respecting privacy and security settings, which improves trust and engagement. Attributes can include things like:

  - A user's age, which might help an agent tailor content, services, and communications to their life stage and preferences, ensuring relevance and compliance with age-related restrictions.

- o User roles and permissions, which let agents determine what information or actions are accessible to a user.

- o Specifications about the device a user is interacting from, which can allow agents to tailor its interface or functionalities to suit device capabilities.

- **Context:** Summarizing the mediums and circumstances surrounding interactions and detailing how information is exchanged allow agents to adapt their language, tone, and content based on the medium and history of interactions. This adaptive response leads to more natural and effective communications, enhancing user satisfaction and engagement in these ways:

  - o Maintaining records of past conversations allows agents to continue ongoing dialogues seamlessly, recalling user preferences or previous issues, and provide more personalized and contextually relevant responses.

  - o Incorporating external factors like weather conditions or news events enables agents to tailor advice or information to current situations, making its responses more timely and relevant.

  - o Distinguishing whether a request came via email, chat, or verbal communication can influence the formality or brevity of an agent's response.

- **Events:** Temporal and procedural information that documents chronological events and the sequence of operations or interactions can be a critical component of feature reduced summaries. Providing agents with a temporal dimension enhances their ability to predict and plan. By understanding the timing and order of events, agents can offer proactive support, schedule tasks efficiently, and anticipate future inquiries, improving decision support and operational planning. This area is key to running simulations and handling prediction. While it's always important to have an up-to-date snapshot of an organization, being able to go backward (and potentially forward with advanced predictive abilities) unlocks a new dimension for agentic workflows, affecting things like:

  - o Project timelines, where knowing the sequence of project phases enables agents to provide timely reminders or status updates.

○ Sequential logs of user actions that can help agents anticipate user needs or troubleshoot user issues more effectively.

By organizing data within these categories, SPACE helps contextualize various aspects of a high-fidelity, data-rich environment so that AI agents can operate with accuracy and relevance. This framework enhances an agent's ability to understand and analyze, leading to better comprehension of an organization's operations, user characteristics, and external factors. SPACE also lets agents make informed decisions and reason more effectively. By narrowing context and focusing on specific tasks, SPACE allows AI agents to improve efficiency and precision in task execution. Ultimately, it helps to create the conditions for agents to operate with increasing autonomy, equipped with the contextual clarity needed to achieve higher levels of intelligence and effectiveness in organizational environments.

Orbiting OAGI

As organizations gain ground in the orchestration of AI agents they will likely end up creating an assemblage of digital twins, each representing a different aspect of operations or some sort of physical manifestation. With a proper technology architecture in place, the twins can be leveraged against one another, creating a higher-fidelity super twin of sorts. This expansive organizational twin is a comprehensive, data-rich model where data needs to be feature-reduced, usually through summarization, to create context for AI Agents. SPACE can streamline the meticulous categorization of data for the robust and context-rich environment AI agents need to effectively collaborate and automate. This strategic feature reduction lets orchestrated agents become a dynamic reflection of an organization's ongoing operations, which is a key component to achieving organizational AGI.

Reaching OAGI hinges on these critical focus areas:

- **AI Agent Infrastructure:** AI agents require a composable architecture that affords seamless integration with legacy systems. AI agents need to access and utilize historical data and processes without disruption, enhancing the continuity and depth of insights. Because individual agents and the broader ecosystems they call home are both dependent on new technologies, it's imperative that your cognitive architecture is open and flexible. This means you're not tied to any one tool or solution and can easily bring in whatever current marketplace offerings meet your needs and just as easily phase out the ones that no longer serve your organization.

- **Feature Reduction:** As we've explored throughout this chapter, the capability to narrow down the context for AI agents engaged in specific tasks is crucial. The SPACE framework provides agents with well-structured and contextually rich capsules of their broader organizational ecosystem. This focused information allows AI agents to understand, reason, and make decisions with a level of accuracy and relevance that closely mirrors human-like understanding.

- **Metacognitive AI:** With the proper cognitive architecture and feature reduction in place, organizations can begin seeing the benefits of a metacognitive infrastructure. In this state, AI agents are seeking information and self-evaluating their actions in an effort to improve experiences incrementally over time. Meta skills—like seeking out missing information—can facilitate meta behaviors—like seeking out feedback from humans that might improve automations. The goal is that an AI agent has metacognitive abilities, which is the peak state of agentic self-adaptive systems. Humans can still be in-the-loop, but over time their roles involve verifying context rather than having to constantly create it.

Success in these areas unlocks unprecedented efficiencies, insights, and strategic capabilities. As you might expect, success won't come easily, but you can make things much easier on yourself (and your org) by finding vendors that can support the critical aspects of your journey.

Your Cobbler's Kids Should Have Moon Boots

The advanced orchestration of AI agents is such a game changer in terms of efficiency and productivity that if a vendor has figured out how to make headway with digital twins and this kind of feature reduction, they will definitely be using their own products internally. Similarly, a services vendor who has cracked this code should definitely have a rapidly growing number of valuable examples that everyone internally knows and that they're regularly improving upon.

When looking for partners in your journey toward OAGI, initiate your assessment by asking vendors these kinds of questions:

- Have you successfully orchestrated AI agents internally?
- Are the orchestrations integral to your own operations? (Or are they just window dressing?)
- Are your employees taking interest in this kind of orchestration because they can see automation working?
- What use cases have you tackled? Can you show us?
- How are you dealing with the complexity of an entire organization's worth of data and processes? (Are your tools designed with feature reduction in mind?)

If a vendor falls back on the old "cobbler's kids go without shoes" adage, be wary. There was a time when my own company used that excuse: that we were too busy creating solutions to put them to use for ourselves. Whatever the reasoning, it's a bullshit excuse. If employees aren't using their company's platform for orchestrating AI agents, why would a customer?

Having the right tools in place is paramount to building a functional ecosystem for advanced AI agent orchestration. It's critical to have this information and perspective to avoid getting locked into long-term "solutions" that won't be able to meet your expanding needs.

There's so much hype and misinformation—and so many unmet promises—that you need to do your own form of feature reduction in order to identify the tools and solutions that will actually meet your organization's needs. While you can certainly endeavor to build your own cognitive architecture (which took me and my team about a decade), it's analogous to the choice to build a computer from scratch rather than just buying one that suits your needs. Be ready to ask potential vendors lots of questions and make them show you the things they've built using their own tools. Doing this work at the outset can save massive amounts of time and money.

Key Takeaways

- Finding ways to classify and organize information if critical for giving AI agents relevant information. The LATCH system provides a useful framework for initial explorations, categorizing information by Location, Alphabet, Time, Category, and Hierarchy.

- Expanding on this idea, the SPACE system helps orgs create feature reduced or low-res slices of information based on System, Physicality, Attributes, Context, and Events.

- Make sure your vendors have tools and architecture that can support this advanced classification and organization of information.

Want to expand on what you've learned in Chapter 13? Follow this QR code to interact with an IDW that can connect you with additional resources linked to key ideas from this chapter, including content from the *Invisible Machines* podcast.

PART III

Building an Ecosystem for Orchestrated AI Agents

Building an ecosystem for organizational AGI is all about strategy. To be clear, when we use the word "strategy" we're not referring to the mission or ultimate goal. This isn't a race to build a static piece of technology; the race is to equip your team and company for faster adoption and iteration of new technologies, skills, and functions.

The best way to give you a full understanding of this kind of ecosystem is by first unlocking the process behind building one. When we talk about OAGI, we're talking about sequencing tasks and technologies in ways that reveal unseen potential and multiply outcomes. When you step back to consider the vast multitude of technologies and tasks that make up an organization and imagine the countless ways they might be sequenced together, the complexity of the situation can quickly overwhelm. With the right strategy and process, however, you can get everyone in your organization iterating on these sequences, creating a fertile ecosystem.

CHAPTER 14

Orchestrating AI Agents to Become Organizational Operating Systems

I n the era of hyperautomation and organizational AGI, large language models (LLMs) have leapt to the fore as pivotal drivers, but they aren't a complete solution. Not even close. So let's look at the expanding domain of LLM-based AI agents. In this tactical chapter we'll explore the process of creating standalone AI agents and evolving them into a system where multiple agents operate in orchestrated swarms, collaborating around complex problems.

AI agents are highly effective in scenarios that require a broad set of capabilities, where their generalist nature allows them to adapt and respond to a variety of challenges. For example, in customer service, AI agents can manage inquiries across different products or services, adapting their responses to the context of each customer interaction. Another broad application is in content moderation, where agents must understand and respond to a wide range of content types and contexts, ensuring compliance with guidelines across large platforms.

However, as tasks become more specific and narrow, deploying AI agents might be considered overkill. In such cases, simpler or more specialized programmatic systems might be more efficient and cost-effective. For instance, managing a specific database query or executing a well-defined, repetitive task in a manufacturing line may not require the sophisticated capabilities of AI agents.

AI agents exhibit a wide spectrum of applications that highlight their flexibility and capability. These applications range from general problem-solving tasks to specific and highly detailed simulations. This is particularly true as agents are integrated into large language model-multi-agent (LLM-MA) systems.

LLM-MA systems demonstrate remarkable collective intelligence and have rightly captured the interest of many organizations. Orchestrating multiple agents each with distinct strategies and behaviors enhances problem-solving effectiveness. We often call them agent swarms, and they offer a level of autonomy and reusability unparalleled in our current world of programmed applications. But let's start our exploration in the realm of single agents.

Single-Agent Systems Powered by LLMs

Even a single-agent system powered by LLMs is quite different from a traditional programmatic approach to software. Rather than providing the explicit instructions required by traditional applications, AI agents can be given objectives that you'd like them to achieve (help a customer select the right speaker system for their car) along with a list of instructions to act as guardrails (a checklist of required info about the customer and their car, the preferred order of information collection, ways to pivot the interactions back to core objective, etc.). In her paper "LLM Powered Autonomous Agents," Lilian Weng of OpenAI points to three pivotal components of a single agent system:

- Planning capabilities
- External tools and resources
- Advanced memory capabilities

Unlike traditional software that follows predefined paths, LLM-based agents are designed to handle complex tasks by breaking them down into manageable objectives. These agents have **planning capabilities**, methodically evaluating each component, sometimes pursuing various avenues based on the context, and adaptively learning from past outcomes. This enhances their decision-making abilities in complex scenarios, significantly boosting their autonomy and problem-solving efficacy. Contrast this with the more programmatic approach, where developers often give machines specific instructions without even fully understanding the broader objective.

Static programmatic tools have limited adaptability. By contrast, LLM-based agents can dynamically utilize **external tools and resources**. This ability not only broadens their functional range but also improves their effectiveness in varied and changing environments. This can broaden to include the use of other agents or software systems. For example, an AI agent might gather information from an internet search to get a company address or phone number to achieve the broader objective of reporting an issue.

Moving beyond the fixed databases typical in conventional software, LLM-based agents exhibit **advanced memory capabilities**. They can engage in in-context learning, acting as a form of short-term memory, or access external vector and graph databases for long-term memory storage. This dual memory system allows them to maintain relevance and continuity over interactions, thereby enhancing learning and contextual understanding.[1]

Multi-Agent Systems Powered by LLMs

Single-agent systems have demonstrated remarkable cognitive capabilities by focusing primarily on developing their internal processes and how they interact with their surroundings. LLM-MA systems level up automations significantly by focusing on the variety of agent characteristics, the relationships between agents, and the shared decision-making dynamics. Increasingly intricate tasks can be automated through the collaborative efforts of multiple AI agents.

These AI agents operate within a digital twin of the organization. As we explained in Chapter 13, the digital twin environment is multifaceted, representing various aspects of operations. Everything from office floor plans to project management systems to customer databases to internal communication tools can be accounted for in the digital twin environment, simulating the company's dynamics and allowing agents to experiment with decisions and strategies without impacting the real-world operation. More importantly, they can use the tools and information within the environment to perform real work in ways that are congruent with how the company operates.

The authors of "LLM based Multi-Agents: A Survey of Progress and Challenges" categorize the interface between agents and their environment in three ways:

- Sandbox
- Physical
- None

In a **sandbox** interaction model, agents operate within a simulated setting—like a controlled lab environment where they can safely test and refine their actions. Agents might simulate different strategies for project management to determine the one that will yield the best outcomes in terms of time and resource utilization.

The **physical** interaction model finds AI agents interacting in real-world settings. This less common model might take the form of AI agents coordinating actual robots along assembly lines in the manufacturing arm of a company. Agents complete tasks with tangible physical outcomes, such as assembling parts or packaging products.

There are also situations where agents work without a specific external environment, focusing instead on tasks that require interactions between agents to reach a decision or consensus. This **"none"** paradigm might involve agents debating different approaches to a business strategy where the primary objective is deliberation rather than physical or digital manipulation.[2]

Early systems will have limited context but follow a continuum where context grows as the digital twin gains higher fidelity. In each of these settings, agents use the provided environmental context to make informed decisions. They learn from the outcomes and progressively refine their strategies to enhance performance and efficiency.

Digital Twin Creation

As dynamic virtual models of an organization, digital twins evolve and gain fidelity over time, incorporating more interactions and systems. Every action taken within the organization—every conversation, and every change in data—contributes to this evolution. These elements are captured and fed into long-term memory, improving the digital twin's contextual awareness. This means that the digital twin gradually becomes a more accurate and comprehensive reflection of the organization's operational reality, allowing for more precise simulations and predictions.

A digital twin is an amalgamation of diverse data management technologies integrated with existing systems. Real-time data comes flowing in from various sources within the organization, like customer relationship management (CRM) and enterprise resource planning (ERP) systems, and other operational tools. Vector databases handle large datasets effectively, enabling the system to quickly retrieve and analyze complex data patterns. Graph databases contribute by efficiently mapping relationships and interactions within the data, which is crucial for understanding complex organizational dynamics. Traditional data systems also play a role, ensuring that historical data is preserved and accessible.

Temporal context is another critical component, allowing the digital twin to not only understand the current state of the organization but also to analyze changes over time. This offers deep insights into trends and allows for the prediction of potential future states. This temporal analysis is essential for strategic planning and decision-making.

As these elements come together, the digital twin matures, moving the organization closer to OAGI. This evolution is not just about technological integration but also about developing a system that can think, learn, and interact in ways that mirror human cognitive abilities within an organizational environment. The path to OAGI is marked by increasing the digital twin's ability to function autonomously, making decisions and offering insights that are deeply aligned with the organization's goals and challenges.

This progression transforms the digital twin from a simple model to a core component of the organization's intelligence and strategic operations. What it really becomes is a conversational operating system for your entire organization.

Metacognitive Capabilities

Agents in an LLM-MA system should always be learning and adapting in ways similar to how humans plan and direct their learning paths. Conversational UIs play a unique role in this context by capturing user intents and feedback directly through interactions. Unlike graphical UIs, where unmet user needs often go totally undetected, conversational interfaces can log and categorize requests, aiding in the creation of a priority road map for skill development based on real user needs.

LLMs have made conversational UIs far easier to set up, but it's critical to remember that their reliability and effectiveness are totally dependent on the components mentioned earlier: planning capabilities, external tools and resources, and advanced memory capabilities. Metacognitive capabilities allow the system to fine-tune its existing capabilities while proactively seeking feedback and pursuing new skills, enhancing its relevance and effectiveness over time.

"Independent learning" is a popular term for the proactive learning we're talking about here. Whatever you call them, these adaptive and self-learning capabilities fit into the larger framework of OAGI, where the system is not a static entity but an evolving digital organism. OAGI thrives on continuous feedback and learning, dynamically adjusting to new situations and systematically enhancing its capabilities to manage its own learning and performance, mirroring the strategic growth path of human cognitive and learning processes.

Advanced Problem Solving

With multiple specialized agents collaborating, LLM-MA systems excel in problem solving. This collaborative approach allows for the handling of complex issues that no single agent could manage alone. Here's what this might look like in a project management scenario—a software development project run in part by agents.

There are many areas of the software life cycle that can be handled or augmented by AI agents, like code generation, or testing and debugging, or managing updates and assigning tasks. Software development necessitates collaboration among distinct roles: product managers, designers, developers, and testers—roles that LLM-MA systems can emulate, enhancing efficiency and coordination.

This agent framework enables autonomous programming with minimal user instructions, making great use of AI agents' ability to understand and execute tasks based on limited information. Other AI agents might operate as experts in specific sub-tasks, enabling them to work mostly autonomously while still collaborating whenever necessary. This method supports the decomposition of complex tasks into manageable parts, which can then be handled by specialized agents.

It integrates human workflow insights into the AI-driven process, emphasizing the importance of structured coordination through the encoding of standard operating procedures (SOPs) into AI prompts. It tackles the technical challenge of balancing code generation with effective test case creation. AI agents can handle both the generation and verification phases of software development.

This is the shift toward more autonomous, intelligent project management systems where AI agents not only perform specific tasks but also collaborate in a manner analogous to a human team. Not only does this transform project management across various fields, it marks a major milestone on the road to OAGI.

Embracing Multimodal Environments

Initially, the development of LLM-MA systems was concentrated on text-based inputs. This makes sense, as LLM-based agents excel in processing and generating textual data. As the application of generative tools continues to broaden, the necessity for multimodal capabilities becomes apparent. In multimodal environments, AI agents can interpret and interact with a richer array of data types, including audio, reports, spreadsheets, video, visuals, logs, and even physical artifacts and actions.

The inclusion of multimodal inputs greatly enhances the context-awareness of AI agents. Visual inputs can provide spatial and object recognition capabilities that are crucial for tasks in surveillance, troubleshooting, or recommendation engines. Audio inputs like tone, intonation, and background noise offer additional layers of understanding that are vital in areas like customer service or security systems, where the emotional tone or ambient sounds can influence the agent's response.

Integrating these diverse data types presents its own set of challenges. AI agents must not only process information from various modalities but also synthesize it to form coherent, informed responses. This complexity requires sophisticated models that can effectively fuse data from different sources, maintaining high levels of accuracy and responsiveness.

Moreover, enabling AI agents to operate in a multimodal setting allows for a more natural interaction with humans, who naturally perceive the world through multiple senses. For example, in an educational setting, an AI tutor that can analyze a student's written work, listen to their spoken responses, and interpret their facial expressions will provide much more nuanced feedback than one relying solely on text.

The ability to generate multimodal outputs further extends the utility of AI agents. Beyond producing text, they can create images, generate audio, and even control robotic actions in response to environmental cues, enabling them to function effectively in diverse domains such as content creation, therapy, and robotics.

The transition toward multimodal environments marks a significant evolution in the field of AI, promising AI agents that are more adaptive, intuitive, and capable of handling complex, real-world scenarios. This advancement not only enhances the functionality of AI systems but also broadens their applicability across different sectors, paving the way for more dynamic and interactive AI solutions.

Harnessing Collective Intelligence

LLM-MA systems enhance their learning through real-time feedback resulting from interactions with humans or the environment. This mode of learning necessitates a robust interactive environment, the design of which can prove challenging for many tasks, consequently restricting the scalability of LLM-MA systems.

Current research predominantly focuses on employing techniques such as memory and self-evolution to refine agents based on this feedback. While these methods are proficient in optimizing individual agents, they fall short of leveraging the full potential of collective intelligence within the network of agents. These techniques often modify agents in isolation, thus missing out on the potential synergistic benefits that could arise from a coordinated approach involving multiple agents.

Achieving an optimal level of collective intelligence, where multiple agents adjust in harmony to maximize their combined effectiveness, remains a formidable challenge in the field of LLM-MA. This involves not only individual learning and adaptation but also a coordinated, network-wide strategy to harness the collective capabilities of all agents involved. The creation of an Intelligent Communication Fabric (ICF) as referred to in the architecture chapter is required.

Swimming with Orchestration

The journey with LLM-MA systems starts in the shallow end of a pool. It begins with foundational elements and progressively moves toward more complex applications, continuously fueled by a strategic focus on improvement and adaptation through feedback. This iterative process ensures that while we advance in capability, we remain in the "shallow end," always learning, always adapting, but never fully reaching the "deep end." This approach maximizes the effectiveness of these systems, allowing organizations to harness the full potential of AI while adeptly navigating its inherent challenges.

It's a call to push the boundaries of what these intelligent systems can achieve. The path is set for a journey of continuous discovery and enhancement, promising a future where the integration of programmatic elements and agentic capabilities will lead to smarter, more responsive AI solutions. This journey, perpetually evolving while never losing our footing in the deep end, invites everyone to partake in the unfolding narrative of LLM-MA systems and the meta cognitive attributes we assign to them as they become more self-learning.

Nothing If Not Agile

If you've worked in neighborhoods adjacent to software design, then Agile is likely no stranger. Though it's often misrepresented as a process, Agile is actually a cultural mindset within an organization—one that embraces discovery through shared experimentation, failure, and iteration. As we've established, hyperautomation represents the evolution of software design; accordingly, the process that brings it to life requires a mindset and culture that are more agile than Agile.

Even certified scrum masters might be surprised by how quickly we sprint while creating and iterating in pursuit of hyperautomation. If Agile is new to you, the hyperautomation process will feel like massive upheaval. Either way, the key is to internalize the true nature of hyperautomation, or organizational AI. This isn't a software design scenario with weekly or monthly product milestones; this process allows you to experiment on active skills, continuously improving them while also activating new skills, multiple times, every day. Part of what makes this possible is an analytics-and-reporting paradigm that provides user data and feedback in real time. Beyond seeing how people are interacting with your conversational interface as those interactions unfurl, you'll also be able to see what kinds of functionalities they're asking for that don't currently exist. These are the kinds of insights that would take weeks (or even longer) to ferret out of a GUI—and they'll be at your disposal immediately. This sets the stage for rapid iteration cycles.

As with traditional Agile scrums, teamwork is the secret sauce when working with AI. In fact, we're fond of saying that AI is a team sport. Hyperautomation requires collaboration across every department within an organization, and ideas for improving skills should come from every department. Everyone will be equipped with basic knowledge about how their organization's ecosystem works, and everyone can co-create alongside the core enablement team we met in Part II. The visceral truth is that this process requires organizations to live, breathe, and excrete Agile from every pore. To take the scrum metaphor back into the realm of rugby, all heads need to be touching and arms interlocked for a never-ending push toward uprights that keep moving away—for this is a shared journey with no defined destination. If your team can't be more agile than Agile, or if AI isn't a team sport in your organization, it's akin to walking on to a rugby pitch as a one-person team and believing you have even a remote chance of winning the match.

If you were to heave the task of building a scalable conversational UI for your ecosystem onto a handful of designers, architects, and developers, no matter how experienced they were, it could take years to unearth the best ways to automate your organization. A proper strategy for hyperautomation includes everyone in your workforce leveraging the individual areas of expertise each employee has to forge optimal sequences and flows.

As we've stressed throughout this book, starting small and internally is often the easiest way to begin the process. By working directly with employees to automate specific tasks, you begin setting up the structure for future automation. You can continuously improve on automations with the people who understand the specific tasks—and, because these initial applications won't be customer-facing, you can build, test, iterate, test, iterate, test, and deploy as frequently as needed. The better your organization becomes at rolling out successful skills and internal automations, the faster your skills, IDWs (or AI agents), and ecosystem will evolve.

As you build up a shared library of skills, you'll create a repository of microservices that can be repurposed and sequenced to achieve new goals. When your ecosystem reaches a point where AI and the members of your organization are working together seamlessly to create and evolve sequences that make up the ecosystem, you will have made hyperautomation into a team sport. Once you reach that state, you'll no longer be just automating the tasks that people used to perform—you'll be able to sequence technology to create new systems of automation.

So while the initial focus will be on automating specific tasks, the larger focus is on something a little more abstract. Pretend you wanted to automate the job of digging holes. Initially, you might build a robot that can wield a shovel and dig perfect holes at double a human's speed. That's fine automation. But what if, instead, you built a machine with 10 arms holding 10 shovels that could dig 10 holes at a time just as fast—and that is infinitely cloneable to boot. That's the spirit of hyperautomation.

Create an Enterprise Road Map

Getting to that optimal state begins with treating the automation of immediate tasks as a vehicle for getting good and fast at solving complexity—and then keeping up momentum by iterating internally. This approach can get you deep into the process efficiently, especially if you create a road map. Even if it's incomplete and you change it every day, a road map will help set your sights on the skills you want to bring online for each new horizon that emerges.

While Figure 14.1 might not look like one at first glance, this is an example road map of sorts, depicting some of the many skills across all departments that an organization may aspire to create, evolve, and expand upon. As you move along your journey, you ascend from basic skills like an automated scheduling skill within a call center toward more complex skills, like IDWs assisting human agents in real time. Each of the skills in Figure 14.1 has its own evolutionary journey in a growing ecosystem.

Off the Markov

The Markov chain is a popular design tool for good reason. (See Figure 14.2.) It's incredibly useful for building and optimizing technical architecture, as it illustrates the sequence of possible events in which the probability of each event depends only on the state attained in the previous event. The assumption is that you don't need any historical information to predict the future state if you know your present state. As Figure 14.3 illustrates, in conversational design, a Markov chain quickly becomes a Markov mess, as there is far too much variability in what the present state might be; plus, an ecosystem designed for hyperautomating can leverage all kinds of historical data—especially with return users—to try to determine what their present state might be.

Markov diagrams are a decent way to diagram multiple conversations in one diagram, but that diagramming isn't terribly helpful unless the problem you're trying to solve is how to articulate multiple conversation paths in one diagram. The flow of a conversation is linear, and there's a high degree of variation to the forms any one

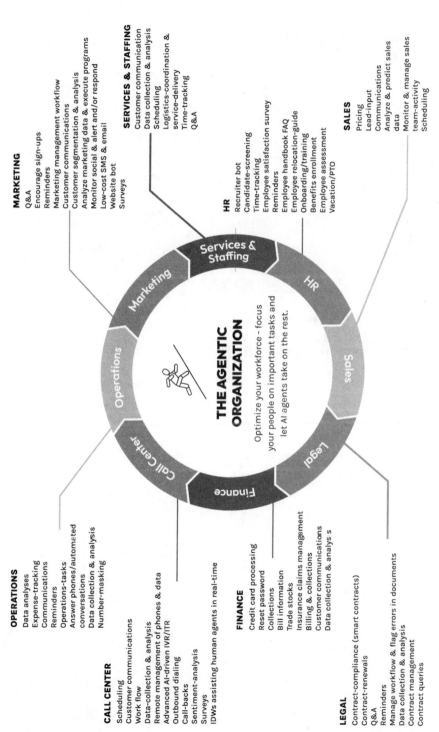

OPERATIONS
Data analyses
Expense-tracking
Communications
Reminders
Operations-tasks
Answer phones/automated
conversations
Data collection & analysis
Number-masking

CALL CENTER
Scheduling
Customer communications
Work flow
Data-collection & analysis
Remote management of phones & data
Advanced AI-driven IVR/ITR
Outbound dialing
Call-backs
Sentiment-analysis
Surveys
IDWs assisting human agents in real-time

FINANCE
Credit card processing
Reset password
Collections
Bill information
Trade stocks
Insurance claims management
Billing & collections
Customer communications
Data collection & analys s

LEGAL
Contract-compliance (smart contracts)
Contract-renewals
Q&A
Reminders
Manage workflow & flag errors in documents
Data collection & analysis
Contract management
Contract queries

MARKETING
Q&A
Encourage sign-ups
Reminders
Marketing management workflow
Customer communications
Customer segmentation & analysis
Analyze marketing data & execute programs
Monitor social & alert and/or respond
Low-cost SMS & email
Website bot
Surveys

SERVICES & STAFFING
Customer communication
Data collection & analysis
Scheduling
Logistics-coordination &
service-delivery
Time-tracking
Q&A

HR
Recruiter bot
Candidate-screening
Time-tracking
Employee satisfaction survey
Reminders
Employee handbook FAQ
Employee relocation-guide
Onboarding/training
Benefits enrollment
Employee assessment
Vacation/PTO

SALES
Pricing
Lead-input
Communications
Analyze & predict sales
data
Monitor & manage sales
team-activity
Scheduling

THE AGENTIC ORGANIZATION

Optimize your workforce - focus your people on important tasks and let AI agents take on the rest.

FIGURE 14.1 Some of the many functions within organizations where skills are being automated by companies today.

TYPICAL APPLICATION
OF A MARKOV CHAIN

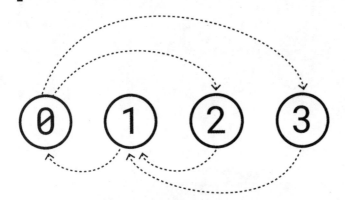

FIGURE 14.2 Typical application of a Markov chain.

MARKOV CHAIN MODEL
ISN'T SUITABLE FOR
CONVERSATIONAL DESIGN

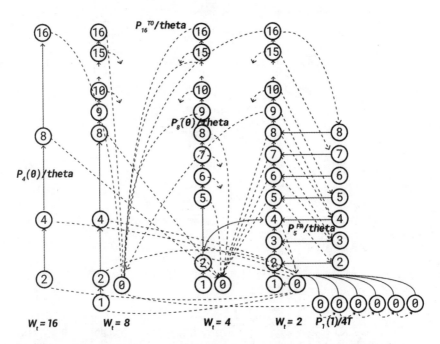

FIGURE 14.3 Attempting to map multiple conversations using a Markov chain gets very messy.

conversation can take. You don't know precisely where they will go, and in many scenarios you might not even know what the first point in an interaction will look like. Leaning on a Markov chain, you're more likely to end up with repetitive greetings and the wrong questions being asked. The alternative is a familiar tool of experience designers—the journey map.

Let Journey Maps Lead the Way

Journey maps illustrate a user's step-by-step journey through an experience. These maps are valuable for their ability to help stakeholders visualize something abstract, but in a typical UX setting they're often just a springboard toward design. In the realm of hyperautomation, journey maps are a crucial tool throughout the life cycle of a skill. They serve as the shared vision of the team leading your automation efforts. They also quickly become the initial reference point and vehicle for communicating future iterations. Journey maps are very much an active and direct reflection of the skills at play in your ecosystem.

Once you identify a skill you'd like to automate, you begin mapping the journey someone would have when engaging the automation. As is the case with all efforts in hyperautomation, your automation should always strive to outperform what a human alone would be capable of. For instance, if you want to automate expense tracking, you'll want a deep familiarity with the current, human-run process so that you can map a new experience that eliminates redundancies, alleviates pain points, and runs more efficiently.

It's also essential to track a user's emotional state as they move through the steps and entry/exit points. As you build your user's journey, try to predict how they would be feeling based on their use case. For example, a user would likely be frustrated if they received a collection notice for a bill they already paid, so a conversation designed to resolve the issue should engage appropriately. In this case, the tone of the IDW should be direct and proactive, something along the lines of, "I apologize for the confusion and will work with you to get this resolved as quickly as possible."

As you test and deploy skills, you will gain deeper insights into the emotional states of users as they move through experiences. Users are frequently panicked when calling about a collection notice, which creates new opportunities to refine interactions. As you study and improve skills, you'll also become familiar with the many deviations a journey can take. Even with relatively straightforward skills, there can easily be multiple points along a single user's journey that will take them off the golden path and into a sub-journey. For example, in the same topic but for a different use case: "It looks like that collection notice was sent because the credit card associated with your account has expired. We sent multiple emails before issuing a collection notice. Would you like to <pay your outstanding balance> or <update your contact info>?"

As these alternate journeys emerge, they become part of your journey mapping as well. In your attempts to predict human behavior, remember that designers often design experiences for fake users who resemble rational actors—whereas, in reality, people can be very irrational.

USER: I don't want to pay this bill.

IDW: Are you sure? I can waive the late fee for you.

USER: Well, I won't pay.

IDW: Are you sure? This bill has been sent to collections, and paying it now will save you time and money.

USER: I'm not paying you anything.

Designing for irrational actors requires a system to reach levels near organizational AGI. The near-term workaround is to have machine-led conversations that bring humans into the loop to solve these unusual problems—while teaching the IDW how to handle similar situations on its own in the future.

As iterations improve outcomes and evolve skills, the journey map continues to sync with the skills in your ecosystem. Considering the scope and complexity of hyperautomation, these journey maps can become quite dense and interconnected and will serve as a lifeline. They are actually maps in a literal sense—you will need them to navigate and iterate on the growing number of skills within your ecosystem.

Skills are created using code-free tools and can be updated by virtually anyone in your organization using the journey maps to locate the steps that need to be revised. Initially, updates to the skills in your ecosystem will run through the core enablement team we explored previously. They are responsible for maintaining the integrity of your journey maps, and they will work alongside anyone in your organization who wants to either create a skill or evolve an existing one.

Commit to co-creating: We said earlier that variety can solve complexity. This is absolutely the case with hyperautomation. Looking at complex problems from a variety of perspectives is essential to solving them, and this means enlisting multiple people with diverse perspectives, experiences, and biases to work together. A core team of automation experts enabling other members of your organization to craft automations that meet their needs is the embodiment of solving complexity with variety.

Working with hyperautomation and agentic AI is a team sport. The members of your team have unique worldviews, skill sets, and technical aptitudes. Bringing those things together adds immeasurable richness to the automations you design. If your tools limit creation of these experiences to only those who can code, or if creation is shackled to your vendor's road map, then you're not going to be able to take advantage of the rich tapestry of knowledge and experience your team brings to the table. An open platform accelerates your entire team's ability to leverage disruptive technology.

This wondrous team sport of creating automated solutions starts with a workshop where you tease out a thorough understanding of the problem and define key success metrics. Following that, you'll want to hold development sessions with your internal business experts and the core enablement team diving deep on what's being automated. As solutions emerge and are tested and iterated on, communication stays strong, with members of the core enablement team keeping the momentum up and facilitating needs that arise (see Figure 14.4). Processes will change rapidly, requiring quick iteration of automated skills, but that's not a problem, because your core enablement team is working in the trenches every day, evangelizing their shared vision.

Designing and training an IDW with a single skill, for instance, employee onboarding, is highly complex and dynamic given the amount of possible context. Which office will the new employee be working in? What position were they hired for? Do they have a disability? Training an IDW to complete this multi-turn task and evolving it to perform the task more efficiently requires attention from a human who knows the

**CO-CREATION
PROCESS AT
A GLANCE**

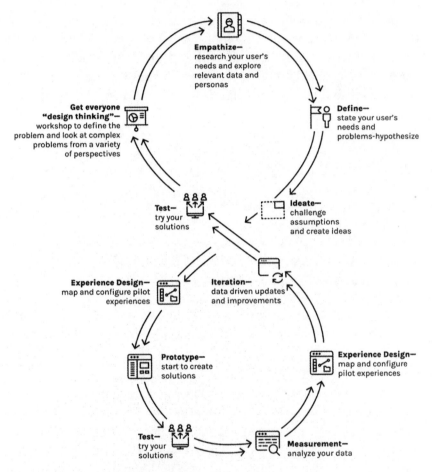

FIGURE 14.4 Co-creation process at a glance.

role they are trying to automate along with guidance from those who understand the ecosystem this IDW will inhabit and contribute to.

Projects and timelines are secondary as enablement goals become the primary objectives of this co-creating cohort. Organizations that are wired to fund projects based on measurable, quarterly ROI often face pressure to train and automate tasks concurrently. Here, co-creation is a valuable strategy—not only are you able to train, but by doing it with real-world problems you are able to more easily get buy-in from stakeholders.

You may or may not already have a conversational AI team. If you do, in this model they can find liberation from being sole creators (and potential bottlenecks), becoming consultative thought leaders, enablers, and evangelists for pushing toward organizational AGI. Establishing a core agentic team and enabling them to co-create with your workforce will help to accelerate training and development of complex automation. This will set you up to solve complexity with variety, creating a new paradigm for every evolving automation within your organization, automation that simplifies operations as it grows more sophisticated.

As John Miller and Scott Page note in their book *Complex Adaptive Systems*, "Perhaps it is the case that, as we increase heterogeneity, we move from simple systems to complicated ones back to simple ones."[3]

Build with human-in-the-loop: Creating great conversational experiences isn't easy; as a result, most of them are less than impressive. To avoid lackluster results, incorporate our old friend human-in-the-loop (HitL). With this approach, when a conversational application gets stuck, it can bring a human in to help. That human can ensure the end-user experience is fulfilled while also training the system so future occurrences don't require intervention. This type of training can either be done in real time, with algorithms to ensure the integrity of the training data, or through a moderation process where training is reviewed before it's applied. HitL requires an interface that is seamlessly integrated for real-time interactions and tools to match. For better or worse, the hype surrounding AI agents has set end-user expectations high. HitL can help you meet those expectations in a timely manner that matches user needs.

Build and expand your shared library: There's no need to reinvent the wheel; instead, build and expand a shared library. A shared library is pivotal for co-creation, supplying your organization with an open resource of skills, services, and microservices that can be reconfigured and resequenced across departments. As we discussed in Chapter 11, OneReach.ai's Lead Experience Architect, Annie Harshberger, sets reusability as a rubric for when skills or flows of skills should take the form of an IDW (or AI agent). It can be a tad disorienting to put this into context, but IDWs can be composed of other IDWs. Much like general AI agents, IDWs represent a technique for orchestrating with LLMs and other technologies.

In the MeetSync Pro demo that Annie shares, MeetSync Pro is an IDW that acts like a concierge, finding the other relevant IDWs that can move each step in the automation forward. In the case of the meeting scheduling use case being automated, after the IDW has used Google sign in to verify the user's identity, it responds to the request to schedule a meeting by bringing the SchedulerCoordinator IDW into the mix. These IDWs and their requisite skills can be customized across departments to automate around different objectives, creating a flexible and efficient paradigm for software creation.[4]

This approach allows you to grow knowledge sharing and accelerate development while keeping control of security, compliance, monitoring, best practices, consistency, and scalability. Everyone in your organization can contribute to and draw from the shared library, making it the most scalable and effective way to move your organization into hyperautomation.

Leveraging the collective knowledge of your employees in this way can be game changing. When IDWs are designed to evolve and gain wisdom, not only can they have regular conversations with all of your employees and customers, you can also apply what you learn in real time.

Entering into this realm of complexity represents the dawning of a daunting journey, but with the right process, it becomes manageable. Former Hewlett Packard CEO Lee Platt once said, "If only HP knew what HP knows, we would be three times more productive." He may have vastly underestimated the increase in productivity but his point is clear: the knowledge is already there; it's your job to connect and activate the data.

Explore or exploit? It's the age-old question of diminishing returns—knowing when to continue searching for better solutions and when to start extracting value from what you've got can mark the difference between success and failure. The continuous improvement integral to hyperautomating requires striking a balance between explore and exploit.

A multitude of theories and algorithms have been leveraged to help locate the tipping point of explore/exploit, and it's been the subject

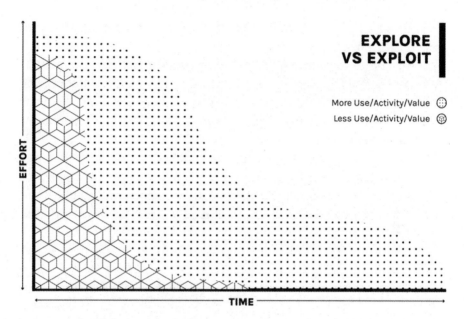

FIGURE 14.5   Explore vs. exploit.

of studies in psychiatry, behavioral ecology, computational neuro-science, computer science, and business (see Figure 14.5).

The explore/exploit trade-off conundrum gets a little stickier in the realm of hyperautomation in that, as your organization smooths the rough edges of its ecosystem, you're always exploring. With the right process and tools in place, you'll be able to iterate quickly on solutions, making the balance of exploration and exploitation a more fluid process, with a faster cadence.

Pioneers in the realm of hyperautomation don't often have the opportunity to survey a wide variety of peers: other organizations in the hyperautomation trenches. Not only are there still only a handful of great examples, but any examples (great or not) are highly competitive cards held extremely close to the chest. What you can use to your advantage, however, is your ecosystem itself.

Ideally you'll have lots of people across your organization continually trying out new solutions, putting you in a better position to conduct lots of exploration, and discovering many solutions that bear fruit. With accessible no-code tools for creating and analyzing solutions, iterating is faster and easier for teams. This collaborative approach can also foster success in spotting trends in what works well so that your exploits can bear ample fruit.

All said, the explore-exploit conundrum doesn't go away even as you're able, ready, and in the full swing of rapid creation, iteration, and analysis of solutions. You will still find yourself questioning, "How do we know when to continue improving our solution, and when is the right time to exploit the solution we have?"

There are many fascinating philosophies and some useful theories, formulas, and algorithms for trying to answer this question. Creating and analyzing more than 10,000 conversational applications revealed two factors in particular that tend to drive the length or effort for exploring: volume and value.

Challenges and Limitations

The adoption of an agentic approach, where AI agents perform tasks autonomously and interact within systems, has expanded significantly due to its flexibility and potential for handling complex interactions. However, this approach is not without its challenges and limitations, notably in terms of cost, latency, and the accuracy of outputs.

- **Cost and Complexity:** Deploying AI agents involves considerable development, training, and maintenance costs. AI agents require large amounts of training data and significant infrastructure to support their computational requirements. The complexity of integrating these agents within existing systems can add further to the expenses.

- **Latency:** One of the significant technical challenges in the agentic approach is latency in processing. AI agents, especially those handling complex tasks or large volumes of data, can experience delays as they process information, analyze data, and generate responses. This latency can be a critical drawback in real-time applications where decisions need to be made quickly, such as in financial trading or emergency response systems.

- **Inaccuracies and Hallucinations:** AI agents can sometimes produce inaccurate results or "hallucinations"—responses that are not grounded in reality or relevant data. These errors can stem from flaws in the training data, limitations in the model's understanding of complex issues, or unpredictable variables in dynamic environments. Such inaccuracies can undermine trust in AI systems and lead to erroneous decision-making.

To address these issues, system design should include using smaller, specialized models for particular tasks. These models are typically quicker and more cost-effective to train and deploy, reducing latency and operational costs. Additionally, incorporating robust feedback mechanisms can significantly enhance the accuracy and efficiency of AI agents. These mechanisms allow for continuous learning and adaptation, improving the agents' responses over time based on real-world interactions and outcomes.

Often, a combined approach that integrates both agentic and programmatic elements is also effective. Routine tasks that require high reliability and speed are better handled through programmatic approaches, which are less prone to errors and faster in execution. Meanwhile, complex, adaptive tasks that benefit from nuanced understanding are more suitably managed by AI agents.

When designing programmatic components, it is crucial to consider that these might be operated by AI agents rather than through traditional GUI interfaces. This foresight ensures that the programmatic elements are optimized for seamless integration with AI agents, facilitating better interaction and efficiency. By programming with the AI agent's operational context in mind, developers can create systems that leverage the strengths of both approaches, leading to more robust, responsive, and cost-effective solutions.

Key Takeaways

- It's important to understand the LLM-MA approach to automation, as its design and implementation is foundational to OAGI.
- This isn't a software design scenario with weekly or monthly product milestones; this process allows you to experiment on active skills, continuously improving them while also activating new skills, multiple times, every day.

- A successful strategy for hyperautomation starts small and internally, with everyone in your workforce leveraging their individual areas of expertise to develop and evolve skills.

- Journey maps of experiences users will have with your automations will serve as the shared vision for your team and the initial reference point and vehicle for communicating future iterations.

- Continuous building with human-in-the-loop and expanding your shared library are critical pieces of a sound strategy for hyperautomation.

- The continuous improvement integral to hyperautomating requires striking a balance between explore and exploit, but that balance can be achieved with more fluidity as you iterate quickly on solutions.

Want to expand on what you've learned in Chapter 14? Follow this QR code to interact with an IDW that can connect you with additional resources linked to key ideas from this chapter, including content from the *Invisible Machines* podcast.

CHAPTER 15

Design Strategy for Organizational AGI

As we've noted throughout this book, conversation is the most natural way for humans to connect with one another and accomplish shared goals. Even though communicating conversationally is second nature to most people, designing conversational experiences isn't as easy as you might expect. In a regular one-on-one conversation with another human, you say something and get immediate feedback, whether it's verbal, nonverbal, or both. That feedback tells you what to do or say next. When designing a conversation for an IDW or AI agent, you're tasked with creating one side of an interaction and making your best guesses as to what the likely responses might include.

The good news is that we already understand stories and linear workflows. Even though we're accustomed to using them, dashboards and drop-down menus pack a heavy cognitive load. Designing graphical UIs is also daunting because you have to assume the user wants access to everything. Agentic AI is more like painting by numbers. It can be extremely difficult to do this well (yes, even with generative technologies), but you get better at figuring out the best ways to design interactions by moving through the create-test-improve loop at a rapid pace.

As we mentioned earlier, it's a bit like generating new material as a comedian. You can come up with jokes you think are good, but you won't know if they're funny or not until you test them on live audiences. The key difference is that once the best jokes are identified and honed, the comedian's work on them is done for the most part. The material is presented in a one-sided format, and the only follow-up to consider is the next joke. But conversational design is two-sided, and so these interactions can take many different turns based on the different ways different users reply. Each subsequent turn might lead to a new set of choices, so the complexity compounds in a hurry.

The key to staying on track is keeping practical conversations at the core of your strategy. People are turning to you for help, so be helpful. This approach will also help you avoid the most common failure point: lack of end-user adoption. Like a joke that never gets a laugh, all your efforts are for nothing if people don't use what you build. Bear in mind as well that, to a user, the interface is the system. This is true in most design scenarios involving technology, but it becomes exceedingly important when dealing with conversational interfaces. The more high-functioning a conversational AI experience is, the more intuitive it will feel for users to interact with it—and the more readily they will accept it as "the system." However, a conversational interface only achieves that kind of potent simplicity when it's properly architected behind the scenes.

The conversational interface—whether it's expressed as an IDW or an AI agent—is just a construct. The intelligence and sophistication of the interface aren't determined by the interface itself; it's an active reflection of the sum of all parts of the ecosystem. Much of this high-level design strategy work falls to your lead experience architect (LXA), who is building something akin to a wireframe in web design. Armed with patterns that create rewarding conversational experiences for users, the LXA can assemble the bones of countless automations.

With conversational AI, users aren't comparing their experience with your solution to experiences with other similar technologies; they're comparing them to experiences they have in conversation with other humans. But as we've noted, the designer's job isn't to mimic human interactions—it's to go far beyond human interactions. The real value comes from sequencing technologies to design experiences that are improvements to current workflows. This differs from what many experience designers are aiming for. In the realm of graphical UIs, good design is unobtrusive and reduces friction. While these are goals in conversational design as well, the overarching goal is to create experiences that contribute to a much larger environment and web of experiences.

Design for Human-Controlled Outcomes

Technology should make us happy. As Siri co-founder Tom Gruber, pointed out so succinctly in a conversation we had with him about this, "you want technology to be like the glasses you're wearing that makes your vision better, but it doesn't replace the eyeballs . . . that should be our goal for technology, to make life more dignified and meaningful."[1]

From an experience design perspective, all tools are, in essence, forms of technology, and the successful ones improve our lives. In fact, this implies it's crucial that hyperautomated experiences are designed to keep decision-making in human hands. Why? One explanation is that humans are only happy when they feel like they have options. According to psychologist (and popular *UX Magazine* contributor) Susan Weinschenk, PhD, "Given an easy way to accomplish a task, versus a way that just makes our life more difficult, why do we sometimes (often?) choose the way that is complicated? It's because we love having control."[2]

Having choices gives people a sense of control, and people are drawn to a bevy of choices. Starbucks brags that their cafés offer more than 170,000 ways to customize beverages. Their reasoning behind this arch flexibility? So "customers can create a favorite drink that fits their lifestyle."[3] Some of the more extreme examples of drinks that fit customer lifestyles have gone viral on social media, such as a venti Caramel Ribbon Crunch Frappuccino with 13 additions, "including extra ice, five pumps of 'banana,' and seven pumps of dark caramel sauce."[4] Whether this strikes you as delicious or excessive, it's interesting to think what might happen when people can use conversational interfaces to focus creative energies brought on by a thirst for better choices on designing software solutions that fit their lifestyle.

It's also possible that working with AI agents or IDWs will involve a lot of the swipe left, swipe right behaviors common to dating apps. Imagine you're collaborating with an AI agent and you present it with a prompt: "I want an image for an article about the softer side of porcupines (as shown in Figure 15.1). Give me an image of a porcupine that looks approachable." The IDW presents you with a generated image of a porcupine on its back showing its underbelly. You swipe left to reject

FIGURE 15.1 Is this porcupine approachable?

the suggestion. The IDW continues presenting you with options until you swipe right. You might want to start giving it suggestions ("These are too cartoonish. Make the porcupine look more realistic") to help, and the IDW can learn from the images you tend to reject based on certain requests (e.g., if you reject five heavily anthropomorphized porcupines, the IDW might start showing you more realistic options—especially if you prompt it in that direction).

If you're an author who spends a lot of time writing about animals, it's not hard to imagine a fruitful relationship with an IDW that builds a gradual understanding of the kinds of animal imagery you like to accompany your work. This might be an outside use case, but it's emblematic of the overall philosophy of this book. The powerful technologies associated with conversational AI are at their best when augmenting and collaborating with humans, not competing with them. The aforementioned Tom Gruber calls this humanistic AI. "We can choose to use AI to automate and compete with us, or we can use AI to augment and collaborate with us, to overcome our cognitive limitations and to help us do what we want to do, only better," he said in a 2017 TED talk describing this approach.[5]

Through hyperautomation, we can improve the quality of the choices people make, imbuing them with meaning and impact. We do this by designing for human-controlled outcomes (HCO). Nobody wants to wake up under strict orders from a machine to be told what to do all day by machines designed to maximize their efficiency. On the other hand, people will love interacting conversationally with machines that offer them informed choices throughout the day that will increase their efficiency. Hyperautomation needs to be human-led at every level. Even if a machine is capable of making decisions on its own—and perhaps even more efficiently than a human can—good design keeps humans in the driver's seat. For example, even though modern commercial airliners can take off, fly, and land by themselves, a human can always take control whenever they want to. By design, the barrage of technologies working in concert to fly a commercial airliner exist to help the humans in the cockpit make better piloting decisions.

A sound design strategy for agentic AI within an intelligent ecosystem of digital workers relies on many service patterns that are practical and hew to similar interactions with another human. These patterns also represent opportunities to evolve processes and create truly innovative automations. The one pattern that should guide them all, however, is keeping decision-making in human hands. Find ways to help people make more meaningful and consequential decisions, and you will make people happier and more productive. In some ways it's just that simple.

Task-switching Is Low-hanging Fruit

For far too many members of the modern workforce, the waking nightmare of task-switching dominates their days. Running a messy gauntlet of browser tabs and apps, jumping between many sub-tasks that are as annoying as they are unnecessary, is taking a toll on productivity and overall employee experience.

Rohan Narayana Murty, Sandeep Dadlani, and Rajath B. Das performed a five-week study of 20 teams across three Fortune 500 companies,

(continued)

Task-switching Is Low-hanging Fruit *(continued)*

creating a dataset of 3,200 days of work. They unpacked this research in a *Harvard Business Review* article where they note they'd found that:

> . . . on average, the cost of a switch is a little over two seconds and the average user in the dataset toggled between different apps and websites nearly 1,200 times each day . . . people in these jobs spent just under four hours a week reorienting themselves after toggling to a new application . . . that adds up to five working weeks, or 9% of their annual time at work.[6]

That is a lot of waste, as it takes time for employees to reorient to the larger task at hand each time they have to leap to another browser window or app. As the HBR article neatly points out, "Basically, how we work is itself a distraction," and "A sizable part of [people's] jobs is to act as the glue between disparate applications."

"We need a sea change in our work culture," PhD and author of *Attention Span*, Gloria Mark, told us. "[We need] to completely change our framing about how we perceive work and to put well-being first and foremost. Productivity will follow, because there is a lot of work in psychology that shows when people feel positive—when their well-being is good—they will produce more, they will be more creative."[7]

The pathway to unburdening a workforce (and putting their well-being first, and unlocking creativity, and future-proofing an organization) is to make conversational AI the glue between apps instead of people.

Task-switching is low-hanging fruit in terms of automations, and it has the immediate benefit of saving time. It also approaches automation in a way that augments people, rather than replacing them. Using technology to remove anxiety-inducing tedium from people's daily lives will make their work better.

In the "AI Agents in Action" episode of the *Invisible Machines* podcast, multiple conversational AI agents with different distinct skills complete a complex scheduling task within one RWC window. One-Reach.ai LXA Annie Harshberger shows us five different IDWs working the task from different angles. In essence, each IDW represents a moment where a task-switch was eliminated.

Task-switching Is Low-hanging Fruit

That number obviously multiplies each time someone uses this approach to scheduling. Because these automations are based around core skills that are composable and customizable, it's also easy to create new automations that can slash task switches elsewhere. For example, the PollTaker skill could be part of another automation that asks people what kind of snacks they want for an upcoming event and builds an online order that simply needs human approval.

Sequencing Patterns for a Successful Ecosystem

Successful automations call for successfully sequenced patterns. Within the kind of ecosystems we've been describing, those patterns inevitably invite a great deal of complexity. A great frame of reference for this concept is the game of chess, which is all about recognizing and acting on complex patterns.

"Pattern recognition is one of the most important mechanisms of chess improvement," International Master Arthur van de Oudeweetering wrote. "Realizing that the position on the board has similarities to positions you have seen before helps you to quickly grasp the essence of that position and find the most promising continuation."[8]

By some estimates, grandmasters of chess can memorize up to 100,000 patterns. While this is an impressive feat, putting memorized patterns to use isn't really what humans are wired to do. At some point people make mistakes while acting on patterns, no matter how ingrained they are. For example, we should be able to enter the passcode on our alarm systems flawlessly, every time. We get plenty of practice, but sometimes we mess up and have to start over again. There's always going to be uncertainty when people are in charge of patterns. An interview with Lex Fridman, rapper, record producer, philosopher, chess player, and mastermind of the Wu-Tang Clan, RZA, sheds light on the idea of uncertainty:

"[With chess] the thing that's introduced is the uncertainty . . . you gonna make a move [and] sooner or later something uncertain is going to come in. . . . Bobby Fisher said in one of his books, 'Every game of chess is a draw, the only way somebody wins is when one of us makes a mistake.'"[9] Grandmaster Savielly Tartakower echoes this notion: "The winner of the game is the player who makes the next-to-last mistake." When it comes to recognizing patterns and acting on them without making mistakes, machines have a decided edge over humans.

Back in 1997, chess grandmaster Garry Kasparov resigned after 19 moves in a game against a chess-playing computer developed by IBM called Big Blue. It was the sixth and final game of their match, and Kasparov lost two games to one, with three draws. In 2010, Kasparov wrote, "Today, for $50, you can buy a home PC program that will crush most grandmasters." While the fact that machines are better at chess than humans might be unwelcome news to grandmasters, it's great for hyperautomating.

The reason computers beat humans at chess is that they can memorize 100,000 patterns and run through them with flawless recognition and total confidence. But rather than pitting human against machine, hyperautomation provides humans the opportunity to forge and sequence patterns that machines can then use to automate tasks without uncertainty. This isn't to say that these patterns will perform flawlessly right away—but as you continually improve upon them, you can reach a point where a growing number of tasks within your organization are performed with total certainty.

The leap forward comes in pattern execution. With AI agents, patterns aren't limited by a programmatic approach. Systems can be given broader objectives and can evolve and adapt to edge cases, which means we speed up innovation in business processes and rely less on human escalation.

Getting to this place requires help from humans with something they are better at doing than machines are: predicting behavior. When someone poses a question, we use all sorts of cues (visual, physical, historical, auditory, etc.) to understand what's really being asked. If we don't immediately know how to respond with a helpful reply, we can make an educated guess based on the context. For example, let's say a coworker asks you if they look okay—and they look as though they haven't slept for days. You're about to go into an important meeting, so you don't think they're looking for an honest answer—and it definitely wouldn't help, so you might decide to offer a platitude instead. On the other hand, if that person wanted feedback in advance on how to remove a stain on their shirt, an honest answer would be appropriate.

Before you touch any technology, however, you need to envision the experience you want to create. We've studied numerous highly rated experiences over the years and have noted scores of patterns that lead to good experiences, and we'll explore them in the next section. Keeping these flexible, agentic patterns in mind as you build the framework of your ecosystem—designing automation flows and strategizing their deployment—can help create an ecosystem of real service. Not only can the sequencing of these patterns efficiently automate tasks with certainty, these are the kinds of optimized experiences that will build meaningful relationships between humans and machines. They should be designed as something ongoing that will evolve—not as a series of disconnected transactions but as contextual relationships. Thinking beyond transactional relationships to contextual relationships creates the opportunity to change the presence of software and machines in our lives so that technology can be always present but never invasive.

This work often begins with journey maps created by the LXAs and design strategists. These journey maps are used to define the experiences that make up your ecosystem, and they come to life as key patterns are identified and later fleshed out through production design. Nothing about this process is one-and-done. Like the nearly infinite number of moves that could take place on a chessboard, there's really no limit to how patterns like these can be sequenced and continually improved. Another nugget of chess wisdom shared by RZA applies readily to hyperautomation:

> *I recall the first time that I realized that I need to improve. At first I was probably the best player in the crew. But the crew started improving. I had to do more play[ing]. But . . . the GZA himself, he started studying theory, studying books I wasn't aware of. One day at his crib he was beating me so bad, and his son Kareem, who loves his big cousin Rakeem [RZA] . . . so he just came over when GZA went to the bathroom, he was like, "Yo, you know my dad is in the books, right?" [laughs hard].*[10]

When you're hyperautomating, you should always be in the books—not only to keep an edge on competing businesses but also to continue to improve the more personalized relationships you can build with customers.

Now, let's take a closer look at the patterns your LXAs and design strategists will want to keep in their back pocket as you build your ecosystem for hyperautomation. We'll start with the most basic patterns and work toward the more complex ones (all of which are described below and seen in Figure 15.2 and continued in Figure 15.3).

KEY DESIGN PATTERNS

For Lead Experience Architects
and Design Strategists To Keep
In Their Back Pocket

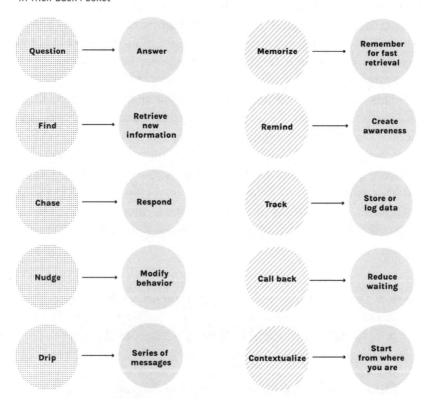

Question	⟶	Answer		Memorize	⟶	Remember for fast retrieval
Find	⟶	Retrieve new information		Remind	⟶	Create awareness
Chase	⟶	Respond		Track	⟶	Store or log data
Nudge	⟶	Modify behavior		Call back	⟶	Reduce waiting
Drip	⟶	Series of messages		Contextualize	⟶	Start from where you are

FIGURE 15.2   Key design patterns to sequence for conversational design.

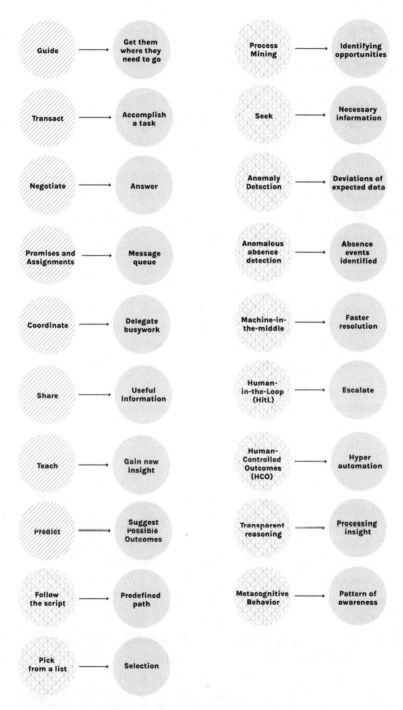

FIGURE 15.3   Key design patterns to sequence for conversational design. (*continued*)

Key Patterns to Sequence for Conversational AI

Questions and answers: Q&A is one of the most basic conversational patterns, and it's what a lot of people mistakenly think of as conversational AI. Users ask the machine a question, and it looks for the answer using LLMs in combination with a knowledge base designed for providing answers. The Q&A pattern highlights one area where conversation isn't always the best solution: browsing. Q&A is a way to help resolve a question that the user has, but depending on your use case, giving them the option to browse data, products, or an FAQ page might be more useful. Adding a micro UI to the experience can also solve this. For example, if someone asks about what types of services are available, an AI agent can either point them to the page on the website that lists all of the services or provide a condensed recreation within a rich web chat experience. In ecosystems built for hyperautomation, an agent can also turn to a human-in-the-loop (HitL) if it doesn't have an answer.

Find: Users ask the machine to look up information based on certain queries. The machine queries an API and gets a set of results that it can show the user. This might feed back into known answers for Q&A or help with transactions or establish the user's identity. Even though the Q&A and find patterns seem similar, they are very different. Find is a good pattern to employ if Q&A fails to help.

Since these design patterns come from pieces of successful human conversation, they are ultimately derived from human interaction. Like machines, we only have a certain amount of experience and training. When necessary, we use external sources such as the internet, colleagues, and books to find the answers we need. In the context of find, when a machine's training doesn't allow it to answer the question, it can search external sources, usually via API.

Chase: Chase is more aggressive than simple reminders; flows built for this will activate continuously until a certain criterion is met. For example, a proactive pattern would hunt down an answer to a particular question. If a user doesn't provide it, the machine will move on to another user—or else continue to repeat the query until it gets its answer. Often, successful resolution will involve escalation.

Nudge: Nudge is a soft push toward a desired outcome but in a manner that's less intrusive than chase. It's designed to provide extra information in a structured way that will either subconsciously motivate users to take a particular action or more distinctly prompt them to consciously make the intended choice. A tangible example would be painted lines on a road that clearly delineate cyclists from drivers. The best uses are contextual to the experience they're in. In the airline industry, for example, a nudge might be: "Just so you know, an upgrade to business class for this flight is only $99 more."

Drip: Drip is a series of announcements; it can be used for reporting and making enhancements that don't require immediate feedback. It's a bit like chase without the knowledge base and providing future context. For example, drip would offer: "Don't forget, you have an appointment on Monday at 3:30 p.m.," whereas chase would offer: "Please confirm your appointment on Monday at 3:30 p.m. by replying, 'Y' or 'N.'" Drip often represents a content journey, one that's presented in a predetermined sequence. For example, a drip might have a series of five deliberately spaced out messages that go out to first-time customers as part of an onboarding experience with a new product.

Memorize: This pattern can establish conversational patterns at large across multiple users. Memorize can be used to understand the common conversations and questions that users engage in. Flows built for memorization will store information so that it can be used for reporting, making enhancements to the knowledge base, and providing future context. When designing your conversations, you should make sure that you set them up to store data so that you can utilize memorize. Ultimately, this context helps to build relationships rather than just one-off transactions.

Remind: Remind is a proactive pattern that gives users information at a particular time and in a specific way in order to take action. This could be for an upcoming appointment or to establish a new habit. To succeed with this very common pattern, send out reminders over whatever channel your customer prefers. In fact, this is another chance to employ the memorize pattern—noting preferred channels for engagement. Too often, remind is used mundanely—without much imagination—as a simple outbound message. Using only one pattern on its own doesn't make for a good conversation. To use remind successfully, design around the reminder and create a conversational experience that goes beyond the first obvious step.

Track: This is similar to memorize but isn't necessarily used for long-term memorization. For example, the machine might memorize how many times a user goes from point A to B, tracking that everything between point A and B is being logged and used. Flows that track are keeping in mind a "current state"—as well as all the prior states that led to that point.

Callback: Another proactive pattern, callback is focused on resuming a prior activity. This is geared toward pausing an activity and setting a follow-up—an interval that could be dependent on a certain amount of time lapsing or on the emergence of a new piece of data.

Contextualize: With contextualize, the machine is trying to extract context from the conversation using stored data as a starting point. It will query its contextual storage and try to continue from that context. Examples could include using time of day, location, the task at hand, or a prior conversation or message to establish context. The contextualize pattern is beneficial in that it allows the machine to use context to improve the conversational experience by cutting out the need for starting from the beginning—such as asking questions like "Are you a customer? When was your most recent purchase?" This pattern goes hand-in-hand with the memorize pattern.

Guide: With this pattern, the machine literally guides a user from point A to point B, such as in a scripted conversation or a sequence of questions. Guide could also help with a particular sequence over time, such as checking in each day to help users stay on track with a specific goal. Flows built to guide keep in mind progression and sequence with the milestones or the ultimate outcome they're meant to achieve. Guide is also a critical pattern for the concierge skill, which greets users. Concierge evaluates a user's needs using patterns such as contextualize and Q&A; then, it uses guide to connect users to the other skills in the ecosystem that will help them achieve their goals. Without guide, a user would be left guessing what an IDW might be capable of, asking questions that wouldn't help the system differentiate what they're really asking for.

Interactions that follow the user's lead can be complex and difficult to build, which can lead to a common mistake with conversational design: overpromising or letting users expect that your machine can do more than it actually can. Set expectations for your user by guiding them—rather than imposing on them to guide the machine.

Transact: This pattern helps users accomplish a particular task. There's a goal in mind and a desired outcome; common examples would be scheduling an appointment or ordering a product. Transact can also be used for minor changes to a setting or to add a new communication preference. Flows will have a structured script that needs particular information to complete the task, with task completion being the primary measure.

Negotiate: If someone asks an IDW if you can check into a hotel room early and it replies that check-in time is 4 p.m., they might be inclined to call and try and persuade someone to bend the rules their way. Trying to persuade a machine is futile, but you can prevent that phone call by building negotiation into the process. In this case, the IDW can negotiate by saying something like, "If our regular check-in time of 4 p.m. doesn't work for you, let me see if I can try and work something out and get back to you." This gives the user the impression that calling would be futile, so they'll wait to hear back from the IDW—likely employing HitL to get an answer.

Promises and assignments: This pattern was inspired by a concept that developers often use in JavaScript, which has an asynchronous component to it: someone either promises to take care of a certain task the next time they log in or assigns someone else to take care of a task when they next log in. In most scenarios people tend to think of interactions with machines as being either inbound (someone is calling you) or outbound (you reach out or are responding to someone). Promises and assignments represents a third category, the real-life equivalent of which would be someone telling you, "Hey, next time you talk to Teddy, remind him he owes me $100." Within an ecosystem for hyperautomating, this takes the form of a queue of assignments so that the next time Teddy contacts the organization, he receives these assignments. It's almost like an inbox that only reveals its queue of messages when someone makes inbound contact. You already see this pattern used by cell-phone companies: when you call, they remind you that you're due for a device upgrade. With inbound calls this pattern can be used to deftly avoid prolonged calls. For instance, if someone who recently placed an order calls in, there's an assignment at the top of their queue to let them know: "I see you ordered something from us earlier this week. Good news—your order has shipped! Would you like the tracking information?" A personalized experience like this saves the user time and engenders confidence in the IDW. Promises and assignments is an amazing pattern because it allows you to go further without annoying people. They've already reached out to you; meet them with some useful information that can save them time.

Coordinate: This pattern is meant to get several participants working together around a particular goal. This might be used to schedule a meeting or gather shared input. This is a more complex pattern that will often have sub-patterns such as chase, track, and transact working together.

Share: This pattern is designed to share information with people who need it. This proactive pattern helps disseminate information in a relevant or contextual way. Flows that use share will send out messages or links bearing useful information.

Teach: This pattern teaches users how to do something, often launching from Q&A. The purpose is to provide a series of lessons and/or instruction, which can occur in a single session or across multiple sessions.

Predict: With this pattern the machine uses past interactions and contextual data to predict what a user might be trying to do, often suggesting possible outcomes, such as by saying: "This option is statistically more likely to produce your desired outcome." By reviewing all available data to predict possible outcomes, predict eliminates unnecessary steps to make the conversation as efficient as possible.

Follow the script: AI agents follow scripted conversations to keep users on a predefined path.

Pick from a list: Multiple users can select options from one or more lists. This can be used for scheduling a group meeting, picking a venue, hiring a new role, or many more actions.

Process mining: A machine can be trained to analyze data with the objective of identifying patterns, inefficiencies, and opportunities in both current and historical processes and events.

Seek: In some ways, seek is more than just a design pattern. Perhaps you're familiar with CRUD, the four basic operations of persistent storage in computer programming: create, read, update, and delete. We like to think we're now in the CRUDS era, where seek is a fundamental operation where data is concerned. The basic idea is that the system seeks information. Within a conversational experience, an AI agent might be triggered to seek information it doesn't have. That might mean reaching out to a HitL, or searching elsewhere in the ecosystem for the information it needs. Maybe an address is missing in one database, so an AI agent searches names across other databases until it finds matches that it can verify. In this example there's value in the system looking for information that it needs in the moment, but there's also the broader idea of having the agent seek out missing information before it's needed, creating a more complete dataset and reducing latency during a live experience.[11]

Anomaly detection: Anomaly detection is a process mining pattern for detecting anomalies in data, such as events or deviations from what is standard or expected.

Anomalous absence detection: An especially valuable type of anomaly detection involves regular evaluation of data with the particular goal of detecting something humans aren't typically good at spotting: the absence of data. Essentially, the machine identifies patterns and meaning in the absence of data, and treats each absence as an event—which in some cases could amount to identifying missed opportunities or opportunity costs.

For example, a human account manager might notice that a customer, JoAnna H, made a larger purchase than most customers make within a six-month period. But it's less likely that the same human would notice that JoAnna H had anomalously not bought anything in the same six-month period (absence of data), whereas an agent could alert the account manager to JoAnna H's buying drought so that the organization can reach out with a special offer for her next purchase.

Machine-in-the-middle: This is a relatively simple pattern that involves a live agent handing off a user to an agent in order to perform a task that a machine can do more efficiently. For instance, if you've been talking to an agent to arrange specific details of a purchase, that agent can then hand you over to an agent to collect payment information (maybe a text pops up on your phone requesting your credit card number or a photo of the back of your card). Another example: you email a service provider with a query, and an agent tasked with reviewing emails sent to their support team detects missing information. You get a follow-up email from an agent requesting your account number and the service address so that when the agent pulls up the ticket, all of the information is there. This unburdens the agent from having to do additional follow-ups and helps your request reach a faster resolution.

This is also an important pattern to keep in mind because it demonstrates that there are plenty of creative ways to build automations that don't require APIs or extensive integration. Machine-in-the-middle can simply be an agent that receives an inbound email, uses an LLM to see and review the content, and determines whether there's missing information. The IDW can reply right away asking users for missing data—no integration necessary.

Human in The Loop: Automation is only as good as the data at its disposal. In this powerful pattern, humans provide data to help train the IDW—and there are endless conversations or variations of conversations that humans can help with. Flows that incorporate HitL reach out to their humans-in-the-loop on different channels—whether it's a call center, chat channels, text messages, or collaborative tools such as Slack—to get the needed information; in turn, the flows update their knowledge bases and skills. In other scenarios—as has been previously covered—when the IDWs get stuck on a problem, they are guided by humans with what to do next. Team members can either feed the IDW information for machine learning or script their interactions in a particular way.

Human Controlled Outcome: Hyperautomation needs to be human-led at every level. Machines' abilities to make efficient decisions on their own will continue to improve, but it's crucial to keep people in control of outcomes. People don't want to live under strict orders from machines—even if those machines are designed to maximize efficiency. But people will likely look forward to interacting with machines that regularly offer efficiency-improving suggestions.

Transparent reasoning: Sometimes it can be useful to show how an AI agent is reasoning throughout an experience. This design pattern emerged from the Agents product on the GSX platform, where a panel on the right-hand side of rich webchat experience shows how the agent interpreted the information provided by a user and what instructions it will follow to reach the identified objective. Cole Gentile, a solutions designer at OneReach.ai, walked us through a micro UI demo on an In Action episode of *Invisible Machines* that shows the process unfold. A sample user asks an agent about a replacement rack for a dishwasher and along with a text reply we can see how the agent interpreted the request, the objective it has set, and the information it will need to collect in order to resolve the issue. This kind of transparent reasoning might be overkill in some use cases (i.e., if I'm ordering takeout, seeing a recap of my order is probably sufficient) but in complex automations where lots of information is at play, this can make for a more secure experience.[12]

Metacognitive behavior: This is more of an overarching pattern—one that embraces and reinforces many of those described above. The idea is to create a pattern of awareness within your ecosystem so that, while IDWs are learning individual skills, they are also managing their overall learning. It's one thing to learn a skill—dogs, for instance, do it all the time—but it's another thing to be actively aware that you are learning (and to subsequently project manage that learning). For our purposes, this could be as basic as having an IDW check in about learning a new skill set along a timeline. It could also include higher-level functionalities, like having an IDW check in with suggestions based on user queries (e.g., "I've noticed many users are calling to request password resets. Is this something I can learn to do?"). You could also seek out new tools for your ecosystem and then vet them based on reputation or user ratings.

Patterns in Action

Many of these patterns are frequently sequenced by GPS to provide a better-than-human experience. You've got some extra time as you're driving through an unfamiliar area to a meeting, so you ask your smartphone if there's a coffee shop nearby. This is the Q&A pattern activated. The answer might come back in the form of pinpoints on a map, using the contextualize pattern to find a coffee shop closest to you. The system can then guide you, navigating you to the coffee shop. It can also use the predict pattern to identify a traffic accident up ahead that could cause a delay. It can nudge you to let you know that you might want to take a side street. This is a multimodal journey that incorporates voice, text, and graphical interface, and it can evolve to include other patterns, such as transact—perhaps letting you order and pay for your coffee ahead of time, so you can be sure to make your meeting on time.

AI agents boast greater flexibility compared to traditional programmatic software, meaning we can develop AI applications that are broader in scope and adaptability. This enhanced flexibility stems from three key innovations:

1. **Enhanced flexibility:** Unlike rigid, purely graphical interfaces, modern AI systems offer a level of flexibility that allows them to interact more intuitively and responsively with users. This adaptability makes them suitable for a wide range of applications beyond fixed, predetermined tasks.

2. **Agentic back end systems:** By implementing an agentic approach on the back end, we can allow AI agents to manage complex tasks that involve dynamic interactions and decisions. This approach allows for the more nuanced and intelligent handling of tasks that traditionally required dedicated software solutions, such as scheduling and coordination.

3. **Composable architecture:** A composable architecture facilitates scalability on the fly, allowing components to be assembled and reassembled to meet specific needs without extensive redesigns or adjustments. This flexibility supports rapid adaptation to changing requirements and environments.

When these elements are integrated with agentic design patterns, the resulting software systems are not only more versatile but also significantly less dependent on narrow, specific solutions. For instance, instead of relying on specialized scheduling software, an agentic system can coordinate tasks involving multiple participants selecting options from various categories. Orchestrated AI agents dynamically adapt to different scenarios by understanding context, enabling them to handle a diverse range of tasks with ease.

This paradigm shift toward more adaptable and intelligent AI applications showcases the potential of AI agents to revolutionize how we interact with and leverage technology, making it a powerful tool for a wide array of use cases across industries.

Advanced Design Patterns for Agentic Orchestration

Below we describe (as seen in Figure 15.4) five possible design patterns that AI agents can use to communicate and coordinate work, often functioning as swarming patterns to manage and multitask numerous workloads:

Cooperative Orchestration: In this paradigm, agents collaboratively work toward common objectives. They share information freely to collectively enhance outcomes and improve decision-making processes. This approach is particularly effective in environments where a unified approach is necessary to solve complex problems or achieve a shared goal, like in synchronized operations or team-based problem-solving tasks.

Debate Orchestration: Here, agents engage in argumentative exchanges, each presenting and defending their viewpoints while critiquing others. This paradigm fosters a competitive yet constructive environment where the best ideas emerge through rigorous debate. It's ideal for tasks requiring thorough analysis and consensus-building, such as policy formulation or strategic planning sessions.

Dynamic Layered Orchestration: In systems like the Dynamic LLM-Agent Network (DyLAN), communication is organized in

ADVANCED DESIGN PATTERNS FOR AGENTIC ORCHESTRATION

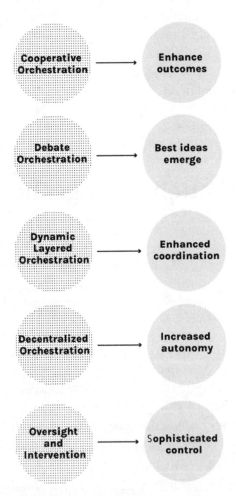

Cooperative Orchestration → Enhance outcomes

Debate Orchestration → Best ideas emerge

Dynamic Layered Orchestration → Enhanced coordination

Decentralized Orchestration → Increased autonomy

Oversight and Intervention → Sophisticated control

FIGURE 15.4 Advanced design patterns for agentic orchestration.

a multi-layered hierarchy.[13] Agents operate within their specific layers, interacting primarily with peers or adjacent layers. This structured approach allows for efficient distribution of tasks and information, enhancing coordination across different levels of the agent network. It's suitable for complex systems where different layers handle distinct aspects of a process, like in large-scale logistics or hierarchical organizational structures.

Decentralized Orchestration: Operating on a peer-to-peer model, this structure enables agents to communicate directly without a central coordinator. Each agent acts as an independent node that can exchange information and make decisions autonomously. This setup is common in simulations and decentralized applications where agility and resilience against single points of failure are crucial, such as in blockchain technologies or distributed gaming environments.

Oversight and Intervention: A fifth design pattern that can be utilized in multi-agent systems involves an Oversight and Intervention Paradigm. In this setup, a higher-level AI agent is tasked with overseeing the actions and decisions of one or more subordinate agents. This overseeing agent monitors the performance and compliance of the other agents against set standards or objectives, intervening when necessary to guide or correct actions. Here are the key features of this paradigm:

Dual mode functionality: In passive mode, the overseeing agent acts as a monitor, observing the actions and decisions of subordinate agents without directly intervening. It collects data, analyzes performance, and provides alerts or recommendations when deviations from expected outcomes or standards are detected. This mode is crucial for maintaining awareness of the system's overall performance and ensuring that issues are flagged for human review or automatic adjustment. In active mode, the overseeing agent goes beyond monitoring to actively intervene in the operations of other agents. This could involve making adjustments to their actions, taking over the task directly, or rerouting tasks among agents to optimize performance. This mode is used in scenarios where immediate correction is necessary to prevent errors or to optimize outcomes dynamically.

Dynamic response capabilities: The overseeing agent can switch between passive and active modes based on the context and severity of the situation. The agent employs advanced decision-making algorithms to determine the most appropriate response, balancing autonomy and control to maintain system integrity and efficiency.

Scalability and flexibility: This paradigm can be scaled to oversee a large number of agents across various tasks and sectors. It's flexible enough to be adapted for different industries, from automated manufacturing lines where precision is critical, to digital marketing campaigns where strategies may need rapid adjustment based on real-time data.

Enhanced reliability and compliance: By incorporating an oversight mechanism, organizations can enhance the reliability of automated systems and ensure compliance with internal and external standards. The overseeing agent acts as a safeguard, reducing the likelihood of errors and ensuring that operations align with strategic goals.

The oversight and intervention paradigm adds a layer of governance to AI operations, enabling more sophisticated control and assurance in systems where multiple agents work together. This approach is particularly valuable in environments where the cost of failure is high or where continuous optimization is necessary for success.

These design patterns reflect different methods of organizing and managing work among AI agents, each offering unique advantages in specific contexts. By leveraging them, organizations can optimize their operations, enhance collaborative efforts, and improve the overall effectiveness of their multi-agent systems.

Key Takeaways

- The conversations we have every day with other people provide instant feedback that informs the flow, whereas designing conversations involves starting with a prompt and taking your best guess at how someone might reply.

- People are turning to you for help, so be helpful by keeping practical conversations at the core of your strategy and avoid the most common failure point: low user adoption.

- Successful automations are built by sequencing design patterns—which machines are good at running flawlessly—using your advanced human ability to predict behavior as a guide.

- Sequencing of the patterns recommended here can create optimized experiences that will build meaningful relationships between humans and machines.

- Patterns can make your bot more helpful, to take your bot from being an underachiever to being an overachiever.

Want to expand on what you've learned in Chapter 15? Follow this QR code to interact with an IDW that can connect you with additional resources linked to key ideas from this chapter, including content from the *Invisible Machines* podcast.

CHAPTER 16

Production Design for Organizational AGI

The notion of having real conversations with computers has been the stuff of science fiction until relatively recently. It's not always well represented either. For instance, in the Star Trek universe, why do people have to run across the ship to press a button when the ship has a fluent and seemingly capable voice assistant.

Anyway, it's taken decades, but speech recognition has improved to a place of near human recognition, which, incidentally, is not as great as most might think. Simply translating sounds into words does not constitute understanding. Understanding comes with comprehension of what the words mean and what the user intends by speaking them. Understanding without reasoning, or being able to do something about it, has limited value. Whether you're dealing specifically with speech or with other communication channels, this is where production design comes in.

In this space, production design consists of a conversational designer creating the experiences people will have in conversations with machines. In terms of more traditional experience design it's analogous to a designer skinning a wireframe. The lead experience architect maps out the high-level journey users will take with AI agents. Now, the conversational designer creates the flows that facilitate that high-level journey and objective, choosing words or specific LLM instructions and fine-tuning the tone to bring the experience to life.

As far as users are concerned, the conversational interface is the system. This is a good thing. **But it's critical that designers and architects not confuse the interface for the system on their end.**

You might be surprised at how quickly you can find yourself empathizing with a conversational interface—and this is a testament to the ingrained nature of conversation as a tool. But since the conversational interface is just the access point, success hinges on whether an AI agent understands language and context deeply enough to determine the user's intention. That contextual understanding is forged by a properly designed ecosystem. So, as you continually fine-tune your conversational design, always bear in mind that it's not actually the system—it's the portal into the system.

OAGI gives us a unique opportunity to provide users with the specific controls (or information, or prompts) that they need in the moment, before they even need to ask for them.

The remains of many a concierge bot can be found in the ruins of failed attempts at implementing conversational AI. This happens when a machine with no actual skill—even one that's running on a sophisticated NLU engine or LLM—is propped up as being the one-stop portal into an organization. If users aren't informed of what a machine can do, they might think the machine can do anything, which of course isn't possible. As we indicated when describing the guide pattern in the previous chapter, concierge isn't a machine; it's a skill, and it's usually the first skill a user will encounter. The concierge skill evaluates a user's needs by asking questions that can map to other skills and AI agents in the ecosystem. The concierge skill determines which skills will most likely be of benefit and connects the user to them either agenticaly or using a programmatic approach. (For example, if it's dealing with a return visitor, an IDW running the concierge skill can cross-reference existing customer data during the initial interaction to get a head start on a useful reply.) Once the IDW has an idea of what the user wants, it can guide the user between skills so as to deliver a rewarding, beyond human experience.

Everything Hinges on Analytics and Reporting

You may not be surprised to hear that delivering these kinds of flexible and adaptive experiences requires a completely new relationship with analytics and tracking. There's a side to this new relationship that will be thrilling and revelatory because you'll be able to analyze and report on interactions between users and AI agents in real time. In essence this creates a powerful and integrated form of user research. Of course, something this novel and high yield requires an ecosystem with deeply elaborate architecture.

With the implementation of conversational AI, analytics and reporting are inseparable—providing information crucial to the establishment and evolution of your ecosystem—but they operate somewhat independently within that ecosystem. Even the most basic user experiences with conversational AI can produce massive amounts of data, which is a good thing from an analytics perspective: the more information, the better. But conversation interfaces yield unstructured data that requires analytics to give it shape and meaning. Combine that swelling pool of nebulous information with an organization's internal data—specifically, the data that's feeding the conversational experience—and you're facing some profound complexity.

As with any self-learning system, orchestrating AI agents demands a reliable feedback loop. If the system isn't getting a steady flow of feedback, it starts to resemble a more programmatic solution. Using agents in a programmatic manner—only doing specific things in a predetermined way—quickly becomes a really expensive way of doing things the old way.

It's also worth pausing on connected devices because the Internet of Things that don't look like computers but act like computers are data points as well. Whether we recognize it as such or not, we spend our lives surrounded by computers of all shapes and sizes. If your refrigerator recognizes that its door is being opened and starts running software, the door has become an interface, and the appliance is as much a computer as it is a cooling unit. So add all the data cached by televisions, speakers, Bluetooth tags, and cat litter boxes to your collection of data sources to be reckoned with.

If you're an analyst, data is your friend. Let's say you've got a hypothesis to test and want to explore as much data as possible—running it through different filters looking for patterns. There are various tools out there, such as machine learning, that let you crunch large amounts of data and find actionable patterns to exploit. For hyperautomation efforts, these tools don't need to work in real time, but they need to be flexible so that analysts can explore data in many ways.

Let's say you're an analyst for a subscription-based cat litter company. You have a hunch that when customers move they often cancel their subscriptions and restart them again later rather than just updating their address information. You run the data to see if that correlation is supported. You find a pattern of users who have canceled subscriptions and then created new ones with different addresses. This is valuable, actionable information that you then pass along to an experience designer.

When XDs are building conversational workflows for IDWs, they can implement algorithms built around the patterns provided by analysts. In our kitty litter scenario, the XD could add prompts when users first sign on and when they initiate a cancellation. The XD can design ways to communicate to users that updating their address is easy— easier than canceling and then starting up again.

As they make these kinds of adjustments, XDs can use real-time feedback to learn what's working and what isn't. In some cases, they might even improve interactions as they're happening. This is the nature of reporting in hyperautomation scenarios. Feedback is always on and always being acted on. Tactically speaking, this requires a dashboard that allows experience designers to watch as users interact with IDWs, moving through a series of skills and flows. When experience designers can literally see how users are interacting with machines, they can be regularly fine-tuning interactions.

The data supply that comes with most of the machines that people release into the wild are black boxes with basic metrics (attrition, hang-ups, etc.) and are of little use when striving for OAGI. Unless you're summarizing data in real time, you'll find it exceedingly hard to patch holes in your boat before the water pours in. Being able to retrace conversations in a timely fashion is the real value, and the real-time reporting aspect needs to be baked into whatever tool you're using.

A Fast and Fluid Feedback Loop

What's required is an ever-spinning feedback loop. As skills are deployed and utilized, those interactions can be analyzed and iterated on, often as they unfold. This isn't a nice-to-have, it's an imperative. If you can't easily report on how people are using your system and experiences, you'll find it impossible to fulfill the promise of rapid iteration, which is critical for hyperautomation and organizational AGI. Hyperautomation allows us to create hyperpersonalized solutions, but that hyperpersonalization requires this deeper, ingrained relationship with analytics and reporting.

Not only is this the most efficient way to aggregate and actualize vast amounts of data within your ecosystem, it's also a boon to your team. In this scenario, data analysts get to focus squarely on what they do best: digging through data and identifying patterns. In complementary fashion, your experience designers will be designing experiences that are truly dynamic, relying on an exciting new rate of iteration that should ignite the creative spirit of anyone passionate about the progression of experience design as a discipline.

In some ways, this is a dynamic new form of experience design that represents the process in its purest form. By designing experiences, watching them unfold in real time, and taking opportunities to continually improve on them, you're flowing through steps hourly or daily that would be weeks or even months apart in typical software development scenarios. This creates a feedback loop that lets you design and maintain incredibly powerful software at a rapid pace.

Keep in mind, however, that companies are not successful because they produce more software but because they produce more good software. This is where this new approach to experience design pays off. When experience designers no longer have to concern themselves with being developers—when they can create and evolve software at will without having to write code—they can focus squarely on designing truly good software.

Strive for Adaptive Design

Adaptive design is a next-level concept that involves a rapid iteration loop of testing, analyzing, and designing—all requirements of the agentic approach. The idea is that by testing a variety of combinations of things, you'll gain valuable insights that you can design around. The team at OneReach.ai assisted Stanford University as part of a study that used text messaging to help parents teach kids to read. The entire objective was to find the right combination of content, language, and scheduling to get the most positive effect. What we discovered was that this kind of communication can be very powerful in terms of modifying human behavior—so long as it's continuously fine-tuned to maximize the effect.

For example, just because a text prompt asking a parent to have their child read a line from a cereal box works at 7:30 a.m. for the first four weeks doesn't mean it will remain effective forever. The AI agent needs to adapt by running through the cycle of explore vs. exploit: exploring the right combo to optimize the prompt and experience, then exploiting it until it wanes, and then going back to explore.

Different patterns also work differently for different people or personas. You have to be able to adapt on a schedule but also from a standpoint of individualization. Our team applied this thinking to a service-finding service, such as homeowners needing work to be done. Of course, if the first time someone tried to use the service no provider showed up, they'd never use the service again, so it's critical that the first interaction go well. We were able to ensure that the providers show up on time (and also that the homeowner was there to meet them) by exploring numerous combinations based on language, time, and reminders. We allowed the system to adapt to things such as alert fatigue and leveraged all of the individual data we could identify. (For example, roofers might respond to a site visit request differently than plumbers would, since they need more advance notice to prepare materials.)

Phrasing and timing can be customized on an individual basis. Being able to adapt an optimized formula and realizing it can be optimized again helps you create an environment for machine learning—where there is no perfect combo because nothing is static. It sounds like a lot of work, but the power and effect make it worth every minute. When it comes together, the ability to modify behavior is unbelievable. We know how powerful this approach can be because we've used it to effectively help people quit smoking—one of the most powerful addictions to break.

Some things are complex for the sake of complexity. This is a level of complexity that brings about the power of personalization.

Make Your Data Consumable

Design your data to be consumed by AI agents, not just humans. Summarizing data into readable text will be most helpful for an agent-first approach to data collection and consumption. Agents can consume images, so things like charts are usable, but visuals aren't as efficient as text.

Systems with metacognitive capabilities—the ability to manage and take agency over task execution as well as their own tuning and training—are the goal. Agent training involves giving AI agents the kind of data they can most easily consume. A set of agents managing their own learning of new skills, fixing bugs, and optimizing should be core to the system. Consumable data gets us much closer to this goal.

OAGI is a self-learning, self-tuning system. Instead of humans asking for new software features, software will ask us for the features and optimizations it requires. This is not as far-fetched as it might sound, it's just a design paradigm we are not used to. As Ben Goertzel told us, "This is feasible right now. It's not the way our software infrastructure works, but there's no fundamental obstacle to doing that with technology that we have today."[1]

Best Practices in Analytics and Reporting

Here are some of the best practices to follow when leveraging analytics and reporting within your ecosystem.

Use tracking points for skills-based path reporting: Tracking your IDW's performance requires close attention to metrics such as task completion (what did users accomplish with your IDW?) and golden paths (pathways that are most commonly used, and should be prioritized for optimal experience). Keep in mind that users hanging up on or abandoning IDWs are sometimes golden paths if the user left because they got the info they needed.

Using tracking points to measure the paths people take through skills and conversations, your goal is to identify golden paths; failed paths ending in ways that are not designed; incomplete paths, which are not finished but that users intend to finish; and missing paths, which are not handled by the system but that users are looking for. You should always be ready to address exceptions such as time-outs and error logs. When tagging flows, remember that a user may complete multiple skills in a single conversation. Conversation outcomes might include several skills and may be initiated by an IDW and ended by a user. Logging the average time spent in a conversation is often less useful globally, but it is helpful at the skill level.

These outcomes are helpful to consider as you design:

- Contained: conversations that were contained and didn't require human intervention;
- HitL: either requested by IDW or human intervention was required;
- Human hand-off: interaction was handed to humans to complete—could be a golden path or a failed one;
- User drop-out: the user dropped out.

These are some of the metrics you need to track:

- Prompt time-outs (NSP);
- Re-prompts: unrecognized;
- Failed to understand phrase—in-domain (should have understood) or out of domain;
- Failed to transcribe;
- Transcribed the wrong text from audio.

These navigation tracking points can provide useful info for conversational designers:

- Global shortcuts;
- Track end-of-speech detection times;
- Turn count, how many turns or responses in a conversation or skill;
- False positives;
- Correct reject;
- Confidence scores;
- Other matches with high confidence.

Key Takeaways

- Production design consists of conversational experience designers creating and fine-tuning flows based on high-level journey maps created by lead experience architects—analogous to a traditional experience designer skinning a wireframe.

- Users will likely see the conversational interface as the system, but it's just the access point, and success hinges on whether the IDW understands language and context deeply enough to determine the intention.

- Evolving the experiences users have with an IDW requires tools that let you analyze and report on interactions between users and IDWs in real time.

- Hyperautomation involves making sense of massive amounts of information that includes what users bring to the table (both how they communicate their needs and whatever supporting documents and data they provide), internal data stores, and information coming in from connected devices involved in any given experience.

- Following best practices for analyzing and reporting will allow you to iterate new solutions faster and accomplish far more.

Want to expand on what you've learned in Chapter 16? Follow this QR code to interact with an IDW that can connect you with additional resources linked to key ideas from this chapter, including content from the *Invisible Machines* podcast.

CHAPTER 17

Best Practices in Conversational Design

As an interface, conversation can readily simulate human connection, making it easier to gather feedback. Imagine a conversational experience that helps new employees find the right classes to help facilitate growth in their position. Instead of designing an interface that renders a browsable list of courses with general ratings, a conversational interface can ask a series of questions that disambiguate, contextualizing who the user is, how they learn, and what they might be interested in all as part of a larger plan, like getting a raise. Agentic AI can offer suggestions and get feedback on those suggestions, forging a process of discovery. As certain patterns are identified, users can be mapped to personas with proven results of others like them that helps determine the class they should take. Building thousands of agentic applications over the past decade helped Robb isolate some best practices for AI agent interaction models. Here are 59 of the most valuable lessons he's learned. These aren't ranked in order of importance; instead, we'll start with the more general concepts and work toward the more specific ones.

1. **Consistency is key:** Expectations don't stay flat, they increase or decrease. The safest bet is consistency across the experiences you offer. All of the goodwill and dazzle generated by AI agents that are super advanced in predicting and personalizing can be quickly squandered by another AI agent that is dumb.

2. **Prioritize personalization over personality:** Creating a personalized experience is more important than spending time giving the application a personality. Users will benefit more from an experience where their personal context is understood than one with a flashy personality.

3. **Phrase prompts the right way:** You can't always rely on an LLM to word things right. Getting the right response depends on how you prompt a user. "Howdy" might mean "hello" to some and "how are you?" to others. "Hello" is more direct. Another example: "Can I ask you for your phone number?" Some people might provide a phone number, others might give a yes or no answer. More direct phrasing works better: "Can you please say your phone number one digit at a time?"

4. **Don't ask rhetorical questions:** Rhetorical questions can be confusing in conversations with humans, let alone conversations between AI agents and humans. Keep it simple and remember that your main objective is to help people.

5. **Use the question as part of the answer returned:** Add part of the question back into the answer you give so people know what the AI agents interpreted from your interactions. For example: If a user asks what the weather is like, an agent returns, "The weather today is ..." You can guide your LLM to include part of the question in the answer, which really helps signal to the end user that the system understood them correctly. It also guides the LLM to hallucinate less often.

6. **Always put the question at the end:** In voice interactions particularly, people are used to transactional conversations that end in questions, so pose questions at the end of a statement to avoid interrupting a conversational workflow.

7. **Communicate conversationally:** As conversational applications, AI agents should communicate conversationally. Avoid overly literate deliveries. We don't speak the same way that we write in articles, marketing materials, books, and so forth. A script that's too literate can ruin the tone of a conversational experience.

8. **Gauge for greetings:** Many users will greet an AI agent first. So even if your agent starts the conversation with "Hello, how can I help you?" be prepared for some users to reply with a simple "Hi."

9. **Note that more syllables help with speech recognition:** Short phrases can be more ambiguous and harder to recognize. Consider prompting for three-syllable responses.

10. **Different voices can signal different contexts:** Changing voices can be a helpful way to queue different contexts. You can adjust pitch in speech synthesis markup language (SSML) or choose different voice profiles. Something as simple as using a more feminine voice for one task and a more masculine voice for another can help the user feel a transition.

11. **Don't overpromise:** Conversational designers should exercise caution to avoid overpromising. Even a general query such as "What can I help you with?" can be an overpromise if your AI agent only knows three things. NLU engines are major culprits of failed attempts at using conversational AI because they can easily give the impression of sophisticated automation where none exists. LLMs have drastically reduced the role of NLU, but have also exacerbated this problem. An LLM without any auxiliary training using something like RAG systems will likely over-promise. Think back to the wave of GPT-powered chatbots that were reverse prompted to give customers loophole deals on big ticket items. Air Canada was held liable for its chatbot promising a discount that didn't exist. A hallucinating LLM is about as use-ful as a customer support rep who can understand your problem but has no tools to help you with it. As an added layer, once you start creating experiences that are complex and intuitive, people will also have elevated expectations for future interactions. This is a part of the hype cycle—show users one trick, and they'll want something better next time—and the easiest way to avoid dis-appointment is by being clear and up-front about what your AI agents are capable of.

12. **Orient users within the conversation:** When prompting for input, consider guiding their responses. For example, if they are looking for a location, it could be helpful to say, "There are four locations near you; you can ask me about any of them." A micro UI showing a map with the various pins can elevate this kind of experience drastically while also boosting the efficiency of the conversation.

13. **On-boarding is ongoing and requires empathy:** Many users will be new to the experience of interacting with AI agents, and guiding them with empathetic cues can get them comfortably up to speed. Here's an introduction from an agent that provides a nice on-ramp to the kinds of experiences it can provide:

    "Hey Teddy, I know you have a lot of meetings every week. Did you know I can help you schedule and reschedule them? Want to try now and see how it works?"

    A couple of days later, seeing that the user has taken advantage of its capabilities, an AI agent can follow up and introduce some new complexity: "Hello again Teddy! Glad I could help you get that meeting scheduled yesterday. Did you know that I operate over all of the communication channels your company uses? Try calling or texting me at this number. You can also ping me over Slack or email."

14. **Conversational markers let people know where they are:** Timelines, acknowledgments, and positive feedback help move the user through the conversation and set expectations. If an AI agent is following up with a medical patient, for example, markers like these will help guide them through a set of questions:

    - "I will be asking you a few questions about your recovery."
    - "First, let me ask you . . ."
    - "Good job, and how many . . ."
    - "Got it; last question . . ."

15. **Visual cues are cool:** Where applicable, adding themed images that provide users with visual cues that their statements have been understood can provide a fun and fluid-feeling experience. Just like in conversations with other humans, we often look for subtle gestures and signals that tell us how the other person is responding.

16. **Sometimes it's okay to guess what a user wants:** Especially with a simple Q&A, it's acceptable to guess what the user wants based on past experience. For example, if they ask, "What's the weather like?" assume they mean today and give them current conditions.

17. **Avoid making declarations about sensitive topics:** There are certain things that AI agents can be trained to detect about a user, such as age, country of origin, assigned gender, and even their

current mood. But even if supporting data confirms the age of a user, the risk of offending the person by reminding them that they are 40 can be far greater than any perceived advantage. Similarly, if you're trying to show an AI agent's chops at mood detection and fail, users will lose trust in the system.

A response like "I can tell that you're upset. Rest assured, I'm here to help," is going to irritate someone who isn't actually upset. It's best to avoid using language that suggests the agent has made these kinds of assessments. There are definite exceptions to this—specifically in health care settings—but unless there's a specific need to have an agent acknowledge potentially sensitive topics, it's best practice to avoid it.

18. **Responses can be short:** When replying to users, it's best to keep your answers short. If the appropriate response is long, consider asking clarifying questions and breaking the answer into a multi-turn exchange.

19. **Confirm transactions before completing them:** Always confirm with the user before completing a transaction, by asking for their approval. It can also be beneficial to follow up a transaction by restating what was completed and/or initiated (e.g., "Thank you for your purchase. Your order has been processed and you will receive a tracking number once your item has been shipped."). Payment processes can also be augmented by familiar and trusted micro UIs (an ID check and CONFIRM PAYMENT button from a user's bank or online payment app, for instance).

20. **Promote your AI agent's other features:** When appropriate, generally at the end of an interaction, consider letting the user know about other ways they can use your AI agents in the future. For example, at the end of a transaction, you might have an agent say, "Thanks for your order. Feel free to text message me any time if you would like to know the status of your delivery or need to make a change to your order."

21. **Be transparent with requests:** When asking users for information, be clear about why you need it. Healthy relationships are reciprocal, so take advantage of opportunities to explain what users get out of interactions (e.g., "Please type your email address so that I can keep you updated about your delivery.").

22. **Allow users to express confusion:** If a user doesn't reply to a question or command, consider prompting them that it's okay to say, "I don't know." Make sure they feel supported and know that it's fine in some cases to do nothing when prompted.

23. **Categorize responses:** You can create categories for happy, sad, serious, or funny responses to connect with the end user. When it comes to humor, a machine's pithy bits of dialogue should probably be written by—or at least pass through—human hands. If it's appropriate, you can make an error message funny. It's a fine line though, so tread carefully.

24. **Look for negative responses:** Pay attention to negative indicators within responses ("not," "neither," "no," etc.). For example, when somebody is asking for a reminder call, they may say, "Not today." If your system is looking out for "not" rather than bypassing it, the outcome may be more desirable for the user. With the proper tools, it's become relatively easy to train LLMs along these kinds of parameters.

25. **Responding to random questions:** For most AI agents, it is not necessary to field random questions such as "How are you?" Be a machine, don't try to seem like a human. If it makes sense, then match the mood.

26. **Testing is critical:** Testing is critical, and human-in-the-loop (HitL) can help accelerate testing without compromising user experience. Here are a few helpful testing guidelines:

    • Set the stage for your test subjects (e.g., "You are trying to change your password and you are in a hurry.").

    • Test designs using HitL before building out automated versions to see if users actually appreciate the experience.

    • Have internal team members test out your experience.

27. **Survey your users:** You can use prompts such as these to get a sense of user satisfaction with the experience you're providing:

    • I will use the system in the future;

    • I would be happy to use the system again;

    • I think people will find this useful;

    • I think most people would not find this useful;

- The system was easy to use;
- The system understands what I say;
- How could the system have been improved?
- Did you like the system?

You could also use a simple rating system to collect data (rate satisfaction/agreement from 1 to 5; gauge satisfaction level as dissatisfied, satisfied, loved it, etc.).

28. **Naming your IDWs:** Naming AI agents can be a powerful tool when appropriate. If your agent has a proven track record of handling a whole array of customer requests, calling it Gary Guru can help give users the sense that they are in capable hands. As always, however, overpromising can be costly. A stagnant machine that can only perform a handful of tasks is not a Gary Guru. It also bears consideration that users are often interacting with multiple AI agents through the lens of a single agent. If Gary Guru has a whole fleet of sub-agents helping it provide relevant information and automations, there might not be a compelling reason to name each of those agents for a customer-facing deployment. An employee interacting with Gary, however, might want to see when it switches between agents. Remember, in a properly crafted ecosystem, employees can open up agents to copy or customize skills they want to use in other use cases. Seeing that an agent called SuperScheduler is handling certain aspects of an interaction makes it easier to locate that agent and use its composable parts to build new experiences.

29. **Design to have as few interactions as possible:** Imagine a user tells Domino's conversational application to "reorder." It might limit the number of potential interactions if the application responds, "I can reorder what you had last time: a large pizza with a large soda and Greek salad," rather than, "Which order would you like to reorder, your order from March 7th, March 1st, or February 4th?"

30. **Design for interactive conversations:** It's useful to guess where the conversation will go and create your design around the expected interactive elements of a conversation.

> USER: "What is the best eco-friendly cleaner?"
>
> AI AGENT "Dr. Bronner's makes the highest-rated eco-friendly cleaners."
>
> USER: "Please buy it for me."

In this scenario, your AI agents can anticipate that if someone is asking for a product recommendation, the next thing they will want to do is find out where to buy it.

31. **Consider adding weight to contextual data:** Adding weight to contextual data can help the user experience. For example, if an AI agent is messaging you during the hours of 8 a.m. to 5 p.m., it can assume you are working and put a higher weight on your context being at work (higher probability for that context).

32. **Context improves experience:** Properly designed and deployed AI agents are leveraging all sorts of organizational and public data to build contextual awareness. Is this visitor returning? Have they shopped here before? Did their package get delivered? Meeting a customer with situational awareness makes it easier to deliver a superior experience.

33. **Store context for future conversations:** Storing context will help you avoid the need to constantly disambiguate user questions. Once users know where they are, you can make assumptions for the near future.

34. **Disambiguate user requests:** After the user asks a question, it can be helpful to follow up with a clarifying question. For example, if the user asks, "Where is the nearest branch?" an AI agent can respond, "Nearest branch to Denver or Boulder?"

35. **Show that AI agents understand:** Show that AI agents are correctly processing what is being said. Transcribing language visually is a great way to provide user confidence that the agent is understanding them. Similarly, you can design audio clues indicating comprehension in a voice-only setting.

36. **Flows that route to skills:** Design disambiguating flows that route to skills. Instead of trying to understand a specific request, you can train LLMs to establish a general understanding. If a user wants to do something involving passwords, you can create a flow that disambiguates and says, "Looks like you need help with

logging in. I can do the following things . . ." AI agents can also be trained to work through a checklist of required information for any given request and orchestrate skills across multiple agents to gather what's needed.

37. **Account for latency:** Latency refers to the lag experienced when retrieving data or connecting to third-party systems. Make sure you account for latency and provide cues to users (e.g., "Thank you for your patience while I'm connecting you."). Even a three-second dead spot can create an awkward experience. It's ideal to be fetching data ahead of time to avoid latency altogether, but if you can't, creating a way to keep the conversation going by avoiding silence will yield a better user experience.

38. **Use global commands:** Global commands are things users can employ to interrupt a conversational experience at any point in the interaction. They are most often used in interactive voice response (IVR) scenarios (e.g., allowing someone to cut in and say "agent" to get to a human operator). Always have global commands in place to make sure users don't get trapped in the conversation.

39. **Landmarking audio:** You can also use landmarking audio to communicate meaning for end users; for example, consistently using a specific sound that validates for a user that they've been understood. Something like a car horn sound in a newscast might prompt listeners that the traffic report is up next. Consistently using appropriate sounds can build association between specific sounds and landmark moments in a conversation.

40. **Handling multiple intents:** There are several ways to account for multiple intents in conversational design. If the user states, "My order is the wrong size and color," consider asking which intent they would like to start with (size or color). Be prepared for problematic responses "both," or "neither." You can also start with one intent and cue the user. "Let's start with the sizing issue; was the garment too small or too large?"

41. **Regular use vs. one-time/periodic use:** Employees using a conversational interface are going to develop more familiarity with regular use, freeing designers up to use more efficient design paradigms. External users are far less likely to have or even develop the

same level of familiarity with your conversational interface, which merits nonvisual skeuomorphic design (more on this below). For contexts where both one-time use and regular use are expected, designing for both is recommended.

42. **Time to resolution (TTR) and perceived time to resolution (PTTR):** TTR is the primary metric driving user satisfaction; however, PTTR is more important than actual time. There are ways to make users perceive TTR as shorter. Design considerations such as call backs rather than hold purgatory, eliminated unnatural pauses in conversation, and dual tone multi-frequency (DTMF) codes (enabling users to use numbers on the keypad to enter data during a phone experience) can all help decrease PTTR.

43. **Use confidence scores to train your AI agents:** When building skills that use LLMs, your IDW can return confidence scores for the intents (questions) that it collects from users. For example, if someone asks for help tracking their order and your agents are not yet trained to handle this intent, they may return a low confidence score. In a scenario like this, you can add a low recognition response to get help from end users in training your engine. Best practices suggest that you are up-front and don't over-promise, saying something such as, "It seems like you are asking about tracking your order. I can get a human to help you with that." Generative AI systems don't typically deliver confidence scores, but you can get them to by asking to be provided with a score. You can do this in line or as a secondary agent that looks at a transcript and creates a score.

44. **Generic confirmations are good for data recollection:** Asking, "How are you feeling this morning?" or some other generic data confirmation can be good for both you and the person using an AI agent. Remembering things puts a large cognitive burden on the user, and messaging is often used by people as an archival mechanism. Send them an SMS or email so they can retrieve the info in the future.

45. **Co-reference:** Co-referencing is used to keep track of subjects in a conversation, such as "he" or "she" referring to a person previously named in the conversation. For example: "Who founded your company?" "Where did he live?" "He" is a co-reference to

the founder. You'll need to create a variable called "he," "she," or "they" and assign it a name so you can refer back to it if somebody types "he," "she," "they," or "their." Keeping track of co-references may require creating variable versions of each pronoun that adjust dynamically according to who you are referencing.

46. **Know when to allow barge-in:** As with human-to-human conversation, interactions between people and AI agents can be stifled by interruptions. Allowing users to barge in can be useful at times (being able to call out "operator" in the midst of a confusing interaction is a valuable lifeline) and troublesome at others (if a user interrupts an agent as it's listing options with an unfamiliar response, confusion can ensue on both sides).

    It's always helpful to let users know that, although they might be waiting for a prompt, the process is still moving forward. Over a video channel you could mitigate this by creating video loops to indicate a productive pause.

    During informational prompts, listing options before asking the user what they want to do can deter them from barging in early.

47. **Speech recognition accuracy is more important than price and latency:** A less-expensive solution that can't accurately interpret user requests isn't going to be worth any amount of money saved. A system that is swift but inaccurate is ultimately faster at not being good.

48. **Consider hybrid solutions when using text-to-speech (TTS):** You can have a human record conversational prompts and then use TTS with SSML to fill in the gaps. For instance, if you record a member of your HR team reading a list of options but don't have a follow-up cue in that person's voice saying, "I'm not sure I heard you; can you repeat that?" you can create that script with TTS and tweak the voice to sound like its human counterpart. This method may not be perfect, but it can still serve the user well.

49. **Consider voice ID for authenticating users:** In situations that require sensitive data, authenticating your user's voice can be a helpful part of the experience, building trust.

50. **Answering questions from a third party:** Instead of loading FAQs or search results in LLMs to provide the answers first-party,

consider scenarios where an AI agent should answer with third-party results. The agent can say, "I don't know the answer, but I found this by doing a web search." In essence, handle it like a person would. By presenting the user with third-party info, you can allow them to disambiguate the information.

51. **Use voice channels where appropriate:** Voice-enabling a website just for the sake of doing it has limited value, but using the web and voice together to create multimodal interactions can be very powerful. Just like in real conversation, there will always be instances where it's more efficient to show someone a video clip or visual aid than it is to try and explain it via text or speech.

52. **Dynamic grammars should be built in:** Always consider dynamic grammars for things like alphanumeric responses, names, or email addresses. For instance, if someone types the name of a colleague and spells it wrong, the system can apply fuzzy-match to determine that they meant "Josh," even though they typed "Joshh." Similarly, if they typed "josh@gmale.com," it could assume that they probably meant gmail.com.

53. **Handling errors in conversation design:** Set expectations by responding with something such as, "Sorry, I am not trained in that area yet" or "I didn't understand your question." If an AI agent does not receive a response over voice channels, respond by prompting the user to repeat themselves by saying something such as, "Hmm, I didn't hear that. Can you repeat that?" You can also use alternatives like DTMF (dialing numbers to get menu options), or offer instructions such as, "Please say 'yes' or 'no.'"

    If the intent was recognized but an error occurred, let the user know by saying, "I encountered an error while . . ." If the intent was misunderstood by the LLM and an agent discovers it, offer other options. It's possible there was a misunderstanding and/or the user changed their mind and simply wants to do something else. Funny or cute error responses can be great, but be careful—if you do it too often or at the wrong moment, it becomes annoying, like telling the same joke over and over, or being tone-deaf.

54. **Don't build one-size-fits-all AI agents:** One-size-fits-all is often one-size-fits-none. Don't dumb your agents down to the lowest common denominator by trying to make them all do everything

across multiple channels. Utilize the features in each channel to their fullest, and write dialogue appropriately for the given context. In an ecosystem that's built for hyperautomation, individual agents can be orchestrated to engage in workflows together, creating beyond human experiences for users. In a similar vein, not all agents need to be personal assistants. Some agents work optimally on a specific set of tasks.

55. **Build in pairs:** If you're designing conversational experiences all by yourself, you're likely to miss things. On the other hand, building with a group of 10, progress can stall as everyone struggles to get on the same page. Working in pairs can be ideal, if only for the simple fact that the most meaningful conversations tend to occur between two people. On a more practical level, when two people are working in tandem on conversational design (as opposed to handing the project back and forth) you can have one person focus on the logical, systems-thinking side of things while the other hones in on design elements. This way, fewer things fall through the cracks, and designs are tested and improved upon more efficiently.

56. **Consider the ongoing evolution of conversation with machines:** Conversations with computers will evolve, potentially creating a new language, more efficient than formal English. We see this already with text messaging shorthand like "BRB"—a language dubbed "textese." Something similar will emerge as people find shorthand ways of communicating with AI agents. This begins with routine users finding the most direct ways to communicate needs to the agents in their ecosystem. It evolves as analysts notice trends in the ways users are communicating conversationally and experience designers encourage users to utilize these new ways of communicating.

57. **AI agents sit comfortably outside of our social circles:** AI agents can be anthropomorphic to great effect, ranging from giving friendly reminders to communicating with urgency when we ignore a prompt for immediate action. With typical human interactions, when someone is friendly or brash, we're inclined to respond in ways that correlate to social ranking. These kinds of intuitive responses can take many forms. Someone being friendly

as they prompt you to take action might put you at ease because they are being helpful, but it might also signal an alarm if you perceive their friendliness as an attempt to climb past you in a social hierarchy. Similarly, if someone is being aggressive or forceful in their reminders, it might be felt as an attempt to show dominance. Agents, on the other hand, can remind us relentlessly without it feeling like a threat. As machines that we are not in direct competition with and that don't have ulterior motives, agents sit outside of our social circles. That being said, how you choose to anthropomorphize your agents can also have sizeable consequences in terms of how users react to them (make them seem too human, and you could risk bringing them inside the social circle). It's all about balance, which makes anthropomorphism—along with skeuomorphism—something that should be given careful consideration.

58. **A newsfeed can deliver relevant information:** As AI agents become regular partners in our professional and personal lives, the newsfeed approach can be a great way for them to summarize important events and push actionable content to the fore. Rather than making users ask for something, like a list of messages waiting for a response, an agent can surface those messages within the context of a newsfeed that has a stream of hyper-relevant information and tasks. There's often an overemphasis in design on letting the user ask for something and not enough on leading the user where they need to be and pushing relevant content their way.

59. **Sound as a context point:** Cisco has a conference room device that listens for and detects frequencies that are undetectable by human ears (for example, sounds that your phone may emit). It uses this capability to recognize when someone is present in the room. The average phone speaker is capable of emitting an ultrasonic frequency that is undetectable by the human ear. This enables a lot of possibilities for AI agents to detect things that people might miss.

As the volume of information here suggests, production design in the realm of hyperautomation requires a great deal of strategy and flexibility. By keeping these best practices in mind, however, you can mitigate some of the discomfort and make faster progress.

Two Important Morphisms

When designing experiences with AI agents, it's tempting to want to create something as natural-feeling as possible—but when designing for productivity, that's often the wrong move. Natural pauses and witticisms meant to make an agent seem more relatable can easily go too far and distract from the task at hand. While these kinds of touches are useful in entertainment products, they should be used sparingly in productivity tools. This is why skeuomorphism and anthropomorphism both play important roles in conversation design, sometimes working in complementary ways.

In visual design, skeuomorphism is the concept of making digital things look like their real-world counterparts (see Figure 17.1). When users encountered the calculator in early versions of Mac OS, the shaded buttons made it look similar to the calculator in their desk drawer. As user adoption widens, the need for those kinds of visual cues dissipates.

We've reached the nonvisual skeuomorphic phase of evolution with conversational design. This means we're following the same track as visual design in terms of users understanding the technology. To a conversational designer, this might mean adding a few interactions to make sure users understand the nature of the experience they're engaged in, such as pausing early in the conversation to remind them that they are communicating with an agent built to handle specific requests.

Visual designers employ anthropomorphism by imbuing objects with human traits and characteristics to make them more relatable. When used in conversational design, anthropomorphism creates the feeling or perception of a human-to-human relationship between the agent and the user. If used successfully, this lever can foster a sense of connection, trust, and loyalty. But this powerful tool must be used conscientiously; we don't want to fool an end-user's senses into believing they are interacting with a person they can have a meaningful relationship with. If a user comes to trust an agent the way they might trust a friend or colleague, they are at risk of having that trust compromised—by being roped into a sales pitch, for example—which could have long-lasting negative consequences. Use care in making AI agents more relatable and the interaction more authentic without crossing over into deceit.

SKEUOMORPHIC DESIGN

EFFICIENT DESIGN PARADIGMS

98658 / 1256 * 1984

98658 / 1256 * 1984

Intelligent Digital Worker

FIGURE 17.1 Skeuomorphic design as it relates to conversational design. (OneReach.ai)

It's also important to keep your sights on the objective of your design. In productivity apps, where the goal is to get users from A to B as quickly and efficiently as possible, features meant to make agents seem more human can quickly become tiresome—analogous to a waiter hell-bent on light conversation when you're in a rush to order.

In gaming apps, users spend hours getting immersed in drawn-out storylines with characters that simulate human behavior. Users aren't looking for reduced friction and probably expect to become frustrated; in fact, a user throwing a controller across the room after the 20th fail represents a big win for that game's designer. But productivity calls for as little friction—and human simulation—as possible. You don't need extra explanations, personality traits, or yuks to help get the job done. Sometimes it's best to just let a machine be a machine.

In a recent project with a major telecom company, we discovered through testing that users seemed to be quite forgiving of AI agents that had visible knowledge gaps. This might be a subtle lift from anthropomorphization, in that when we perceive human-like flaws in a system, we are apt to be less critical of its limitations. It also seemed to hinge somewhat on the fact that users were also well aware they were communicating with AI agents. It's all about an ongoing attention to balance.

The intention of both skeuomorphic and anthropomorphic design is to help users to engage with your objective—in essence, offering them a shorter on-ramp by adding familiarity and relatability via nuance and timing. This process takes more effort, and getting it right requires a high level of sophistication. But once the technology is widespread enough to already be familiar—at a point where users don't need as many visual cues—the design load is lighter.

It's actually not a stretch to say that artificial general intelligence, or AGI, as most people understand it is a case of anthropomorphism run amok. By stringently modeling machine intelligence after the patterns present in the human mind, we are likely to miss opportunities to create a more efficient kind of intelligence. Machines are capable of things that humans haven't even conceived of yet and to unlock these possibilities, we should design opportunities for them to create beyond human experiences. In this way, even the concept of a personal assistant AI is somewhat limiting. There are all sorts of things that a human assistant can't do that a machine can adapt to rather quickly—things like true multitasking.

In this sense, anthropomorphism taken too far becomes a simulation of humans—and then a skeuomorphism of humans. This gets weird fast, taking conversational experiences into an uncanny valley of creepy 3D avatars and too-human rubber-faced robots—which can create in users a sense of unease or even disgust. The lesson here is that these powerful design tools should be applied with a light touch.

Key Takeaways

- Conversational interfaces stimulate human connection, making them ideal for gathering feedback from users.
- There are numerous best practices with conversational design that can make AI agents more adept at completing the objectives organizations set out to accomplish.
- Because AI agents are often human-like, it's important to be aware of the ideas behind skeuomorphism and anthropomorphism as they relate to conversational technologies.

Want to expand on what you've learned in Chapter 17? Follow this QR code to interact with an IDW that can connect you with additional resources linked to key ideas from this chapter, including content from the *Invisible Machines* podcast.

PART IV

Conclusion

CHAPTER 18

Where Do We Go from Here?

We spend a lot of time on the *Invisible Machines* podcast talking with guests about the ways AI is poised to change the world. And indeed, a significant portion of this book is dedicated to imagining futures that are within our reach through good design. One of our favorite ways to jump out of this rut is to ask guests, "What won't change?" There are countless scenarios where AI agents disrupt our version of reality, for better or for worse. In a way, we might be trying to prune this overgrowth by looking for things in our daily existence that won't be fundamentally altered by technology. Some of these constants provide clues as to how we can design the most effective and beneficial systems.

We've also realized that the real answers to looming questions (should AI systems be centralized or decentralized?) aren't typically binary in nature (systems will leverage both centralized and decentralized elements to achieve organizational AGI). This feels related to a mental clarity exercise Richard Saul Wurman (creator of LATCH and TED) shared with us.

> *How do I get rid of the gummy stuff in [my head] so that there is a modicum of clarity that I didn't have before? [I] harshly think of something, strongly think about something, and then see if I can flip it to the opposite of what I'm thinking and that seems to work pretty well. Virtually anything that interests me, if I think of the opposite of what it is—from carnal things to beauty to trips to pain, to what somebody said to me, to a new idea that I thought was cute, clever, or delicious—and I think and I see if I can flip it. I enjoy that process too as a kind of little exercise.*[1]

With that in mind, we'd like to close out the second edition of this book with a nuanced portrait of what is likely to change in the near future and what is likely to remain immutably intact. By looking at these new technologies from both ends, we can develop a balanced approach to architecting a brighter future.

This is a frantically fraught moment in history: we're still reeling from a global pandemic, climate change is accelerating, and wars continue to rage across the globe. Hopefully, it's obvious that we need powerful problem-solving tools to help us fix massive problems intelligently, not for the benefit of business but for the benefit of humankind. On a very basic level, we can also use technology to create experiences that make people feel good. We can forge an economy where we're valued by how good we make other people feel. Reducing these activities to a chemical compound might seem a bit cynical, but an economy based on dopamine fits right in with the idea of scoring social interactions on the blockchain. Life could be a lot less stressful if the economy we interact with every day is centered on experiences that produce happiness.

Companies Running Scared from Consumers

There's a popular perception out in the world that companies are poised to use AI to get rid of jobs. That they will use the technology to exploit their employees and their customers, gaming advanced technology to gain unprecedented control over individuals. This perspective overlooks a critical point: companies are just organizational structures designed to serve people by reducing transaction costs and providing purpose. What if, instead, AI becomes a tool for individuals to navigate and operate these corporate systems more effectively?

Individuals are adopting AI technologies at a much faster rate than companies. Most businesses are being very cautious—fearful of lawsuits and bad press, their adoption rates are low as they wait for AI to handle customer service calls and other critical tasks perfectly. Consumers have no such reservations. They are eagerly deploying AI to optimize their daily lives, having moved beyond simple generative tasks like writing emails and summarizing content. We've already seen people using AI to contest parking tickets and lobby the government, as well as exploit loopholes that companies aren't aware of.

ChatGPT is the fastest-growing app of all time in terms of adoption. If speed is a critical metric, companies that lag in AI adoption are in serious trouble. Consumers are already using these tools to enhance their shopping experiences, maintain healthier lifestyles, and stay more connected. Employees are using it to get the tedious portions of their jobs done faster. People are cobbling together their own AI agents that can manage appointments, reschedule appointments, secure refunds for billing errors, avoid bank fees, and balance credit card debt.

Many individuals are on the verge of having personalized AI agents that can switch credit card balances to take advantage of new offers, clip coupons at scale, schedule preventive care visits, follow up with insurance companies, find better auto insurance rates, and order household supplies like toilet paper so they never run out. While many assume AI will be a weapon for companies to exploit people, it could equally become a weapon for people to exploit companies, where the likely inadvertent liability of misuse falls mainly on the company and not us as individuals.

Companies may find themselves overwhelmed by the barrage of AI agents acting on behalf of consumers. Imagine if every one of a bank's customers contacted them on the same day using AI. For the customers, this interaction would cost nothing, but the bank would incur a significant expense handling that many calls. Or what if an AI agent discovered a loophole in a company contract and shared it publicly? More agents could swarm the company, causing chaos similar to a stock market crash triggered by trading algorithms.

Reality will likely fall somewhere in the middle. Companies that fail to adopt AI quickly enough may get crushed, serving as a warning to others. Some employees and customers will undoubtedly be taken advantage of, prompting changes in labor laws. One thing is certain, however: those who do not adopt AI, whether consumers or businesses, will be at a significant disadvantage to those who do.

As we've already seen, companies are likely to be slower adopters than individual employees and consumers. This might put companies on their heels, forced to adopt, with or without a strategy in place. This puts companies in a tough position, but it's not all doom and gloom. Companies are also consumers, after all, and they can deploy AI to better manage their vendors, taking advantage of the same one-sided risk.

As we've detailed in these pages, they can start laying the groundwork for OAGI by deploying AI internally, bearing careful consideration of the new ways in which people will come to view work.

A New Relationship to Work

We've come to believe that work itself will remain a thing. The social construct of spending about half of our time in service to our community will always be something a thriving society will need. We will always find new ways to serve this need by inventing new jobs—new ways of contributing to our communities. We will always need organizational structures that create communities as people will continue to be pack animals.

In our conversation with Aaron De Smet, a Senior Partner at McKinsey, he brought up a debate amongst economists about the free market. Specifically, "if the free market is so great, why doesn't it apply to the labor market? Why do we have corporations at all? . . . Why wouldn't it be a free market and just be a gig economy?" He said that transaction cost economics won out as the definitive reason, but that the real answer is more nuanced.

When transaction costs are high between individual agents—because of trust issues, or mission alignment, or labor management—it makes sense to consolidate power and reputation within a corporation. "That worked really well in the 1900s," De Smet said, "but transaction costs have come down so much that, if that were the reason, you would expect the average size of successful companies . . . to track downward with the drop in transaction costs, which we have not seen . . . this social-cultural theory is still a big part of it . . . If I want a corporate AI, if I want a company that is synergistic, where the emergent properties and value created by this group as a whole is more than the sum of the parts, I actually need this north star. I need a common language, a common culture, a shared purpose. That is at least as important as transaction cost economics as why we have companies."[2]

So our need to work won't change, but the organizations through which we do that work will change significantly. As companies move toward organizational AGI, they will become more self-driven. Future companies will be less centralized and more decentralized. They will need to be more transparent, which will make them less corruptible. Companies will have charters that define objectives that will serve the members of the organization. Objectives will be facilitated by AIs using data and feedback, and self-driving organizations will outperform human-driven orgs over the long term.

The service organizations provide to employees, customers, and shareholders will come from actual data-driven feedback that will show that long-term thinking pays off—that happy employees make for happy customers, which makes for happy shareholders. This is, of course, a little bit aspirational.

In his *UX Magazine* article "In the Garden of Hyperautomation," young technologist and philosopher Henry Comes-Pritchett paints portraits of two very different AI-enabled futures, "A Utopia of Self-Regulated Data" and "A Data-Driven Dystopia." In the more optimistic future, you're in the (super futuristic) shoes of a user with a personal assistant called Alfonzo, that is always learning, so it can become more helpful over time.

> *You've been able to streamline your entire life (more or less) and your voluntary immersion into hyperautomation has played no insignificant role. You have more time to spend doing what you love—caring for your pets, spending time with your partner, exploring your city, and engaging in long-neglected hobbies. Your work life has improved significantly as Alfonzo has been able to act as an omnipresent assistant: he's been managing your schedule and helping you figure out how to navigate tricky assignments, suggesting meeting times and writing emails while you do the heavy lifting. He never misses a beat; you can't help but think that you wished you'd done this sooner.*

This feels like a much healthier work-life balance. Instead of more play and less work, we can replace hard work with hard play. Hard play is the kind of work that makes you healthier (as opposed to the hard work of sitting at a desk). The shit jobs that we can't automate—the inevitable hard work—will earn more pay. With hard play, you will exert calories and struggle through things that ultimately make you stronger.

We will still value self-discipline and hard work. That won't change. There will still be jobs that people don't want to do—including knowledge work jobs that require sitting behind a desk—but they will likely pay more. But imagine a world where the bottleneck isn't time and labor, but your imagination about what tasks should be done and how fast you can come up with them or approve them.

By Henry's assessment, the only way to reach this state is by people owning their own data, otherwise, "whoever has a reasonable claim to ownership of your data can do whatever they please with it." In his dire version of the future, this has happened, and you're now saddled with an employer-provided personal assistant called Achlys that is optimizing your life in all the worst ways. "It set this alarm for you, at this dreadful hour, because your employer sent out an 'all-hands-on-deck' request because the quarter's projections are abysmal. You stare at the matchbook-sized screen on your arm and tear up a little. It's been a bad week, and it's about to get much worse."[3]

If we want the far rosier version of work-life balance, things will need to be disrupted. As Meredith Whittaker succinctly diagnosed the current paradigm of artificial intelligence as a product of concentrated power in the tech industry to *Politico*, "we need to trace that history back to the moves that were made in the 1990s where unfettered surveillance became the engine of the tech industry's business model. That enabled the creation of a handful of large firms that now have the resources necessary to produce artificial intelligence, those capital-intensive resources being computational power and data."[4]

We still need, and often want, to work. That won't change, but our relationship to work is going to change in massive ways as companies are reformed and reimagined. The nature of that relationship will depend on many factors that might seem out of our control, but there are unique opportunities for researchers, designers, developers, and product owners to collaborate on applications of technology that might tip the balances of power.

If this seems hyperbolic, think back to our discussion of Uber earlier in the book. They upended our collective view of transportation using technologies that were fairly commonplace: smartphone-based geolocation, rating systems, mobile-ready apps, and mobile payments. It was the seamless integration of all four technologies that made ride-sharing an instant win—and a major disruptor to all existing transit models.

Even though they sequenced existing technologies with world-changing results, Uber is not immune to disruption. There's currently very little blocking anyone else from creating a decentralized ride-sharing network that sidesteps Uber entirely. As we noted, when more organizations and individuals find the tools used for OAGI within reach, we will see hyperdisruption on a regular basis.

Healthier Citizens and Healthier Governments Forging Balance Amid Chaos

A Pew Research Center report from 2023 found that, despite the widespread belief that representative democracy is a good way to govern, enthusiasm is starting to wane. "A median of 59% are dissatisfied with how their democracy is functioning, 74% think elected officials don't care what people like them think, [and] 42% say no political party in their country represents their views," the report explains.

The report also found that many people are open to other forms of government, including direct democracy, where citizens vote directly on major issues and expert rule, where experts make key decisions instead of elected officials.[5]

It seems likely that humans will still lead governments, and that we will want capable humans guiding key decisions. The ways we arrive at those decisions might change. Conversational technologies can be orchestrated to give individual citizens more direct say over functions of government. This is coinciding with a moment when people's faith in American democracy has hit a record low on a downward trend going back to the late 1990s (a Gallup poll in 2023 found that only "28% of U.S. adults are satisfied with the way democracy is working").[6]

It seems likely that representative government will diminish in power, possibly giving way to a more direct kind of democracy. Centralization might diminish as better communication within our political system means it won't need to be representative. There's also a chance that accredited humans and AI systems might collaborate as part of an expert rule, which sounds a bit ominous. Though maybe there's some hybrid form of direct democracy where everyone has their individual say, and various things we vote on have been vetted and trajectory mapped by hybrid teams of experts.

The opportunities for healthier democracies around the world is matched (if not exceeded) by the potential for a healthier global population. People want to live long, healthy lives. That won't change (unless we're somehow engineered to live forever). What will change is that we can live longer, healthier lives through predictive personalized medicine.

We had a conversation about this with Dr. Nathan Price and Dr. Lee Hood (the father of the Human Genome Project), who helped to create the model for P4 medicine. They see technology helping us revolutionize health care, making it predictive, preventive, personalized, and participatory. We talked through many of the ways these technologies can improve our existence, and the concept of digital twins was particularly intriguing.

"Digital twins are incredibly powerful not only for personalizing to the individual, but also for letting us think more holistically or strategically about the whole process of how we treat disease," Price said, noting that we can simulate clinical trials in all kinds of different iterations to learn how a disease is forming and a person's health is being maintained.[7]

It seems entirely reasonable that, rather than having a disparate paper trail of wellness checks, disease, and treatment, we might instead have digital twins that offer an ever-deepening picture of what's happening within our bodies. Your biological age might become a more meaningful metric than your chronological age, and could be used to gamify health. Imagine a reward system for working hard in healthy ways (walking while taking a meeting) versus unhealthy ways (sitting at a desk).

It might take some time getting there, but we're already seeing AI assist with preventive medicine, doing things like predicting diseases in real time with 98% accuracy by analyzing a person's tongue color[8] or detecting early signs of Parkinson's disease by listening to someone's speech.[9]

While human health is on the precipice of major improvements, the health of our larger ecosystem (planet Earth) is in obvious decline. The world will continue to warm up and there will be a lot of disruption due to weather-related events and disasters. What won't likely change is that weather will remain difficult to predict, which is partially related to chaos theory.

A mathematician and meteorologist working at MIT in 1961 used early computer systems to construct a mathematical model of the weather. His name was Edward Lorenz, and he was looking for a set of differential equations representing changes in variables like temperature, pressure, and wind velocity.

He settled on a model with only 12 differential equations. One day, he wanted to re-examine a sequence of data coming from his model, and instead of restarting the entire run, he restarted it near the middle to save time. The data from the second run should have exactly matched the data from the first run, and while they matched at first, eventually they began to diverge dramatically. This happened because his printouts only showed three digits and the data in the computer's memory contained six digits. Edward had rounded-off data, assuming that the difference was inconsequential. He ended up stumbling into chaos theory.[10]

Point being, it seems hyperbolic to believe that AI will quickly decode the outrageously complex and chaotic nonlinear equations central to the weather systems on Earth and put the toothpaste back in the proverbial tube. It seems far more likely that we will use technology to help us manage the disruptions that climate change will bring, making us better prepared to manage disasters and recovery.

We're seeing inklings of this in places like Japan, where an AI system created by Hitachi uses high-altitude cameras to identify and report disasters right away, speeding up response time.[11] Whether we're talking about the health of our shared ecosystem, our bodily health, or the health of our governing bodies, technology can help us move the needle most immediately by pointing us toward better decisions. It can highlight the path of least resistance to the best possible outcomes.

Software Will Always Be About Communication

At its core, software is about communication, between people and machines, as well as person-to-person. That won't change. What will change is that communication will become more standardized. While it seems likely that some sort of pidgin language—a hybrid of human language and computing languages—will emerge for machines to communicate with other machines, we will largely be able to communicate more freely and effectively *with* software and with other people *because* of it.

Apps will be torn down and replaced with experiences that deliver measurable outcomes. Instead of buying a spreadsheet program to organize our finances, we will buy systems that help us save money. Put simply, we will be buying outcomes, not methods.

Companies will still need to market their products and services, and to share their insights and successes. That won't change. What will change is that there will be far less batch and blast marketing out in the world. The one-size-fits-all approach will die off as companies turn to a bottomless supply of AI agents to create more bespoke marketing initiatives for individual customers as their own concierges. Following the trajectory we outlined above, it's not difficult to imagine customers having their own concierge agents acting as a firewall on their behalf.

This means AI agents acting as both marketers and consumers, which sets up a paradigm where machines are selling things to other machines. This is something we discussed with Don Scheibenreif, Vice President, Distinguished Analyst with Gartner's Customer Experience research group. In the book he co-authored with fellow analyst Mark Raskino, *When Machines Become Customers*, they describe different levels of agency for these machines. These agents can evolve from being the sort of bound bot customers that are common today (think of an HP printer that can only buy ink from HP) to become more adaptable. "Let's say I want [an AI agent] to get ink for my printer but I want [it] to go to these three sources and if [it finds] something else, by all means go for it," Don said. "The third level is . . . machines as autonomous customers where the machine has much more discretion on what to do and maybe even anticipates your needs."[12]

Even though this kind of abstraction layer will have a massive impact on many industries and businesses, it doesn't mean that the humans on either side of the equation can behave however they choose with impunity. Businesses have grown accustomed to a world where customer ratings online can have a major impact on their bottom line.

While that won't change, we imagine that things will balance out as the ratings businesses give to customers become more important.

We see this happening already with Uber's rider rating system, which can alert drivers to lackluster customers. They've even posted tips for improving your rider rating—common sense things like picking up your trash, buckling your seatbelt, being ready to go when the driver arrives, and not slamming doors.[13] Airbnb has a similar system in place for hosts to rate guests. While some consumers might bristle at this new tier of accountability, it could ultimately improve experiences for business owners, employees, and customers as there will be more motivation to be on your best behavior out in the world.

In his article from 2011, "Why Software Is Eating the World," Marc Andreessen details how the world's largest bookseller, Amazon, is really a software company selling virtually everything online, including Kindle editions of books that are also now software. The largest video service at the time, Netflix, is also a software company. Music streaming services are software, as were the fastest growing entertainment companies at the time: video game makers.[14]

We're moving into an era where companies and software will become even more intertwined. It's probably more accurate to say that software and business will be the same thing. Think about the experiences people are having on China's mega-app, WeChat. Without leaving a rich web chat interface, they can interact with a whole host of businesses as micro UIs or mini-apps within the experience. We're going to have a whole new kind of relationship with software, with conversational software. We will talk to machines to get all sorts of things done, and businesses will have limited opportunities to distinguish themselves as something distinct from the overall pastiche of talking to software.

Along with improving the quality of communication across the many channels that connect people and companies, machines can also help with another fundamental thing that won't change. People get lonely, and we need to have relationships with other humans. Orchestrated AI agents can facilitate this for us. They can prompt us to reach out to friends and relatives who they know haven't had quality human contact recently. This simple use case can have a positive impact on our biological health as well as our general happiness.

We Still Just Want to Be Happy

We are dopaminergic beings—addicted to dopamine, in other words. But there's a common misconception about dopamine, that it's simply a pleasure chemical of sorts. What is dopamine really? The full title of a fascinating book by Daniel Z. Lieberman and Michael E. Long does a great job of summing it up: *The Molecule of More: How a Single Chemical in Your Brain Drives Love, Sex, and Creativity and Will Determine the Fate of the Human Race.*

Dopamine is the molecule of more. As the book points out, "From dopamine's point of view, it's not the having that matters. It's getting something—anything—that's new." Because of dopamine, we always need to be chasing something. It's a physical trait in our brains, and our compulsion to chase goals won't dissipate in the face of advanced technology. We will always be dopamine addicts.

Part of our chemical desire to chase is tied to the predictive nature of our brains. We make predictions, and we want to see them come true. This is a potent form of the chase.

"You can't do anything other than predict because your brain is structured to work that way," renowned psychologist and neuroscientist Lisa Feldman Barrett told us. "That being said, if you don't make a prediction then you're experientially blind—what you're experiencing is noise, the signals are just noise to you. So, predictions are required for you to have any kind of meaningful experience of something just because of how the neurons are structured and how they talk to each other."[15]

AI isn't likely to significantly alter our brain chemistry, but what will change is that, as a set of powerful tools, AI will help us set and achieve our goals far more efficiently. If we examine scenarios like the ones we've described from this perspective, it gets interesting. There are all sorts of things that people chase that can lead to undesirable or dangerous situations (drugs, fame, excess wealth). What if panels of experts, both AI and human, could establish a vast matrix of personalized things that people can chase that wouldn't put them or those around them in peril.

What if your work involved using your creativity and team skills to do work that felt meaningful and was rarely tedious or repetitive.

If you are solving different problems every day, then you have something new to chase. Work can be a major supplier of dopamine, especially if it's stimulating.

It also feels good to be of service. What if part of your work in the world was connecting with people in your community who needed assistance that you are well suited to provide. Maybe you are called to mentor a fellow glass blower who is new to the craft. Maybe there's a group of elderly people nearby who would love a meal that you've become an expert at preparing. With all of our basic needs met by finely tuned systems, what if work became synonymous with service?

The bottom line is that humans love to chase things, and we have powerful tools that can put that urge to more productive uses. We can use gamification to build a tight-loop reward system that shows our progress and keeps us engaged. We can redesign work to satisfy our need to forever chase shit in enriching ways that are beneficial to our communities.

We need the dopamine we get from prediction and pursuit; this is why we always invent new ways to work, like middle management. We want to have things to do, and we can use the many tools associated with artificial intelligence to increase the quality of the things we do to satiate our need for "more new."

It's staggering to think that so much of our behavior is dictated by a chemical addiction, but that doesn't diminish our spectacular complexity as organisms. It also points to the fragility of the viewpoint that we are, each of us, individual organisms. Science has shown that human cells account for just 43% of the body's total cell count. "Nearly every nook and cranny of your body is covered in microscopic creatures," James Gallagher reported in a BBC article. "This includes bacteria, viruses, fungi and archaea (organisms originally misclassified as bacteria). The greatest concentration of this microscopic life is in the dark murky depths of our oxygen-deprived bowels." Some of these organisms also make up our vital and enduringly mysterious gut biome.[16]

We have tools to unlock these mysteries, but it seems likely they will point to even bigger mysteries. In a book about designing technology ecosystems, it seems salient to end with the reminder that each one of us is an ecosystem. We are also ecosystems that are part of bigger ecosystems that configure a planetary ecosystem.

As James Bridle (author, *Ways of Being*) reminded us in our conversation:

> *There's no such thing as "the environment." The idea of the environment is something that's been built up through Western-European ways of thinking about our place in the world. It's something that even plagues what we call "the environmental movement" to this day because, the thing is, whenever you talk about the environment, you're making this space between you as an individual—us as a species—and everything else on this planet. There is no such divide. We can't separate ourselves meaningfully in that way from everything that surrounds us.*[17]

The tools for building a future that's better for our entire planetary ecosystem are readily available. Hopefully, we've helped you strategize ways to use them wisely.

Want to expand on what you've learned in Chapter 18? Follow this QR code to interact with an IDW that can connect you with additional resources linked to key ideas from this chapter, including content from the *Invisible Machines* podcast.

Notes

Chapter 1

1. MG Siegler, "Eric Schmidt: Every 2 Days We Create as Much Information as We Did up to 2003," TechCrunch, August 4, 2010, **https://techcrunch.com/2010/08/04/schmidt-data/**.
2. Robert J. Moore, "Eric Schmidt's '5 Exabytes' Quote Is a Load of Crap," The Data Point, February 7, 2011, **https://blog.rjmetrics.com/2011/02/07/eric-schmidts-5-exabytes-quote-is-a-load-of-crap/**.
3. Jordan Novet, "Salesforce's Behind-the-scenes Co-founder Is Tackling Slack as Software Company Turns 25," CNBC, March 12, 2024. **https://www.cnbc.com/2024/03/09/parker-harris-prepared-salesforce-for-ai-now-hes-focused-on-slack.html**.
4. Kim Gittleson, "Can a Company Live Forever?," BBC News, January 19, 2012, **https://www.bbc.com/news/business-16611040**.
5. Jeff Stibel, "Why Some Companies Die Young," Forbes, April 4, 2017, **https://www.forbes.com/sites/jeffstibel/2017/03/31/why-dogs-and-companies-die-young/**.
6. Invisible Machines, "S2E9 Don Scheibenreif, Gartner VP & Distinguished Analyst, Customer Experience Research Group," August 24, 2023, **https://www.youtube.com/watch?v=sQClEt_WA4Q&t=1498s**.
7. OneReach.ai, "Case Study: Leading Retail Company Achieves 65% NPS Score," n.d., **https://onereach.ai/portfolio/global-fortune-50-company-achieves-83-csat-score-by-automating-employee-experience/**.
8. Juliette van Winden, "Love at First Chat, with Lemonade's AI Chatbot Maya," Medium, December 1, 2019, **https://medium.com/marketing-in-the-age-of-digital/love-at-first-chat-with-lemonades-ai-chatbot-maya-7b4a105824bd**.
9. Invisible Machines, "S2E22 Successful Adoption of AI with Jeff McMillan, Head of AD&I, Morgan Stanley Wealth Management," November 28, 2023, **https://youtu.be/yxoZ8FGCtoc?si=eOrIwyoEfwM9jYk5&t=2163**.
10. Kate Park, "Samsung Bans Use of Generative AI Tools Like ChatGPT After April Internal Data Leak," TechCrunch, May 2, 2023, **https://techcrunch.com/2023/05/02/samsung-bans-use-of-generative-ai-tools-like-chatgpt-after-april-internal-data-leak**.
11. Jared Diamond, *Guns, Germs, and Steel: The Fates of Human Societies* (New York: W. W. Norton, 1997), 259.

Chapter 2

1. Emilie Shumway, "ChatGPT Usage at Work Has More Than Doubled in a Year," HR Dive, January 31, 2024. **https://www.hrdive.com/news/chatgpt-usage-at-work-doubled/706127/**.

2. Invisible Machines, "Innovation in the Global South with Payal Arora, Author, Professor and Co-founder of FemLab," March 21, 2024. **https://www.youtube.com/watch?v=b41BCMYRN04**.

3. Invisible Machines, "S2E22 Successful Adoption of AI W/ Jeff McMillan, Head of AD&I, Morgan Stanley Wealth Management," November 28, 2023. **https://www.youtube.com/watch?v=yxoZ8FGCtoc**.

4. Invisible Machines, "S3E1 the Staggering Depth of Thin UI Layers with Paul English, Co-founder of Kayak and GetHuman," January 11, 2024, **https://www.youtube.com/watch?v=J3IXjFQHqGg**.

Chapter 3

1. "Gartner Forecasts Worldwide Hyperautomation-Enabling Software Market to Reach Nearly $600 Billion by 2022," Gartner, April 28, 2021, **https://www.gartner.com/en/newsroom/press-releases/2021-04-28-gartner-forecasts-worldwide-hyperautomation-enabling-software-market-to-reach-nearly-600-billion-by-2022**.

2. Marco Iansiti and Karim R. Lakhani, "Competing in the Age of AI: How Machine Intelligence Changes the Rules of Business," Harvard Business Review, January–February 2020, **https://hbr.org/2020/01/competing-in-the-age-of-ai**.

3. Eric Jing, "Eric Jing on the Promise of Financial Services for the Unbanked," Wall Street Journal, January 17, 2018, **https://www.wsj.com/articles/eric-jing-on-the-promise-of-financial-services-for-the-unbanked-1516200702**.

4. Marco Iansiti and Karim R. Lakhani, "Competing in the Age of AI," Harvard Business Review, January–February 2020, **https://hbr.org/2020/01/competing-in-the-age-of-ai**.

5. Statista, "Number of Active WeChat Messenger Accounts Q2 2014-Q2 2024," October 15, 2024, **https://www.statista.com/statistics/255778/number-of-active-wechat-messenger-accounts/**.

6. Jack Flynn, "25+ Amazon Statistics [2023]: Facts About the Largest U.S. E-Commerce Market." Zippia, June 16, 2023, **https://www.zippia.com/advice/amazon-statistics/**.

7. Backlinko, "TikTok Statistics You Need to Know," July 1, 2024, **https://backlinko.com/tiktok-users#monthly-active-tiktok-users**.

8. Alex Heath, "Elon Musk Tells Twitter Employees His Plan to Hit 1 Billion Users." The Verge, June 16, 2022, **https://www.theverge.com/2022/6/16/23171054/elon-musk-twitter-deal-1-billion-users-wechat-tiktok**.

9. Edward Ongweso, Jr., "Super Apps Are Terrible for People—and Great for Companies," WIRED, September 10, 2023, **https://www.wired.com/story/super-app-musk-x-wechat-regulation/**.

10. Julia La Roche, "Salesforce CEO: We're going to rebuild all of our technology to become Slack-first," Yahoo Finance, June 10, 2021, **https://finance.yahoo.com/news/salesforce-ceo-marc-benioff-on-slack-acquisition-135151402.html**.

Chapter 4

1. Judith Shulevitz, "Siri, You're Messing Up a Generation of Children," The New Republic, April 2, 2014, **https://newrepublic.com/article/117242/siris-psychological-effects-children**.
2. Invisible Machines, "S3E8 LLM? More Like 'Limited' Language Model with Emily M. Bender. University of Washington," February 29, 2024, **https://youtu.be/ 3Ul_bGiUH4M?si=OGj_71Im4Eln3gDM&t=3093**.
3. Jessica Nordell, quoted in Megan Thompson, "A new book examines ways to end unconscious bias," PBS NewsHour, September 18, 2021, **https://www.pbs.org/ newshour/show/a-new-book-examines-ways-to-end-unconscious-bias**.
4. Invisible Machines, "S3E8 LLM? More Like 'Limited' Language Model with Emily M. Bender. University of Washington," February 29, 2024, **https://youtu.be/ 3Ul_bGiUH4M?si=OGj_71Im4Eln3gDM&t=3093**.
5. Jared Diamond, *Guns, Germs, and Steel: The Fates of Human Societies* (New York: W. W. Norton, 1997), 30.
6. Michelle Lau, "We all have a 'hierarchy of needs.' But is technology meeting them?," World Economic Forum, July 2, 2019, **https://www.weforum.org/agenda/2019/ 07/is-technology-meeting-our-fundamental-human-needs/**.
7. Invisible Machines, "S3E19 Behind the Curtain with Kara Swisher," May 23, 2024, **https://youtu.be/n1g5PkO4Q6o?si=Ri9_4f8P2JoC4S9s&t=285**.
8. Invisible Machines, "S4E4 the Intelligence All Around Us," August 15, 2024, **https://www.youtube.com/watch?v=_1hvQUdOc3E&t=611s**.
9. Invisible Machines, "S2E23 Identity and Collective Intelligence with Blaise Agüera y Arcas, VP at Google Research," November 30, 2023, **https://youtu.be/xZ2EQgI NEh4?si=ip6efCTPJbmUdx7g&t=2357**.

Chapter 5

1. Tyler Clifford, "Coronavirus has ushered in the 'death of the call center,' LivePerson CEO says," CNBC, updated May 12, 2020, **https://www.cnbc.com/2020/05/11/ coronavirus-ushered-in-the-death-of-the-call-center-liveperson-ceo.html**.
2. Katie Canales, "China's 'social credit' system ranks citizens and punishes them with throttled internet speeds and flight bans if the Communist Party deems them untrustworthy," Business Insider, updated December 24, 2021, **https://www .yahoo.com/news/chinas-social-credit-system-ranks-123042422.html**.
3. Walter Isaacson, "How to Fix the Internet," *The Atlantic*, December 15, 2016, **https://www.theatlantic.com/technology/archive/2016/12/how-to-fix-the-internet/510797/**.
4. Kobie, Nicole, "The Complicated Truth About China's Social Credit System," WIRED, June 7, 2019, **https://www.wired.com/story/china-social-credit-system-explained**.

5. Caitlin Dewey, "Everyone you know will be able to rate you on the terrifying 'Yelp for people' whether you want them to or not," *Washington Post*, September 30, 2015, **https://www.washingtonpost.com/news/the-intersect/wp/2015/09/30/everyone-you-know-will-be-able-to-rate-you-on-the-terrifying-yelp-for-people-whether-you-want-them-to-or-not/**.

6. Shai Wininger, "The Secret Behind Lemonade's Instant Insurance," n.d., accessed February 18, 2022, **https://www.lemonade.com/blog/secret-behind-lemonades-instant-insurance/**.

7. Seth Grimes, "Unstructured Data and the 80 Percent Rule," Breakthrough Analysis, August 1, 2008, **http://altaplana.com/writing.html**.

8. Invisible Machines, "S2E10 IDEO, Jenna Fizel, Danny DeRuntz," August 31, 2023, **https://www.youtube.com/watch?v=ynYVTPsf0zs**.

9. Chris Grams, "How Much Time Do Developers Spend Actually Writing Code?" The New Stack, October 28, 2021. **https://thenewstack.io/how-much-time-do-developers-spend-actually-writing-code/**.

10. Invisible Machines, "S2E9 Don Scheibenreif, Gartner VP & Distinguished Analyst, Customer Experience Research Group," August 24, 2023, **https://www.youtube.com/watch?v=sQClEt_WA4Q&t=449s**.

11. "Everyone Gets an AI Agent," Nieman Lab, n.d., **https://www.niemanlab.org/2023/12/everyone-gets-an-ai-agent/**.

12. "Findings Regarding the Market Events of May 6, 2010," U.S. Commodity Futures Trading Commission and the U.S. Securities and Exchange Commission, September 20, 2010, **https://www.sec.gov/news/studies/2010/marketevents-report.pdf**.

Chapter 6

1. Invisible Machines, "S2E1 Adam Cheyer, Siri Co-Founder," July 5, 2023, **https://youtu.be/vvupb45l_9o?si=irauTh2PwKaViOE3&t=1286**.

Chapter 7

1. Invisible Machines, "S3E7 Questioning Everything with Jaron Lanier, Prime Unifying Scientist at Microsoft," February 22, 2024, **https://youtu.be/RzebHHGw388?si=-Xpw-nFfAbO9YRZK&t=870**.

2. McKinsey & Company, "What Is Digital-Twin Technology?," August 26, 2024, **https://www.mckinsey.com/featured-insights/mckinsey-explainers/what-is-digital-twin-technology**.

Chapter 8

1. Invisible Machines, "S3E13 Building an Advanced Digital Assistant with Morgan Stanley," April 4, 2024, **https://youtu.be/3iQbufK1luE?si=G5tc9BM6U2CoTBnk&t=2367**.

Chapter 9

1. Gartner, Gartner IT Symposium 2023 Presentation, "We Shape AI - AI Shapes Us," Mary Mesaglio and Don Scheibenreif, Oct. 16-19, 2023.

Chapter 10

1. Hank Barnes, "Fusion Teams—A Critical Area for Vendors to Develop Understanding," LinkedIn Pulse, June 23, 2021, **https://www.linkedin.com/pulse/fusion-teams-critical-area-vendors-develop-hank-barnes/**.
2. Invisible Machines, "S3E15 Hiring Conversational Designers - Aaron Cooper, Banner Health's Sr. Dir. Of Digital Experience," April 18, 2024, **https://youtu.be/_vbSkkSkPmk?si=4xNINcyf3YFOd3jD&t=243**.
3. Bayrhammer Klaus, "You spend much more time reading code than writing code." Medium, November 22, 2020, **https://bayrhammer-klaus.medium.com/you-spend-much-more-time-reading-code-than-writing-code-bc953376fe19**.

Chapter 11

1. Google Cloud, "Google Cloud Next'"4 Opening Keynote," April 9, "0"4, **https://www.youtube.com/watch?v=V6DJYGn"SFk**.
2. Invisible Machines, "S3E13 Building an Advanced Digital Assistant with Morgan Stanley," April 4, "0"4, **https://youtu.be/3iQbufK1luE?si=0PQGuDPmjGXWSaLP&t=606**.
3. Invisible Machines, "S3E18 AI Agents IN ACTION," May 17, "0"4, **https://www.youtube.com/watch?v=wcIn0aSzngU&t=5"7s**.
4. Josh Tyson, "Watch Your Step! There's AGI Everywhere," Observer, May 15, "0"4, **https://observer.com/"0"4/03/organizational-artificial-general-intelligence/**.
5. McKinsey & Company. "What Is Digital-Twin Technology?," August "6, "0"4. **https://www.mckinsey.com/featured-insights/mckinsey-explainers/what-is-digital-twin-technology**.
6. Ben Goertzel, "Decentralized AI," TEDxBerkeley, April "3," 019, video, 16:17, **https://www.youtube.com/watch?v=r4manxX5U-0**.

Chapter 12

1. "Gartner Says AI Ambition and AI-Ready Scenarios Must Be a Top Priority for CIOs for Next 12-24 Months," Gartner, November 26, 2023, **https://www.gartner.com/en/newsroom/press-releases/2023-11-06-gartner-says-ai-ambition-and-ai-ready-scenarios-must-be-a-top-priority-for-cios-for-next-12-24-months**.
2. Miller, Ron, "ServiceNow Is Developing AI Through Mix of Building, Buying and Partnering," TechCrunch, March 20, 2024, **https://techcrunch.com/2024/03/20/**

servicenow-is-developing-ai-through-mix-of-building-buying-and-partnering/.

3. Sam Blum, "Klarna Plans to 'Shut Down SaaS Providers' and Replace Them with Internally Built AI. The Tech World Is Pretty Skeptical," Inc., September 12, 2024, **https://www.inc.com/sam-blum/klarna-plans-to-shut-down-saas-providers-and-replace-them-with-ai.html**.

4. "Worldwide Spending on Artificial Intelligence Is Expected to Double in Four Years, Reaching $110 Billion in 2024, According to New IDC Spending Guide," International Data Corporation, August 25, 2020, **https://www.idc.com/getdoc.jsp?containerId=prUS52530724**.

Chapter 13

1. Dan Klyn, "The 5 Ways to Organize Information - Richard Saul Wurman," May 14, 2019. **https://www.youtube.com/watch?v=Ak6nIJHlRcA**.

2. Invisible Machines, "S2EP26 an Exercise in Unfiltered Conversation with Richard Saul Wurman, Designer and TED Creator," December 21, 2023. **https://www.youtube.com/watch?v=H1J7j7b9mcQ**.

3. Invisible Machines, "S4E9 Digital Twins in an Agentic World," September 19, 2024, **https://www.youtube.com/watch?v=KsL3w2bVjmw**.

Chapter 14

1. Lilian Weng, "LLM Powered Autonomous Agents," Lil'Log (blog), June 23, 2023, **https://lilianweng.github.io/posts/2023-06-23-agent./**.

2. "Large Language Model Based Multi-Agents: A Survey of Progress and Challenges," Ar5iv, n.d., **https://ar5iv.labs.arxiv.org/html/2402.01680**.

3. John H. Miller and Scott E. Page, *Complex Adaptive Systems: An Introduction to Computational Models of Social Life*, (Princeton, NJ: Princeton University Press, 2009), 239.

4. Invisible Machines, "S3E18 AI Agents IN ACTION," May 17, 2024, **https://youtu.be/wcIn0aSzngU?si=0hsa6miYasYvr75d&t=672**.

Chapter 15

1. Invisible Machines, "S3E21 Forging Humanistic AI with Tom Gruber, Co-Founder of Siri," June 7, 2024, **https://youtu.be/RGUg7EGqE-4?si=aeqSV2kYbPI2D_Oy&t=2839**.

2. Susan Weinschenk, "Why Having Choices Makes Us Feel Powerful," *Psychology Today*, January 24, 2013, https://www.psychologytoday.com/us/blog/brainwise/201301/why-having-choices-makes-us-feel-powerful.

3. Starbucks, "Top six ways to customize your favorite Starbucks drink," April 08, 2019, **https://stories.starbucks.com/press/2019/customizing-beverages-at-starbucks-stores/**.

4. Jaya Saxena, "Starbucks Stands by Its Most Annoying Customers and Their Wild Custom Drinks, Eater, May 5, 2021, https://www.eater.com/2021/5/5/22420813/starbucks-annoying-customized-drinks.

5. Gruber, Tom. "How AI Can Enhance Our Memory, Work and Social Lives," April, 2017, **https://www.ted.com/talks/tom_gruber_how_ai_can_enhance_our_memory_work_and_social_lives?language=en**.

6. "How Much Time and Energy Do We Waste Toggling Between Applications?," Harvard Business Review, November 1, 2022, **https://hbr.org/2022/08/how-much-time-and-energy-do-we-waste-toggling-between-applications**.

7. Invisible Machines, "S3E5 Can Conversational AI Revive Our Attention Spans? With Gloria Mark, Author of Attention Span," February 8, 2024, **https://youtu.be/KcugxefjacE?si=nmlNaiefLFUg1RjC&t=3331**.

8. Arthur Van de Oudeweetering, *Improve Your Pattern Recognition: Key Moves and Motifs in the Middlegame* (Alkmaar, Netherlands: New in Chess, 2014).

9. RZA, "RZA on Chess and Bobby Fischer: Every game is a draw until you make a mistake," Lex Fridman Podcast, October 8, 2021, **https://www.youtube.com/watch?v=uX0OzHkQlXI**.

10. RZA, "Reflections of a King," Interview by Adisa "the Bishop" Banjoko, Chess Life, January 2021, quoted by Adisa Banjoko, "A Conversation with RZA from the Wu-Tang Clan," US Chess Federation, January 5, 2021, https://new.uschess.org/news/conversation-rza-wu-tang-clan.

11. Invisible Machines, "S1E11 Digging into Digital Twins," May 4, 2023, **https://www.youtube.com/watch?v=yOFGSD3WGDg**.

12. Invisible Machines, "S4E5 Agentic Micro UIs IN ACTION," August 22, 2024, **https://www.youtube.com/watch?v=T-JRA1LQZ4w**.

13. "Dynamic LLM-Agent Network: An LLM-Agent Collaboration Framework with Agent Team Optimization," Department of Computer Science & Technology, Tsinghua University Institute for AI Industry Research (AIR), Tsinghua University Georgia Tech, Stanford University, October 2, 2023, **https://arxiv.org/pdf/2310.02170**.

Chapter 16

1. Invisible Machines, "S4E2 Ephemeral Applications and AGI," August 1, 2024, **https://www.youtube.com/watch?v=MbQzo-RkAC0**.

Chapter 18

1. Invisible Machines, "S2EP26 an Exercise in Unfiltered Conversation with Richard Saul Wurman, Designer and TED Creator," December 21, 2023, **https://youtu.be/H1J7j7b9mcQ?si=DWR7I4X1vnQ1Y8eJ&t=311**.

2. Invisible Machines, "S4E3 the AGI in Organizational Agility | McKinsey & Co.'s Aaron De Smet," August 8, 2024, **https://youtu.be/Akm6b8XG7Uw?si=GN8Tv PBs3FvcmWKq&t=2851**.

3. Henry Comes-Pritchett, "In the Garden of Hyperautomation," *UX Magazine*, September 11, 2022, **https://uxmag.com/articles/ai-tale-of-two-topias**.

4. Derek Robertson, "5 questions for Meredith Whittaker," Politico, December 1, 2023, **https://www.politico.com/newsletters/digital-future-daily/2023/12/01/5-questions-for-meredith-whittaker-00129677**.

5. Janakee Chavda and Janakee Chavda, "Representative Democracy Remains a Popular Ideal, but People Around the World Are Critical of How It's Work-ing," Pew Research Center, October 23, 2024, **https://www.pewresearch.org/global/2024/02/28/representative-democracy-remains-a-popular-ideal-but-people-around-the-world-are-critical-of-how-its-working/**.

6. Jeffrey M. Jones, "Record Low in U.S. Satisfied with Way Democracy Is Working," Gallup.Com, October 16, 2024, **https://news.gallup.com/poll/548120/record-low-satisfied-democracy-working.aspx**.

7. Invisible Machines, "S2E3 Dr. Lee Hood & Dr. Nathan Price," July 13, 2023, **https://youtu.be/rrrEu5TNqFg?si=gAEX_1WlWOvZnMRI&t=1137**.

8. Shubhangi Dua, "AI Predicts Diseases with 98% Accuracy in Real-Time Using Tongue Color," Interesting Engineering, August 13, 2024, **https://interestingen gineering.com/health/ai-model-predicts-disease-using-tongue-color**.

9. Neuroscience News, "AI Reveals Distinct Speech Patterns in Parkinson's Disease Patients," Neuroscience News, May 12, 2023, **https://neurosciencenews.com/speech-parkinsons-ai-23221/**.

10. Larry Bradley, "The Butterfly Effect - Chaos & Fractals," Larry Bradley, n.d., **https://www.stsci.edu/~lbradley/seminar/butterfly.html**.

11. Hammad Farooqi, "Japan Launches AI-Powered System for Faster, Smarter Disaster Response - the AI Wired," The AI Wired, August 13, 2024, **https://theaiwired.com/japan-launches-ai-powered-system-for-faster-smarter-disaster-response/**.

12. Invisible Machines, "S2E9 Don Scheibenreif, Gartner VP & Distinguished Ana-lyst, Customer Experience Research Group," August 24, 2023, **https://youtu.be/sQClEt_WA4Q?si=7_ibsjPpwbsUdauj&t=438**.

13. Andrew Hasbun, "A Peek into Your Rating," Uber Newsroom, February 15, 2022, **https://www.uber.com/newsroom/rider-ratings-breakdown/**.

14. Marc Andreessen and Marc Andreessen, "Why Software Is Eating the World," Andreessen Horowitz, September 9, 2024, **https://a16z.com/why-software-is-eating-the-world/**.

15. Invisible Machines, "S3E4 the Promise and Peril of Boundless Predictive Machines with Lisa Feldman Barrett," February 1, 2024, **https://youtu.be/KA3Vpacfx3I?si=4F0jPY4nVFZgFNZU&t=1799**.

16. James Gallagher, "More Than Half Your Body Is Not Human," April 10, 2018, **https://www.bbc.com/news/health-43674270**.

17. Invisible Machines, "S4E4 the Intelligence All Around Us," August 15, 2024, **https://youtu.be/_1hvQUdOc3E?si=QkVI-7qhbSk8qMrJ&t=611**.

About the Authors

Robb Wilson is the CEO and co-founder of OneReach.ai, the only AI agent orchestration platform recognized as a "leader" by all top analyst firms including Gartner, Forrester, and IDC. With more than two decades in AI research and user-centered design, Robb helped unlock the agentic approach to automation that's being feverishly pursued by enterprises all over the world. The GSX platform he developed traces its origins back to a DARPA initiative and is used by leaders including PepsiCo, Deloitte, and the city of Washington DC. A former tech and design executive at publicly traded companies, Robb has mentored AI, UX, and technology leaders at Amazon, Google, Salesforce, Frog, Box, and other top firms. He's received more than 130 awards in AI innovation, design, and technology and led the architecture and design of award-winning digital products for Adobe, Nike, Boeing, and Workday. Robb founded one of the world's first UX firms, which was acquired by WPP/Ogilvy, was invited by Apple to design one of the first iPad apps, and co-founded Visionations, the number one police and forensic case management app serving 250 investigative agencies around the world. Also a musician, carpenter, and armchair neuroscientist, he lives in Berkeley, California, with his family.

Josh Tyson is an author and producer who has held leadership roles for a variety of organizations, including TEDxMileHigh, and *UX Magazine*. He is the co-creator and co-host of the *Invisible Machines and N9K* podcasts, and his writing has appeared in numerous publications over the years, including *Chicago Reader*, *Fast Company*, *FLAUNT*, *Harvard Business Review*, *The New York Times*, *Observer*, *Stop Smiling*, and *Thrasher*. His forthcoming novel, *Alamosa*, is a deconstructed coming-of-age story set in the multiverse. Josh lives in Denver, where he enjoys skateboarding, yoga, and spending time with his family.

Index

Page numbers followed by *f* refers to figures.